Lois Hole *Speaks*

Lois Hole *Speaks*

WORDS THAT MATTER

Lois Hole
Edited by Mark Lisac

Published by

The University of Alberta Press
Ring House 2
Edmonton, Alberta, Canada   T6G 2E1

Copyright © 2008 The University of Alberta Press

LIBRARY AND ARCHIVES CANADA CATALOGUING IN PUBLICATION

Hole, Lois, 1929-2005
Lois Hole speaks : words that matter / Lois Hole ; Mark Lisac, editor.

Includes index.
ISBN 978-0-88864-488-6

1. Hole, Lois, 1929-2005. 2. Alberta—Miscellanea. 3. Speeches, addresses, etc., Canadian (English)—Alberta.
I. Lisac, Mark, 1947- II. Title.

FC3675.1.H64A55 2007   971.23'03   C2007-903521-3

All rights reserved.
First edition, first printing, 2008.
Printed and bound in Canada by Kromar Printing Ltd., Winnipeg, Manitoba.

The University of Alberta Press is committed to protecting our natural environment. As part of our efforts,
this book is printed on New Leaf Paper: it contains 100% post-consumer recycled fibres and is acid- and
chlorine-free.

The University of Alberta Press gratefully acknowledges the support received for its publishing program from
The Canada Council for the Arts. The University of Alberta Press also gratefully acknowledges the financial
support of the Government of Canada through the Book Publishing Industry Development Program (BPIDP)
and from the Alberta Foundation for the Arts for its publishing activities.

Titlepage: Lois Hole, 1998. Photo by Sima Khorrami.

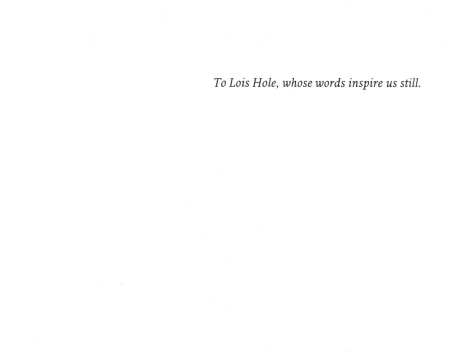

To Lois Hole, whose words inspire us still.

Contents

Foreword

AS THE UNIVERSITY OF ALBERTA looks forward to its centennial in
2008, it is time also to look back at the history of this campus. The
University of Alberta Centennial Series celebrates the university's 100
years of academic excellence with a variety of books about the people
and events that have shaped this institution.

Lois Hole Speaks: Words that Matter, the fourth book in the University
of Alberta Centennial Series, gathers in one volume the speeches Lois
Hole made as lieutenant-governor. In viewing her speeches as a collection for the first time, we can see clearly why and how this remarkable
woman changed public perception of the the the lieutenant-governor's role.
Her quiet determination and her abilty to relate to both young and old
shines through in each of these pieces. *Lois Hole Speaks* captures the wit,
humour and wisdom of a much-loved public figure. In fact, Lois became
known throughout Alberta as "The Queen of Hugs"—a name she earned
during her years as chancellor, when she administered a warm and
personal hug to each graduand. She continued the practice as lieutenant-
governor, adding a touch of warmth and intimacy to an otherwise
austere and remote office. The tradition of the hugs lived on at University
of Alberta Convocations, so that her successor as chancellor, John
Ferguson, was startled at his first Convocation to receive a bear-hug
from a burly male Engineer!

The books in the University of Alberta Centennial Series reflect the
rich and varied history of this province: the first is Donald G. Wetherwell's
*Architecture, Town Planning and Community: Selected Writings and Public
Talks by Cecil Burgess, 1909–1946*. Cecil Burgess was appointed by Henry
Marshall Tory as Resident Architect and Professor of Architecture in
1913. Burgess influenced the planning and development of our campus
for many years and he would be proud to know that his work remains
highly valued to this day.

"I Was There:" A Century of Alumni Stories about the University of Alberta, 1906–2006 is oral history at its best. Ellen Schoeck's labour of love captures the spirit and soul of a century-old institution. She has done so with a rigour for accuracy, and with a passion for its people.

Illuminating the Alberta Order of Excellence pays tribute to the many people who have been honoured for their contribution as citizens and for the examples of individual citizenship they provide for fellow Albertans. The book also showcases Cora Healy-Tobin's artwork for the scrolls given to individuals who have been invested into the Alberta Order of Excellence.

Commissioned specifically for the university's centennial, Professor Rod Macleod's *All True Things: The University of Alberta, 1908–2008*, delves into the community of scholars, researchers and students at the University of Alberta over the past century. Dr. Macleod states that to be able "to reflect on the history of your own institution is a real privilege."

In the centennial year, the University of Alberta will host conversations with the six living individuals who have served as prime minister of Canada. The final book in the University of Alberta Centennial Series intends to bring together in one collection these conversations with our national leaders. The collection will provide readers with unique insights into the way national leaders, past and present, have responded to challenges from members of the higher education community.

As honorary editor of the University of Alberta Centennial Series, I am delighted to present our collective history to our alumni, students and staff in these books as we lead up to our celebrations in 2008.

JAMES S. EDWARDS, P.C.
Board Chair Emeritus
University of Alberta

Preface

I BEGAN THIS PROJECT of collecting and editing Lois Hole's speeches believing it would be interesting and worthwhile. It quickly became apparent that it would be much more. These speeches are a record of a warm and powerful personality expressing deeply held convictions on what it means to be a good citizen and good human being.

Lois Hole spoke with great clarity. She expressed big ideas in everyday language; she talked directly to people rather than speaking over their heads. She spoke repeatedly about what she believed lay at the core of young people's ability to cope with their future and to make that future a better one. She had a wide-ranging and inquiring mind. Her speeches could refer to the best methods of growing vegetables or the film scripts of Charlie Chaplin or the pleasures of the piano or the intricacies of Japanese culture. As she continued in her term of office, new subjects appeared. She had often talked about the principle of caring for one another. Now, she began insisting on the need to extend the principle of caring beyond neighbourhoods and provincial borders to all the world's people.

After choosing the material to include in this collection it was time to interview people who had seen and heard her. Another revelation! One after another, busy people eagerly took time to talk about her. Their voices softened. Their memories seemed to reflect the warmth of her personality. Many prominent speakers can open their listeners' eyes to new perspectives or generate enthusiasm for a cause. Lois Hole was among the few who could bring a light into a room and have it still burning years later among those with whom she came into contact. This quality was all the more remarkable because of her background. While she must have known she was doing some extraordinary things, she never affected to be more than an ordinary person who had been given great opportunities and was trying to put them to good use.

This book contains only a sample of her speeches and of personal recollections. But even a sample is enough to help commemorate Lois Hole and keep alive her most cherished values.

Acknowledgements

DURING HER TENURE as chancellor of the University of Alberta, Lois Hole's office was located opposite the University of Alberta Press offices in Athabasca Hall. Mrs. Hole's wisdom and warmth touched everybody at the University of Alberta Press, so when the opportunity arose to publish a book of her words, the entire Press team responded enthusiastically and brought their diverse professional skills to the project.

The University of Alberta Press would therefore like to thank everyone involved in making this very special project a reality. The Hole family, and in particular Bill Hole, offered their guidance and co-operation in the preparation of this manuscript. Sandra Kereliuk and Bruce Keith provided key insights and details. Mark Lisac provided an enlightening and thoughtful introduction, setting Mrs. Hole's words into context and helping us all to know her better. Several freelancers and temporary staff also contributed significantly: Leslie Robertson copyedited the manuscript, Zanne Cameron proofread it, Helen Dong and Cheryl Mahaffy transcribed Lois Hole's stories from audiotape, and Moira Calder provided the index. At the Press, Peter Midgley and Mary Lou Roy shepherded the manuscript through editorial, Alan Brownoff was responsible for book design and production, Cathie Crooks and Jeff Carpenter saw to the details of marketing the book, while the director, Linda Cameron, kept everyone in sight of the original vision.

Lois Hole on the occasion of being named 1995 Woman of the Year by the Edmonton Business and Professional Women's Club. The award was presented on February 15, 1996 at Edmonton's Royal Glenora Club. [Hole Family Archives]

Editor's Introduction

LOIS HOLE WAS A MUCH LOVED PERSON and a much admired lieutenant-governor of Alberta. She frequently spoke for many Albertans during what was at times a period of intense political debate. This book preserves her words to, and on behalf of, the people she served.

If one thought can explain why people were strongly drawn to her, that thought may be that she enriched people's lives. She was the friendly image of Hole's Greenhouses, the family business that brought life and colour to thousands of homes. She taught gardening to hundreds of thousands more through her books. She influenced major decisions while serving on her local school board and at two universities. When she became lieutenant-governor of Alberta in February 2000, she brought warmth, humanity and relevance to what was often a remote and ceremonial position. She also promptly set about offering a different vision of what the province could become. In place of individualism and money she talked about community and education.

Her views sometimes bent or breached the convention that lieutenant-governors are not to become involved in political debate. Hole knew this. She also learned how far she could go. She rarely spoke about the boundary, but she did tell a group of students in 2004 that, while there was a sound rationale for the prohibition against political activity, she sometimes stepped over the line:

> This apolitical position permits the Lieutenant Governor to repre-
> sent Alberta on ceremonial and state occasions. In other words, even
> though I have political preferences like anyone else, I'm not really
> supposed to express them too loudly. But sometimes I'll sneak in a
> few words in support of public libraries, public education, public
> health care, and the fine arts.

You can practically see her winking an eye at a young audience ready to appreciate an unexpected touch of mischief. Most of her public comments dealt in one way or another with public libraries, public education, public health care, and the fine arts. She never left any doubt about her full support for these institutions. Her definition of not expressing herself "too loudly" usually came down to stating her beliefs without noting that she was implicitly disagreeing with government policy and a strong current of opinion in the province.

How did she get away with breaching convention and tweaking the government's ear? Essentially, she spoke for many Albertans who felt they had no voice in a monotonous political landscape. The Progressive Conservative Party had been in power since 1971 and seemed invulnerable. Many Conservatives nonetheless had occasional qualms about government policy and agreed with much of what Hole was saying. She had also built up a public presence that the government could not readily ignore. The prime minister chooses lieutenant-governors, albeit after carefully gathering advice. Many Albertans were not aware of the niceties and assumed the provincial government had appointed Hole. Her staff knew that Premier Ralph Klein and his cabinet ministers received compliments about their wise choice. The politicians were prepared to put up with occasional irritation from someone who made them look good—and who really was apolitical in important ways. She did not try to affect election outcomes. Nor did she talk about political issues in partisan terms; the people on the pointed end of some of her commentary took what she said as heartfelt advice from a person of goodwill.

Yet there was more to what made Lois Hole different. She had a remarkable capacity to connect with people personally. Whether selling vegetables or hosting an event as the Queen's representative in Alberta, she approached people with a generosity of spirit. When she offered them tips on the best way to grow tomatoes or gave them an extra bunch of carrots at no charge, she made people feel acknowledged and cared for. When she called on them to support public education and libraries, she was saying that their voices were important—that they deserved to be heard.

Crucially, her views grew out of her own experience of life. They reflected her beliefs about what constituted a good life for ordinary families and the communities they lived in. Because she came from a typical Prairie family—as much as any family can be typical—Hole's views expressed the feelings of many thousands of Albertans.

The governments led by Ralph Klein had what political observers often called a "populist" bent. Their popularity rested on the impression of doing things for ordinary people living outside the privileged realms of big business and academia. Hole confronted the ruling politicians with the novelty of a populist lieutenant-governor. She began by meeting people. She almost invariably charmed them all. Kate Evans, one of the hundreds who attended the lieutenant-governor's New Year's Day Levee in 2002, was quoted in the *Edmonton Journal* later as saying, "What a fantastic, warm person she is." Hers was a common reaction. Thousands felt they knew Lois Hole because they had met her at Hole's Greenhouse or during her time as a school trustee. After she became lieutenant-governor, thousands more heard her speak—usually at events small enough where they could make direct eye contact or line up afterward for one of her famous hugs.

Her correspondence reflects countless small moments in which she affected people's lives, beginning well before she took on official public duties. An Air Canada flight attendant from Nova Scotia wrote in 1995 to say, "You very kindly gave me your wonderful book on gardening and I just wanted to send you a big hug of thanks!...I've been asking my guardian angels for help with my green thumb and they sent me you!!!" A businesswoman from Xian, China, said in a handwritten letter in 1998, "How have you been recently? You were the first businesswoman I met in Canada. You are also the Canadian who left a very deep impression on me. Your great enthusiasm towards work and life truly attracted me. Your love to the society really touched me which made me unable to help calling you Mum." And there were many notes like the one, complete with a drawing of a grinning flower, sent by a boy who was apparently thanking her after a class visit to the greenhouse: "Dear Mrs. Hole, Thank you for being so nice and so understanding. The world needs more people like you. And thank you for the flower it's beautiful. P.S. Say hi to your dog for me."

This book presents a collection of speeches that Lois Hole made as lieutenant-governor. It is not complete. More than 800 speeches were recorded in her office files. Many have been left out to avoid duplication and to keep this volume at a reasonable length. However, this is a comprehensive collection in the sense of presenting her most important speeches, along with many shorter ones that illustrate the range of her interests and the range of people she met.

Hole enlisted the aid of a writer, Earl Woods, to prepare her speeches after she took office. The job left too little time for her to write everything personally. The speeches remain her own work. They always began with her ideas; they always took final shape with Hole editing the manuscripts, often in consultation with her immediate family.

Much of the important business of her life was conducted at her kitchen table, in the house (their second on the property) that her husband Ted built on their St. Albert farm. Lunch with her husband, sons Bill and Jim, and Bill's wife, Valerie, was a rarely violated constant in her life. Her staff were sometimes amused by her insistence that she had to be home to prepare "lunch for the boys," who were then in their 40s. The ritual was not about proper nutrition; it was about maintaining close family connections and finding an ideal place to test ideas. Hole usually tackled big decisions by broaching them first in a family discussion over lunch. What to say in a speech and how to say it were often among those decisions—as had been the question of whether she should accept the offer to become lieutenant-governor. She determined that she should take on the responsibility only if she could use it to make a meaningful contribution to Albertans' lives. That contribution included giving serious consideration to her public comments and making sure they counted for something.

Reading the speeches requires a bit of imagination. They were intended for live presentation by a woman whose strong and appealing personality always added to the effect of the words. They were also flexible. Scripted portions were often accompanied by unscripted portions. Those show up in the manuscripts as brief notes signalling to Hole that this was the place to tell one of her many stories from the farm or from other experiences. She would take off her reading glasses, look directly at audiences and transform a formal address into a homey gathering with friends. Some of the stories had appeared in *I'll Never Marry a Farmer*, while others never made it to print. Where possible, some of these stories have been gathered and included in their appropriate place in the manuscript.

While the personal effect can not be reproduced on the printed page, Hole's words take on a new force when they are read rather than heard. She had a knack for expressing her thoughts clearly and simply. Each sentence and paragraph was focussed. Together, the speeches display a robust pattern of ideas. That is not to say that her ideas were always right. Still, she powerfully expressed ideas with which many Albertans could agree, whatever their political allegiance. A stream of correspondence and phone calls came into the lieutenant-governor's office asking for copies of what she had said at any given event.

The other significant point about the speeches being intended for live presentation is less immediately obvious and possibly even more important. Hole often revisited the same themes, constantly elaborating either her ideas or their presentation. She was engaged in a process hugely different from writing a book or saturating the province with a message delivered through radio or television. She intended every word to be delivered in person to an audience occupying the same room or public space. The words are plain and direct. She delivered them to Albertans one at a time, looking each of them in the eye as she was speaking. This personal communication underlined her populist sentiments. When Lois Hole spoke to Albertans she was not reflecting the findings of a focus group or delivering a boilerplate address to get through another public function. She was trying to make genuine contact with every individual within range of her voice. Most responded equally genuinely. She conveyed warmth and sincerity because these qualities were real. She was not acting.

And she was not trying to impose an artificial vision. Here was someone whose beliefs could be called idealistic but who could not be dismissed as a dreamer. She had proven herself a hardworking and nimble business owner. Hole's Greenhouse was an economic as well as a social landmark. She could claim greater business success than many of the politicians with whom she disagreed.

But Hole's ideas were not aimed at fattening Alberta's gross domestic product, although she did not underestimate the value of doing so. She profoundly urged the care and nurture of individuals and the communities in which they lived. She wanted everyone in Alberta to be able to reach his or her potential. By the time she died, she had expanded that vision to the poor of the Third World. Some of the warm reaction to her

Lois at her home in Buchanan, Saskatchewan at 8 years old.

[Hole Family Archives]

Lois (12 years old) and her family: father Michael Veregin, mother Elsa Veregin, twin brother Ray Veregin (right), and younger brother Lorne Veregin (front left). Lois was taller than her brothers until high school.

[Hole Family Archives]

and to her speeches came from a recognition that her impulse was always to build, to create a better future—one that included people who might normally see little hope for any kind of future at all.

As lieutenant-governor, Lois Hole represented Alberta. She had been living in the province for more than 60 years before being named to the post. She was, in many respects, a woman from the Canadian Prairies. Her upbringing left her with talents and sensibilities that were too big and varied to be contained by the image of just one province.

She was born Lois Elsa Veregin in Buchanan, Saskatchewan, in 1929, one of three children of Michael Veregin, who came from a Russian Doukhobor background, and Elsa Norsten, whose background was Swedish. Her year of birth would have surprised many people. Newspaper stories routinely said Hole was born in 1933, while acknow-ledging she did not care to divulge her actual birthdate. She apparently never corrected the mistaken impression, which made her four years younger in the public eye than she actually was. Her family noted with amusement that she became angry when her twin brother once said at a public occasion that he was born in 1929. She never talked with her family about her attitude toward age. Her son Bill noted that she was intrigued when her friend Harriet Winspear turned 100, and he thought her refusal to own up to her real age represented a concern about her mortality.

The Veregin family had come to Canada in 1899, along with thousands of other Doukhobors facing persecution because they had refused service in the Russian military. Hole's paternal grandmother came to Canada on the same ship as the Veregins. The Norstens arrived from Sweden a few years later and homesteaded near Buchanan in 1907.

Young Lois attended public school in Buchanan. The family moved to Edmonton when she was a teenager. She completed her education in Edmonton at Strathcona Composite High School and McTavish Business School. She also earned her Grade 10 piano certificate from the Toronto Conservatory of Music (now the Royal Conservatory of Music). Music would be important to her for the rest of her life. Her mother was a church organist, and Lois occasionally filled in for her and directed the church choir. A religious compromise seems to have been reached between her Doukhobor father and her Lutheran mother. Mrs. Veregin brought up her children in the United Church of Canada.

Young Lois thought about becoming a nurse, but her father encouraged her to look into business instead. She worked part-time in an Eaton's department store while still in school. Afterward, she taught music, then worked at the western Canadian-based Woodward's department store in Edmonton. She quickly turned that job into a promising career, becoming Woodward's first female assistant manager, responsible for, among other things, staff training.

In 1952 she married Edward (Ted) Glancefield Hole, son of Harry Hole, co-founder of Lockerbie and Hole, one of the largest mechanical contractors in Western Canada. Ted knew plumbing and had started engineering studies at the University of Alberta. But he switched interests. In 1952, he graduated from the university with a Bachelor of Science in agriculture. He and Lois married that year and bought 200 acres of prime farmland just outside St. Albert, on a height overlooking the Sturgeon River a few kilometres northwest of Edmonton. Some of the neighbours thought the $100 an acre that Ted paid was twice what

Lois and Ted Hole on their wedding day, September 19, 1952. [Hole Family Archives]

the land was worth; he thought it was a bargain for a prime location blessed with rich, dark soil that could grow just about anything.

The young couple tried all sorts of livestock and crops, with mixed financial success. In her book *I'll Never Marry a Farmer*, Hole described how the light bulb finally came on when she realized people were stopping on the road running past the farm to ask if any vegetables were for sale. The Holes decided to specialize in market gardening. The farm was incorporated in 1979 as Hole's Greenhouses and Gardens Ltd.; it became even more of a local magnet as the local population swelled in the oil boom of the late 1970s.

The stories of that period of their lives focus on raising a young family. Lois and Ted suffered the heartbreak of losing their first child, something Hole never spoke about in public. Karin was born in 1954 and died shortly after birth. Sons Bill and Jim came along in 1955 and 1956. Meanwhile, the young couple met the frustrations of learning how to build the farm business with a cheerful attitude and a belief in learning. They experimented with different crops, consulting library books that visitors would often see strewn on the kitchen table. Neighbours also became accustomed to seeing the Holes out in their garden patch with "hoe in one hand and notebook in the other." The experience was fundamental in scores of talks in which Lois urged Albertans to support public libraries. Library books helped her and her husband figure out how to handle many crops, she said.

The farm thrived. But with urban development closing in around them, the Holes abandoned their vegetable growing in 1991 and converted their business into a retail greenhouse and garden centre. Lois also began writing. *Lois Hole's Vegetable Favourites* was published in 1993. It was followed by more than a dozen other books, including *I'll Never Marry a Farmer*, a highly popular mixture of autobiography and gardening tips. She also became a fixture in newspapers and on CBC radio.

This busy home life had taken a new direction in 1967 when Lois successfully ran for election as a trustee in the Sturgeon School Division. She served as a trustee to 1977 and then chaired the board to 1980. Then she became a trustee for St. Albert School District. Politicians noted her popularity. She said later that all the major parties had asked her to run but that she had never considered doing so. Her main political interest lay in providing "strong support for teachers" and a wide-ranging curriculum—because "to me school trusteeship was where it was all at.... If you did a good job there, things would all fall into place."

A mixed Doukhobor-Swedish heritage was fairly exotic even by western Canadian standards. But a mingling of cultures was common. So was belief in a set of core principles and institutions: family; hard work; one's own ability to get things done by applying effort and common sense; the ability and duty of communities to provide for the common good; the value of education as the path toward a fulfilling life. These were fundamental attitudes on the Prairies.

Family came first. Hole's speeches regularly featured stories about her husband and children. Her experiences resonated with many listeners who could recognize similarities to their own lives. She often cited her parents. Her mother gave her a love of music and gardening and a strong belief in the importance of education. Hole once said, "For my mother, gardening was more of a pleasure than a chore, and she instilled the same feeling in me." She recalled in one of her speeches that her mother thought being well-read was more important than learning to do the chores: "The weeding in the garden could wait, or she'd just do it herself rather than distract me from my studies. I inherited Mother's respect for arts and literature, and I've always agreed with her passionately held philosophy that learning is the most important thing."

Her father emerges from her memories as someone who created her deepest values. Her son Bill said Lois and her father were remarkably alike: "They carried their hands the same way. They had the same rapport with people." And he constantly gave hugs to people, a trait that later became Lois's trademark gesture. Lois recalled her father succinctly in the Introduction to her book *I'll Never Marry a Farmer*:

> *He was a strongly principled man, with deeply held convictions. He raised me to look at life with clear eyes: to judge for myself what was right and what was wrong, and to act accordingly. He also showed me, through his example, the value of good, hard work. (p. 11)*

Less essential to Lois's sense of self but equally telling were two other Buchanan residents who live on in the speeches as vividly as the characters in every novel about small towns from W.O. Mitchell to Harper Lee. They were petite, dark-haired, lovely Miss Jobb, the teacher who opened to her the world of books, and steadfast, goodhearted Mr. Yunick, the mayor who, if someone told him a pothole needed filling, went out and did the repair work himself. Each embodied virtues that Lois admired. They were symbols of her belief in education and community service. She kept recalling them for her audiences six decades after she left their small town; she must have been recalling them for herself at the same time.

Another stock character in the speeches—she also played a prominent role in *I'll Never Marry a Farmer*—was Virginie Durocher. The old Métis woman personified folk wisdom and marginalized communities. Hole talked about her often as an example of how inconspicuous individuals had unexpected riches to offer people around them.

By the time Hole moved to Edmonton she had already developed the personality and attitudes that Albertans responded to. Photographs of her in her late teens and early 20s show an attractive, blond young woman who meets the camera with a self-confident and open gaze. A portrait of her in a satin-finish wedding dress shows her apparently unfazed by the day's excitement.

Life on the farm found her up to nearly any task. Her speeches are full of stories about dealing with disappointments like a broken water pump or a dead cow, and about learning the best strategies for growing crops and making money from them. Nor was she easily intimidated by what others would think. One of her stories had her laughing at the reaction of passersby who watched in astonishment from the road as, hitched up like a horse, she pulled a garden seeder being guided down the furrows by her husband. She told the story as entertainment; it also spoke to a strength of character that made her unlikely to back down if confronted by opposition or ridicule. Even as lieutenant-governor, despite her care to maintain respect for the office, she would not let small issues weigh heavily on her. Runs in her nylon stockings never bothered her much. They were just something that happened to nylons. Her staff constantly checked to make sure she appeared in public with stockings intact. She needed her tougher side after her election as a school trustee. She soon found herself in conflict with a mostly male and mostly older group of school board members who weren't ready for change.

Her inaugural speech as lieutenant-governor recalled her first foray into public life. She told the story briefly, but it touched on several large themes that would reappear again and again in later addresses. She ran because she wanted her two sons to learn French. She had been disappointed to learn that the St. Albert school system, despite being located in a significant francophone community, did not offer a French program. She was clearly no shrinking violet. But just as important, her husband encouraged her. She recalled him telling her, "If you want change, Lois, why not run for that position?" Here was a woman who had her own ideas, but who also had strong support from a husband who was comfortable watching her step onto the public stage while he remained in the background.

The first campaign was simple and pragmatic. There were no grand strategies or political consultants for someone used to pulling carrots from the earth and getting pigs onto a truck. Hole and her friend Laura Henry packed a Thermos and a few cheese sandwiches into her red GM half-ton and proceeded to try to visit every home in the district. She would later recall being welcomed by many farm families who felt strongly about their children's education. But she particularly

Lois while she was school board trustee for the Sturgeon School Division, c. 1969. She was the only woman on the school board right up until she left in 1980. [Hole Family Archives]

remembered one young woman who was raising seven children without many household amenities while her husband invested the family's money in farm equipment—two new tractors for him while she continued getting water from a hand pump. Hole didn't pursue the unequal division of resources further although it bothered her. Many of her speeches made clear her lively awareness of what women contributed to society and how they sometimes received second-class treatment. She said in one speech that the young mother with seven children was willing to sacrifice for her children's future:

> *It was a common theme. None of the people I visited were any less than passionate about education. They knew that a well-educated,*

well-trained population was the best way to ensure happiness and
fulfilment for everyone, especially for their children. The breadth and
depth of those parents' convictions has inspired me to this day.

Some of this golden memory must have reflected her memory of her
own parents. It turned out that not everyone shared her views. It took a
while to bring a French program into the local school system. She found
herself at odds from time to time with older, more conservative, invariably male members of the school board—especially when she cham-
pioned the installation of condom dispensers in high schools. Each time
there was a disagreement, she stood up to other recalcitrant trustees,
arguing simply that what she proposed made sense and would make
students' lives better. Tragic experience lay behind her insistence on the
availability of condoms—the young son of a good friend had died of
AIDS. Her strong-mindedness carried over into the family business.
Some customers angry about the condom issue told her they would
never shop at the Hole greenhouse again. She accepted that risk. More
important was "the greater good." The hard feelings did not always last.
One woman returned to the greenhouse a year later and apologized.

Meanwhile, Hole juggled other priorities. She remained the public
face of the garden business, and she ran the family home as an unofficial
social service agency tending to the troubled children of family members
or friends. Her speeches include only the briefest reference to this activity.
Her son Bill recalls several such interventions. Growing up in the Hole
house meant not knowing who might show up at the breakfast table.
Here was a woman who put her ideals into practice inside her home.

Her influence began to spread. She served on the governing council
of distance-learning institution Athabasca University from 1972 to 1983.
Controversies needed to be ridden out there, too. Hole was among the
councillors who approved moving the university's headquarters from
Edmonton to the town of Athabasca, only about an hour's drive north
but close to the edge of the boreal forest. Arguments raged about the
wisdom of the move. She did not dwell on those times in later years,

< *Lois selling vegetables under the trees beside the house. [Hole Family Archives]*

but noted on a few occasions that the move turned out to be right for the institution.

She was appointed chancellor of the University of Alberta in 1998. That role was satisfying and also prepared her for a larger stage. Sandra Kereliuk, her executive assistant during that period and later, said that serving as chancellor gave Hole a strong sense that the things she was saying made a difference to people. The post gave her a much bigger audience than she had ever had on matters outside gardening. It also gave her the experience and recognition necessary for her final role, although her growing fame as a gardener was filling the same purpose. In the later 1990s she spoke to an estimated 100,000 people in appearances before 600 gardening groups across North America.

She resigned from the chancellor's office in June 2000, four months after being sworn in as lieutenant-governor of Alberta. The vice-regal appointment was controlled by the office of Prime Minister Jean Chrétien. The process was secretive, but word leaked out that the prime minister's staff was surprised by the number of times people spontaneously suggested Lois Hole or enthusiastically endorsed her. Her family later said that Chrétien told her: "When you hear someone's name over and over again, you start to pay attention."

In February 2000, Alberta had reached a point of economic growth and political stagnation. The province had watched an economic boom evaporate when oil prices collapsed in 1986. An approximately 75 per cent drop in oil prices was a decisive final blow after the psychological and financial shocks of the National Energy Program in 1980 and the decade-long 1980s slump in natural gas markets. The economic problems culminated in the early 1990s with another downturn, brought on in part by the Bank of Canada's policy of using high interest rates to lower inflation. There were political shocks, too. Attempts to rewrite the Constitution failed. Provincial budget deficits, fruitless provincial government business loans, and steadily rising unemployment sapped people's faith in their elected leaders.

The atmosphere of political and economic crisis led to the election of Ralph Klein as Progressive Conservative party leader and premier in December 1992 and the election of a very much reshaped Conservative government in 1993. The new government embarked on a program of retrenchment. Spending cuts dominated the agenda. They included an

Lois and Ted Hole meeting Jean Chrétien at a dinner held in Edmonton while he was in his second term as prime minister, May 27 1994. Lois was a strong supporter of the Liberal Party for many years. [Hole Family Archives]

end to notoriously unsuccessful business loans worth hundreds of millions of dollars. But education, health, and culture were the most noticeable targets.

The cuts responded to a sentiment that had taken root among many voters and business leaders, and in the top echelons of the Alberta civil service. People were anxious about more than political failures and economic dilemmas. Nearly half a century of optimism and the more or less steady prosperity that followed the Second World War seemed to be ending. Economic problems that had once responded to policy adjustments now seemed incurable. Governments lost credibility. The primacy of North America as the most favoured place to live in the world could no longer be taken for granted; many people feared that students elsewhere, especially in Asia, were receiving a better education than were children in Alberta.

The result was a bubbling stew of ideas for radical reforms. Welfare was replaced by meagre financial supports and retraining strategies. The welfare reforms were accepted as strong job growth reappeared in the mid-1990s. Other trends were more unsettling. A well-publicized movement seemed ready to undercut public education by turning toward private and charter schools. It wasn't clear whether the government had an appetite for radical change to the public institution that most profoundly affected people's lives. What was clear was that the system was eroding. School budgets were cut. Kindergarten funding was briefly cut in half. Budgets for universities and hospitals fell by much as 17 to 20 per cent. A handful of hospitals closed. In a notorious case in Calgary, one hospital was closed and then blown up. Once again, the government's ultimate intentions were not clear. The premier began talking about a turn to more private care in 1995, but the talk never fully translated into reality. Arts funding was squeezed. CKUA radio, a nearly 70-year-old provincial network offering alternative programming, nearly died after a government pullout; it was saved when listeners rallied to its support. Libraries began to require annual fees to supplement suddenly meagre government support. An anti-tax movement argued that many services should never be publicly funded because governments could never produce high quality and financial efficiency.

These forces tended to dissipate during the 1990s. The provincial spending cuts ended in 1997, just in time for an election. Alberta's economy entered a long period of impressive growth on the strength of sharply rising natural gas exports to the United States, followed after 2000 by sharply rising gas prices and an oilsands construction boom. Yet basic decisions about the future seemed to have been suspended. A political observer could have argued in early 2000 that the province was either about to return to a stronger government presence or about to move further toward privatization. The only certainty in Alberta's political environment was the near-collapse of effective opposition.

Thus, Lois Hole entered the office of lieutenant-governor at a crucial time. Political discourse was fading in quality and relevance. The province seemed to be running out of prominent voices willing and able to articulate Hole's most deeply felt beliefs. At the same time, the winter of 2000 had demonstrated that many Albertans shared at least some of her beliefs. The government was intent on pushing through what was known as Bill 11, legislation to create a legal framework for privately owned and operated surgery clinics. Defenders said it would merely set up rules for a modest system of new clinics that could make health care more efficient. Opponents said the proposed legislation would lead to a large-scale privatization of health care, complete with preferential access for those willing and able to pay for care from their own pocket. Premier Klein called opponents "left-wing nuts."

Debate over Bill 11 broke out across Alberta's normally quiet political landscape. Meetings took place in small towns. Protesters held vigils at the Legislature Building. Hole began learning her new job at a moment of high political feelings. She was sworn in as Alberta's 15th lieutenant-governor in a ceremony at the legislature on February 10, 2000. Chief Justice Catherine Fraser of Alberta Court of Appeal presided. About 600 guests and members of the legislative assembly looked on. Hole took part sitting in a wheelchair; she had broken a heel when she tripped on a podium at an event two weeks earlier.

She said she would try to act as a champion for education, and wondered how she would fit into a ceremonial role derived from Canada's colonial past. "I have thought about that," she told an interviewer a few days before the installation. "But even when the situation calls for more protocol, I think I can always lighten it up with what I have to say, by bringing a little humour into it. I can't really say it will stop me from being the down-to-earth person that I am." Her forecast proved accurate. The first few months showed her that the position could put her into distinctly unhumorous positions, however.

Hole had been lieutenant-governor for five weeks when she spoke to an audience in Red Deer on March 16, 2000. She told them the post involved staying away from political issues. But she went on: "My son asked, 'What will you do with the health bill?'" She said her duties included giving royal assent to bills passed by the legislature, the final stage of approval necessary before they could become law—"except in rare occasions when reservations are considered necessary." She added, "Mr. Klein came to me after I was installed and said, 'Your honour, anything I can do for you, just let me know.' I'm going to."

An enterprising reporter heard echoes of a historic clash in which Lieutenant-Governor John Bowen refused assent in 1937 for key bills supported by Social Credit Premier William Aberhart. Bowen said that bills aimed at controlling banks and that civil rights exceeded provincial jurisdiction. Aberhart's response included turfing Bowen and his family out of the official lieutenant-governor's residence. Bowen's daughter would indignantly tell people decades later that the family had to go to a neighbour's home to call a cab on moving day because the government had cut off their telephone service a few hours before they left.

Hole said in an interview after her speech that she knew she was not supposed to take political stands but that Bill 11 was on people's minds. She intended to bring that to the premier: "I think they're going to resolve it. I'm hearing things and I will tell him what I'm hearing, and I hope it will help him." Klein responded that Hole was "a wonderful person" who would doubtless discuss any concerns with him. He added she had not said she might refuse assent for the bill. But Liberal Leader Nancy MacBeth called her remarks "highly unusual." Political scientists referred to the battle between Bowen and Aberhart. Editorials cautioned her, including one in the *Edmonton Journal* that began: "Lois Hole made a mistake Thursday by publicly commenting on Alberta's controversial private health bill." That Friday she released a short statement confirming she would grant royal assent to the bill if it passed and closed the matter there.

Her family and other associates said later she did not let the experience pass lightly. She realized that she had to find the boundary between constitutional traditions and her own informal style. She would spend the next several months speaking carefully while she thought through the implications of the Bill 11 controversy. She eventually resolved the pull between conscience and official responsibilities by concentrating on a short list of priorities—education, literacy, the value of libraries, and the need to look after the basic needs of fellow human beings. By 2002 she began pushing the boundaries again even in these areas. But by then she was much surer of both her goals and how to express her views in language that would not set off political and constitutional alarms.

Part of her ability to stay away from controversy depended on her strategic sense. Part depended on the persuasive charm that had stood her in good stead as a market garden owner and as a trustee on an occasionally fractious school board. "Just about everybody listened to her," Eric Newell, who eventually succeeded her as chancellor at the University of Alberta, recalled in 2006: "She was one of the most universally loved people. Even the premier. He certainly listened to what Lois Hole said and it wasn't always positive towards him. She had this unique ability to give you a bit of a lecture and you'd feel good about it." Newell had earlier served as chairman of Syncrude Canada Ltd. and had been chairman of the University of Alberta board of governors while she was chancellor. He saw her onstage on a number of occasions. Some of those occasions saw her peering over her glasses and directing comments at a strong-willed politician or business leader. Newell said she could make her point without provoking hostility: "In the kindest way, she was like everyone's grandmother. You didn't think of her in a partisan standpoint. I think she was a Liberal but, you know, you never even thought of her that way. She was a true champion of education.... There was nothing mean-minded about it. And usually the person would be, 'Yes, Lois, I hear you. Yes, we're listening.'"

David Hancock, minister of justice and then of advanced education during her term, said she "brought a new vibrancy" to the position. He was among the many members of government who seemed to have regular chats with her. He also realized the government got more than it bargained for when she was installed as lieutenant-governor—an appealing and experienced public figure who could wield influence in sophisticated ways. Various members of government learned what it was like to sit on a stage when Hole was speaking and realize that she was not hectoring them but nevertheless delivering a message. Hancock said that her listeners' warm response signalled they should rethink their plans: "She let the audience deliver the message for her."

Gary Mar, minister responsible at different times for health and for the arts, thought of her attitude as "passion without profanity." The lieutenant-governor's suite opened off a corridor on the route from his office to the cabinet meeting room. He recalled dropping in "scores of times" for a chat, usually learning something: "She wouldn't hesitate to tell you what she was thinking and it was always welcome. You wouldn't always agree with her but it was always welcome." She would catch his attention with the way she put things: "Maybe not a different perspective. But conveyed in a way that was elegant and eloquent and very well thought out. She might be the last piece of a puzzle in trying to find my own way of expressing a position...through a turn of phrase, a cogent argument." For Mar, she was "a great Canadian" whose ability to translate passions into persuasive, civilized words could serve as a fine example for media and political figures: "I miss her."

Others began to see her as someone who could commit herself personally to what she saw as truly important. She was comfortable in almost any setting. The only kind of event that does not show up in the record is any appearance before strongly conservative groups or individuals. Her schedule would have her talking about women in the trades one day and helping to celebrate the 20th anniversary of a food bank a few days later. She could celebrate the history of Prairie business legend James Richardson & Sons. And she could speak at the annual "mac and cheese" luncheon, which saw Edmonton community leaders dining on macaroni and cheese at a fundraiser for the Inner City Agencies Foundation.

Hole told the "mac and cheese" luncheon in March 2001: "I hope I'm not romanticizing the poor, because that's not my intent. Like everyone else, the man or woman or child in desperate circumstances has both noble and selfish qualities. Like us, he or she is capable of great compassion or wilful disregard for their fellows. They might be polite and humble in their requests for help, or they might be demanding and ungrateful. But it doesn't matter which. The point is, they need help, and as compassionate human beings, it is our solemn duty to provide that aid."

What made the words resonate for her listeners was her willingness to act. Bruce Saville became instrumental in efforts like the inner-city luncheon after earning millions in a telecommunications venture. He recalled that every year after her first appearance, Hole's office would call to say the lieutenant-governor wanted to come back—but not as lieutenant-governor. She would be happy to cook or help serve. "I think she brought a role that's relatively pompous and ceremonial and really brought it to the common man," Saville said. "And that was refreshing and required." He saw her as a person who would say the world is rich enough to feed everyone who's hungry, and that people with the ability to move toward that goal should never just throw up their hands and say it can't be done. Hunger and lack of education result from society's choice to let both continue, Saville said. He heard Lois Hole put those ideas into words in a number of talks: "I just think about them a lot in the things I do."

She also carried her convictions directly into the inner-city community. "People knew her as the flower lady because she donated flowers to all our events," said Hope Hunter, director of the Boyle Street Co-op in Edmonton, a multiservice agency serving poorer neighbourhoods. "She was warm and gracious and lovely.... I think she brought a sense of conscience to a lot of situations. Whether that influenced, I don't know... but certainly people were very heartened by her. They saw her as someone who was well off and influential and speaking up for them." For Hunter, the classic example of Hole's personal touch was the way she dealt with a young woman who had grown up in extreme poverty and tough circumstances. The young woman met Hole at a co-op event. Some time later she had the "phenomenal experience" of seeing Hole remember her at another event. "People were kind of honoured that someone with that kind of pomp and circumstance would come here and honour our community."

She could inject a down-to-earth touch into ceremonial occasions at the highest social levels, too. One of her favourite stories grew out of an adventure early in her time as chancellor of the University of Alberta. She told it often in later years. It had a historical resonance with a classic Prairie tale—the veracity of which has never been tracked down—stemming from a visit to Western Canada in the 1930s by the Prince of Wales. The story has the future King Edward VIII visiting a ranch house for supper. He finishes his main course and the country homemaker who comes around to collect the plates tells him, "Save your fork, prince. There's pie." Hole's often-told story concerning a pie she made for the visiting Prince and Princess Takamado was corroborated by Eric Newell.

Newell attended a lunch at Government House in Edmonton (the former lieutenant-governor's residence that the Bowen family had been kicked out of). The prince had been a student in Canada. A few days before the event, Hole asked him what he remembered best about Canada or Alberta. He responded that he remembered rhubarb pie. So she went home and made him a pie, Newell said. "And she brings it into Government House. And of course the protocol people, they see this thing and (say), 'You can't do that.' They took the pie away from her and put it in another room. Anyhow, she was sitting down at the table and she was sitting with Bill Smith, who was mayor (of Edmonton) at the

Consul General Kiyoshi Shidara and wife visit Lois at the lieutenant-governor's office, April 17, 2002.
[Hole Family Archives]

time … and she was explaining about this pie. And Bill said, 'What do you mean they took it away from you?' He says, 'Go get the pie.' And they did." She presented the pie to the prince and explained that her husband Ted had woken up at four in the morning, taken a piece of it and pronounced it as one of her better efforts. "So that's why I say in a sense she was like everyone's grandma," Newell said.

But a grandma with a bite and an ability to entertain. Everyone knew the formal persona was being set aside when she interrupted the written text of her speeches, took off her glasses and looked directly at the audience as she launched into one of her stories. She could also create dramatic suspense. Newell recalled one speech in which she suddenly turned quite serious and said, "'I want to tell you that I have a dream.' And you could just see the hush over the audience. Everyone was sort of hanging, including myself, wondering, 'Oh, oh, what's she going to say here?'...She had an ability to quiet the audience down. And then she delivered the punch line. She said, 'You know, I dream of the day that teachers and librarians will be paid as much as hockey players.' It had a huge impact on people."

Most of her appearances took place in the Edmonton area. She had to be on hand for official duties and placed great importance on being at home for lunch with her family. Midway through her term as lieutenant-governor the demands of family life increased. Her husband Ted was slipping more deeply into prostate cancer and Alzheimer's disease. He eventually had to be moved into hospital in Edmonton. She made time for the last several months of his life to visit him around supper and watch the evening news on television with him. Characteristically, she endured this trouble without talking in public about it. It was only after Ted died, in March 2003, that she spoke about the experience, and then generally at events having to do with nursing homes or with Alzheimer's disease.

Despite the calls on her time she did manage to enjoy visits to many parts of the province. Her audiences enjoyed her visits, too. It was always a red-letter day when Lois Hole came to town. Nearly two years after her death, people who recalled those visits shared remarkably consistent and similar memories. One of her early excursions was an appearance at a meeting of the County of Camrose Farm Women. "Everybody loved her," Mildred Luz, her host at the event, said. "I guess they responded to her in many different ways because she was a loving, caring person. Whatever she came up with, she really made people think about." Florence Miller welcomed her to a charter night at the Westlock Rotary Club: "I recall everybody was thrilled to have her here. I was impressed with her response to everybody she met.... She was just herself." The crowd paid close attention to her speech. "We felt very honoured to have her here."

Hole must have been especially tickled to visit a Medicine Hat book club formed in about 1927. Nearly 80 years later it was still meeting on the 1st and 15th of each month. The oldest of the 25 members had been in the club for about 50 years. Janice Croissant remembered the visit years later: "She was so wonderful. We were thankful to have her." Hole's call for support of literacy and libraries encouraged a group that already set great store in books and that included two teacher-librarians. "She said in her speech that she wasn't afraid to give Ralph (the premier) the business, too." There were other connections. Like Hole, Croissant came originally from a small town in Saskatchewan: "We spoke about growing up in a small rural county and how it forms your values. And they really stay with you."

A visit to help celebrate the 50th anniversary of the Wildwood Public Library saw her in her element, speaking about a subject she loved in a social environment she knew well. Dave Lindner, chairman of the local friends of the library society, recalled her emphasizing the importance of libraries, "especially the rural libraries that seem to get overlooked." Part of the event featured ice cream that was sold at 50-year-old prices—25 cents for a double scoop. Lindner ordered 200 servings. The crowd, in a town of 350, was large enough that it all disappeared. "At that time it was probably one of the biggest events we had seen." Hole walked about, saying hello and giving hugs. She toured the 1,700-square-foot library and called for support of what she saw as a crucial social institution: "Because in the library, those with sufficient drive and curiosity can uncover the deepest truths, using books to explore the thoughts and actions of others and to inform their own creativity." As usual, she found time to include stories about her garden in her basic message. Lindner said, "I think that's what people liked so much—that she wasn't as formal as she could have been."

Records of her public appearances cover a very broad range. She spoke to library groups, garden groups, students, university and school administrators, military and police audiences, ethnic and cultural groups—a panorama of Alberta society. She could charm nearly 200 people at a dinner put on by the Canadian-Egyptian Society in Edmonton. "Everybody knew her but nobody knew the personal touch she had," Ahmed Idriss, a member of the society's executive, recalled. "People saw that she was a nice lady." She was willing to take risks speaking to groups that others might avoid. One of her appearances took place before the Alberta Alliance on Mental Illness and Mental Health. Dennis Anderson, a past chairman of the group and an Alberta cabinet minister until his retirement from politics in 1993, appreciated her will-ingness to speak in public on a subject that other celebrities had qualms about being associated with. "Without exception, she always brought a

lot of warmth to the gathering," he said. He thought her public statements also rounded off the hard-edged perceptions that had been left by
several years of tough government in the 1990s: "She gave Albertans and
people from other provinces the other dimensions of this province.... At
least she blunted the hard edge of the knife in a few of these issues."
Anderson said two ministers told him they had softened their plans to
cut budgets in certain areas after hearing the lieutenant-governor's
concerns. "I miss her. She had that kind of heart that I wish more people
had."

These connections with Albertans of all stripes returned to her in the
form of thousands of best wishes three years after her appointment. On
February 18, 2003, she read the speech from the throne in the legislature. The annual event had come to be characterized by her warm greetings and hugs for members of the legislature on her way to the Speaker's
chair, and by the tears she shed every time she spoke about Alberta on
these highly formal occasions. On February 20, her office released the
shocking news that she had been admitted to hospital after being diagnosed with peritoneal cancer. The cancer had been discovered during a
minor surgical procedure the previous day. She immediately began
aggressive chemotherapy and assured everyone that doctors had told her
the outlook was good. The warm expressions of support that followed
from many quarters went well beyond formality and general good wishes
for a public figure. David Hancock, then the justice minister, was quoted
offering a typical comment: "When my office was on the third floor...I'd
go past her office to mine and if there'd be a group of school kids there
and she'd be hugging each one of them I'd just get in line and get my
hug to pick up the day." Infrastructure Minister Ty Lund said, "We're
very much saddened by the news. She's doing just a tremendous job of
acting as lieutenant-governor. You hear people all over the province
talking about her." The sadness was doubled when her husband Ted
died a month later at age 76.

Hole wasn't out of action for long. By June she was back in the news
after speaking at a Queen's Golden Jubilee concert in Edmonton's
Winspear Centre. She told the audience of about 1,500, which happened
to include two government-side members of the legislature, that public
education was under increasing attack. "Personally," she said, "I believe
that the destruction of the public school system would be a catastrophe

beyond anything this country has ever experienced." The Alberta government had backed well off its budget cuts of the mid-1990s and its apparent interest in promoting alternatives to the public system. But Hole's comments pinched because the province had endured a bitter, widespread teachers' strike the year before. A "learning commission" had subsequently held public hearings on improvements to the system and had yet to report its recommendations. The strike and its aftermath constituted the largest political jolt since the Bill 11 controversy. The "catastrophe" comment sparked a flurry of news stories. Unlike the case after her comments on Bill 11, Hole took this short-lived controversy in stride. For one thing, she had been saying the same thing for some months; this time it happened to be noticed. She was also more sure now of what she was allowed and not allowed to do. Members of the government in turn seemed more used to her and to what they could expect her to be saying. "I was a little bit embarrassed being put on the spot...but I think what she was trying to get across was that the arts, education, and libraries are important, and we all agree with that," said Tony Vandermeer, an Edmonton MLA who had been in the Winspear audience. Premier Klein said he had no problems with her statement: "She has always been a political person.... She has always been concerned about public education, as we are, too."

Hole's thoughts now clarified and took on broader and more urgent forms of expression. The change had begun the year before and continued into 2003. She had sorted out what she could and could not do and say as lieutenant-governor. Her ideas took on more certain shape, as well. She continued speaking to a broad range of groups but returned more frequently to her defence of public education, literacy, libraries, and the arts. It was increasingly a message she felt was appropriate for any event. Now she more frequently added a call to act on poverty, both in Canada and around the world. She refined her message, changing the wording and adding quotations from people she admired. The speeches tended to become longer, too, more of them delivering a sweeping roundup of all her major concerns.

< *Swearing in new Canadians at the Alberta Legislature, July 1, 2004. Lois's battle with cancer was becoming more difficult. This was her last Canada Day appearance. [Hole Family Archives]*

Her term of office was due to expire in February 2005. That was early in Alberta's centennial year—the province was officially founded on September 1, 1905—and the government was keen to have an extraordinarily popular figure remain in her post to handle hundreds of centennial events through the year. She was equally keen to do the job and was happy when the government asked Prime Minister Paul Martin to extend her appointment. "If I had my druthers, she'll be there forever," Premier Klein said on the fourth anniversary of her becoming lieutenant-governor. Toward the end of February, Martin announced that her term of office would extend through 2005.

She continued her engagements through the summer of 2004 while staff began filling her appointment book for the following year. They expected she might attend as many as 700 events in 2005. That fall, however, she became increasingly tired. Her son Bill recalled a telling moment when she expressed fatigue for the first time that he could remember. She said one night that she didn't want to face another in what had become a long line of presentations of Queen's Jubilee medals. She entered hospital again on the evening of October 26, 2004, a few hours after speaking at the Lieutenant-Governor's Arts Awards. The return of her cancer meant she had to miss the last event for which she had a speech prepared—the official unveiling of a two-storey mural at the Boyle Street Co-op. Her theme was to have been "the importance of caring." The brief address celebrated the men and women at the co-op for compensating for some of the shortfalls and gaps in social programs. "As Canadians and as human beings," she was to have said, "one of our most sacred duties is to protect our neighbours."

Hole said she would return to her duties soon. An office spokesperson said, "This is not serious. There's no cause for alarm." Audiences who had seen her in the preceding weeks had seen a woman looking noticeably drawn and tired, however. It soon became clear that her health was deteriorating rapidly.

One of the events scheduled in the next few months was the official naming of the Lois Hole Hospital for Women. It was an expansion of the Royal Alexandra Hospital in central Edmonton. Hospital officials, acting on the recommendations of her doctors, moved the schedule up. She managed to leave her bed briefly on a chilly November 16 for what was to be her last public event. Her final speech went through a number of drafts and discussions with her family before she settled on the message she wanted to leave with Albertans. She made it about "the power of hope." She expressed her pleasure that the hospital was not only a health resource for women but a symbol of commitment to public health care. She reiterated her belief in education, libraries, the arts, and a strong social safety net. A short passage had a valedictory ring: "I hope that Albertans associate my name with fond memories and good thoughts. I've always done my very best to make people feel comfortable, by giving away a hug or two—along with a couple of plants—and listening very carefully to what people have to say."

She still kept going. She knew that the University of Alberta had just selected a new president, Indira Samarasekera, and asked to meet her. Samarasekera flew out from Vancouver in the second week of December, unsure whether the visit was a good idea. "I was just very nervous," she recalled nearly two years later. "I knew she was very ill." She entered the hospital room accompanied by Pat Clements, the university's former dean of arts. Instead of a wasted figure lying on a pillow, Samarasekera found a woman who had put on makeup and was sitting up in bed, clearly making an effort for what she thought was an important event: "Her eyes were just sparkling." Instead of an awkward period of getting acquainted, there was instant communication. Hole confided that she thought the government commitment to education was not deep-rooted—"because they forget." She urged Samarasekera to keep that message before provincial legislators, and to make sure the university reached out to rural Alberta because doing so would be essential for public support. "I think she sensed how much of a champion she had been in the province.... She sensed she had to ensure there were other champions in the province to carry on what she had been doing."

As the hour-long conversation unfolded, Hole spoke about her surprise at having become chancellor of the university and lieutenant-governor of the province. Samarasekera began to understand what Hole had realized about those posts: "I think the thing she really understood was the importance of the individual, and what a contribution an individual can make.... I think she tried to pass the torch to many people, because she was such a presence and such a force." Hole commented at one point in the visit that Alberta had entered a time of great opportunity and that people must not miss it. Clements began to recite Brutus's speech to Cassius from Shakespeare's *Julius Caesar*: "There is a tide in the affairs of men, / Which taken at the flood, leads on to fortune...." Samarasekera and Hole joined in. "It was an extraordinary moment," the new university president recalled during her installation speech the following September. The two women wanted to go on but Hole was tiring. They agreed they should talk again later in December. By then, Hole was too weak for another meeting. Samarasekera would remember her as the university began building formal relationships with smaller institutions around rural Alberta in the next few years and as the government made advanced education a budget and policy priority.

Lois Hole died on January 6, 2005. A memorial service on January 18 drew thousands of people and an outpouring of the fond memories she had said she hoped people would have of her. CBC radio and all three Alberta television networks broadcast the service. The broadcasts were picked up and shown in many theatres, as well. Participants would comment later on the way the service had attracted government leaders and street people. Thousands of cards and letters arrived for her family. Thousands signed a condolence book. Flags were lowered to half-staff across the province.

Her memory now was tied to the women's hospital and to a legacy fund intended to provide books to Alberta libraries. But it spread far beyond and much more deeply. Alberta's post-secondary digital library, a school, a provincial park, a memorial garden, and scholarships were named for her. CBC television named her the greatest Albertan. Sandra Kereliuk went to work full-time for the family for six months to deal with the cards, letters, phone calls and thousands of tribute requests flooding in. Thousands began donating to the Lois Hole Care and Nurture Legacy Fund and to the Edmonton and Calgary Community Foundations. Groups requested permission to produce tributes ranging from a tree dedication at Trochu to the renaming of the YWCA Women of Distinction Award as the Lois Hole Award for Lifetime Achievement. More than $250,000 poured in within days of the memorial. Much of the money arrived in smaller donations rather than the typical handful of large ones—some organizations received help from the largest number of individual donors in their history. People would stop at the greenhouse and be unable to speak, overcome by tears.

Plaque at the Lois Hole Memorial Garden at the Alberta Legislature, 2006. [Hole Family Archives]

Seeds that Lois had planted began sprouting in less visible, highly personal places. Florence Miller in Westlock said she travelled to Newfoundland later in 2005 and saw a copy of one of Hole's gardening books while buying a plant: "We were down in Newfoundland last year and the lady down there in the nursery said that's her bible." Janice Croissant from the Medicine Hat book club said, "We donated a book to the local library when she passed away." The County of Camrose Farm Women group donated $500 worth of books to the Camrose library; Mildred Luz said strong applause broke out spontaneously when the donation was announced at the group's fall forum. Marjorie Bencz, executive director of the Edmonton food bank, where Hole had spoken twice, asked the family for permission to show a video that Hole had recorded on the subject of giving to the community. It was shown to food bank members in the spring of the year after she died. Bencz recalled, "There was this incredible collective sigh when she spoke. People really felt connected to her."

THESE SPEECHES ARE NOT TRANSCRIPTS OF RECORDINGS. They are from the written record accumulated by the lieutenant-governor's office while Lois Hole was serving in the post. Hole spent much time editing her speeches. However, she was known to stick closely to her scripts and improvise in the sections where she was free to tell familiar stories. Many of the stories were published in her book *I'll Never Marry a Farmer*. In her speeches they served not only as entertainment but as a way of letting her audience feel closer to her. Particularly in her first two years as lieutenant-governor, her speechwriter would insert a one-sentence note indicating where a talk could be interrupted and reminding her which story she might want to tell. The stories from *I'll Never Marry a Farmer* have been excerpted and included in the text in italics to provide the reader with a sense of the story and how it was relevant to the context. The Hole family has helped to reconstruct, where possible, stories that were not printed. Where we have not been able to find at least a version of the story, the notes have been left intact except where they were part of longer sections of text that were edited out.

More than 800 speeches are collected in the office archive. This book contains a representative sample but includes all her major speeches and covers all her major themes. Many brief speeches at routine events have been left out of this collection. Also left out are a number of longer and more important addresses that closely resemble the speeches included in this collection. Many of her speeches were similar to one another, especially when they addressed a favourite topic such as literacy and libraries. The aim here has been to present a full, representative sample without unnecessary duplication. However, a number of the selections focus on the same general subject. They are included to show the evolution of Lois's thinking and the way she explored familiar ideas with new language.

Most of the longer speeches contained the direction "Pause" at a number of points in the script. These have almost all been removed. A few remain as an indication of how speeches were constructed with an eye to dramatic presentation. A number of the speeches have been edited for length and to avoid duplication. An ellipsis (...) in the text always indicates that words have been removed. Where ellipses occurred in the original text, they have been converted to dashes. Most of the dashes in the text were dashes or hyphens in the original.

The short introductions to each speech are printed in italics. So are titles of books cited in the texts. All other words printed in italics appeared in italics in the original text, a device intended to remind Lois to emphasize those words as she was reading.

Thoughts or practices ascribed to her in any of the brief introductory comments were either supported by the evidence in the speeches or reported by her son, Bill Hole, or by Sandra Kereliuk, her private secretary in the lieutenant-governor's office.

In the April 2000 speech titled "A Night of Music," the original version of the speech referred to the "Faculty of Fine Arts." Fine Arts was a department within the University of Alberta's Faculty of Arts; the wording has been changed to reflect what seems to have been the original intent, a reference to the Faculty of Arts.

A handful of minor spelling mistakes have been corrected. A few commonly used words such as "endeavour" and "centre" tended to show up in the original texts as "endeavor" and "center." The spellings have been converted to the British form for consistency and in keeping with the advice in one of Lois's speeches to students that they should prefer the British forms of spelling and pronunciation to the American. Use of capital letters has also been standardized, with two exceptions: the texts of the speeches retain her preference for the forms "Lieutenant Governor" and "Monarchy." Where questions of grammar arose, the original text has been left intact.

The texts usually indicated where the speeches were made. Some place names have been added where locations are known. In uncertain cases, no place name appears at the start of the text.

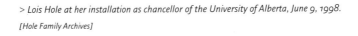

> *Lois Hole at her installation as chancellor of the University of Alberta, June 9, 1998.*

[Hole Family Archives]

Lois Hole
Speeches

Lois Hole and special friend Lou Hyndman at Lois's installation as chancellor of the University of Alberta, June 9, 1998. [Hole Family Archives]

1998

Lois Hole gave her first speech as lieutenant-governor of Alberta on February 10, 2000, the day she was installed in office. She had already made a significant public speech on her installation as chancellor of the University of Alberta on June 9, 1998. She put much effort into this inaugural address. Her family and associates thought it was one of her best, an address that summed up her personality, her outlook on life and public affairs, and her hopes for a young generation.

Chancellor of the University of Alberta

Inaugural Address of Lois E. Hole
University of Alberta, Edmonton
June 9, 1998

Introduction
EMINENT CHANCELLOR, Your Honour, Distinguished Platform Guests, Honourable Clint Dunford, Our Senate, Graduates, Families, and Friends: I must thank Chancellor Lou Hyndman once more for his very kind introduction. This distinguished gentleman has dedicated the last four years of his life to bringing dignity, enthusiasm, and excitement to the role of chancellor. The current fundraising campaign is but one example of how he has helped to raise the profile of the position and enhanced the reputation of the university. Lou, your leadership has shown how effective a chancellor can be in promoting our great university. Everybody, please join me in thanking Lou Hyndman for the tremendous contributions he has made to our university—the University of Alberta.

We are very honoured to have with us a number of distinguished chancellors emeriti, Dr. Jean Forest and Dr. Peter Savaryn. Each of these special people have made very important contributions to the strength and reputation of this fine university. I would also like to say, as I walked in, I saw Louis Desrochers here, and I know he's sitting in the back somewhere. I want to thank you, Louis, for coming. I just would like to say before we give these people a round of applause, I received a wonderful letter from Dr. Sandy Mactaggart, who was in Scotland, and who would have been here if it was possible. Please join me in a round of appreciation for their outstanding efforts.

To our acting board chair Lloyd Malin, I salute you for your wisdom and understanding, and especially for the patience and leadership you have shown during the past year.

I really look forward to working with you, Dr. Fraser; your efforts as president have greatly contributed to our university's status as one of the finest universities in the country and on the continent. Your energy and spirit are inspirational—it's going to be thrilling being a part of your team.

We also have with us a number of distinguished guests, the representatives of other educational institutions from across the province and the country. Thank you all so much for coming to participate in this ceremony. We are indeed honoured to have you here.

The graduates of the Faculté Saint-Jean are present at this convocation today. The Faculté is renowned as a centre of excellence in Canada and merits a special mention.

Finally, I wish to express my sincere gratitude to my nominators, the people who sent such wonderful letters of support and who made it possible for me to be here. Thanks also to our Senate for the confidence, the trust, and the faith they have placed in me as chancellor; and a sincere thanks to all the people who have sent cards and personally congratulated me on this prestigious appointment.

Graduates

CONGRATULATIONS TO ALL OF YOU—you made it. Every one of you has reason to be proud today. You've earned a degree from the University of Alberta in very challenging times. You've made sacrifices, struggled with dwindling financial resources and larger classrooms, dealt with the stress of wondering if you'd find a career after university, but here you are—many of you had to work at two jobs and eat a lot of ketchup and Kraft dinner to do it. You have each earned a University of Alberta degree, and no one can ever take that achievement away from you. I know I speak for everyone in this auditorium when I say that we believe in you. We believe that you *will* find success and happiness, and that in finding these things you will make the world a better place. Your hard work and perseverance has enriched not only yourselves, but everyone around you. That's what getting your degree is all about—by improving yourselves, you cannot help but improve the lives of others. I look forward to seeing the great things that you will accomplish in the coming years.[1]

I now have a story to tell you—I just couldn't miss this wonderful opportunity to tell you a story. It's to do with a graduate from the University of Alberta: our son. I just have to tell you that, as many of you know, we started out rather small. We built a greenhouse; and then another greenhouse; then a third one. By this time, the boys' dad said to me: "You know, Lois, we're not going to enlarge, we're not going to increase or do anything to expand, unless the boys decide to come into the business."

He was very good. He did not insist on them coming in with us. He said: "They will make up their own minds. If they want to come, that's just fine." In the meantime, our oldest son, Bill, who was in his last year at university, got a job working for Woodward's. His job was to make sure that the groceteria didn't run out of carts in the wintertime. Now I want all the ladies who are sitting here, and all the mothers, to realize that this is a mother talking. Keep that in mind, because I also want to tell you that while Bill was there they never ran out of carts. Anyway, Bill came home one day and said to his dad: "You know, Dad, I think I'd like to get a full-time job working for Woodwards. At university, they talked about marketing; they said all kinds of things that I think Woodwards should put into their business. They should be doing this and, you know, if they did that...." And then he went on, all excited with all these ideas he had about what Woodwards could do.

Eventually, Ted said to him: "Okay, Bill, if that's what you want, go right ahead." So the next day Bill went into Woodward's to see the manager, and he said to him: "I'd like to get a full-time job working for Woodward's."

Now remember, this is a mother talking. The manager looked up at Bill and said: "Gee, Bill, I'm sorry. We don't have any full-time jobs." Now I know what that man was thinking. When he looked at this wonderful, handsome, intelligent university graduate, he said to himself, "If I hire him, he'll have my job in a month."

So Bill came home and said: "Dad, they don't have any full-time jobs, so I've decided to come to the farm. What I want you to do, though, is get rid of those three greenhouses. Start a new complex. We'll start it up where we planted carrots before." And I have to say, Ted had always wanted to do this. This was something he always thought would be good—start a complex there, on that patch of carrots. Bill said: "We'll start small. We'll start with seven green-houses. Then, as we go along, we could add to the complex. Maybe we'll put in a nursery; maybe we'll put in a perennial area; we'll do this; we can do that.... Dad, there are so many things we could do, and I know they will work. We'll expand slowly, take our time, and do it right."

So I say to you, look where Woodward's is today. And then look where Holes is today.

I have a second story. I have actually three stories to tell you, and I'll tell them one right after the other because then I have a little bit more to tell you. It's all to do with education, so I thought it was kind of apropos for you.

I was invited to go to a school out in the country—it was actually in Bon Accord—where this teacher I knew phoned me. "Lois," she said, "would you come out and talk to the students in Grades Seven, Eight and Nine on Career Day?"

I said, "What did you want me to talk about? It's Career Day?"

"I want you to talk about your career," she replied.

I said, "What career were you thinking you wanted me to talk about?" Now this was a number of years ago, and she said, "Oh, well Lois, a career of market gardening, of course." I said, "Margaret, what kid in Grades Seven, Eight and Nine in their right mind would want a career in market gardening?"

"Oh Lois, don't worry," she said. "These are farm kids. Besides, there are going to be all kinds of people there. We're going to have a doctor, a nurse, a fireman, an RCMP, somebody from the symphony, two people from the university, a photographer...." She went on listing all these wonderful people who were going to come and talk about their career.

I said, "Margaret, with a line-up like that, these kids aren't going to come to hear me." She said, "Oh, yes they will, Lois. They have to."

So I went.

I'm walking down the hall. I haven't thought of what I can say to keep these children's interest.

And as I was walking, two little girls came along. They were walking, coming to the class that I was going to talk to, and one little girl says to the other little girl: "I have to make twenty more dollars for this special dress" that she was getting for some very special occasion. So I thought, "Oh, now I know what to talk about." So I went in and there was a little girl in Grade Seven who was shaking like a leaf because she had to introduce me. She said: "We are so pleased to have Mrs. 'Holey' here with us today."

I turned to the kids. "Hey, kids," I said. "Want to make some money this summer?" Every kid sat up. I said, "I'm going to tell you how to make some money. You're going to go home and you are going to ask your mother for half of her garden, and in that half a garden, you're going to plant peas, and you're going to plant those peas nice and thick. Then you're going to get up in the morning and you are going to pick those peas."

You'll notice I left an awful lot out between the planting and the picking, but I had their attention and I didn't want to lose it. Then I said: "And when you've got a nice, great big bag full of peas, you will ask your mother to drive you to the nearest big store and when you get there, you will ask the first person you see that works there to ask the produce manager to come out. And when they bring the produce manager out, you will say to the produce manager: "I have this bag of peas I'd like to sell to you." And he will reach over and feel them and know they're so fresh and wonderful.... He'll want them so badly that he'll say to you: "How much do you want for your peas?" And you will say: "TWENTY DOLLARS."

I thought the little girl was going to fall off her chair. Then I said to the kids: "You can sell peas anywhere. People, they just love peas. You can put them in little bags, and in big bags, and medium sized bags. you can take them to the City Market; go door-to-door." The kids got all excited and they were throwing out suggestions and ideas for how they are going to sell these peas. Just then, the bell rang. Now the bell signified that I had to go to the next class to talk to another Grade Seven, Eight and Nine class about careers. There was a little girl sitting in the front row and she put her hand up and she said: "Mrs. Hole, don't tell the other kids about the peas." As I walked out, three teachers followed me out asking me about growing peas.

The other little story that I want to tell you was another Career Day here in the city of Edmonton, when I was invited to go to and speak to Grade Five students. The teacher said to me: "Lois, you don't have to talk to them for very long. Make it quite simple. Talk about, maybe, watering in the greenhouse, or whatever you decide. Something the kids will probably enjoy." So I got there. And the kids looked so tired. They had been listening to people talking to them all day long. There had been the editor from the Journal, the mayor, some aldermen. Different people, all kinds of people, were there to talk to them and they look so tired. And I thought ,"Oh, they are not going to be able to pay any attention." I looked around in the room and just then I spotted two little boys I recognized as two little boys whose parents and grandparents were Italian. I thought, "Oh, isn't this interesting" because they had come out to our place. So I knew them. I certainly knew their grandparents very, very well. And then I looked around a little more and I realized, "My goodness, there are some East Indian children here...Lebanese...there are probably some German children, too...." And as I looked around, I saw some black children, some Oriental children, and I thought, "Oh, isn't this wonderful, all this tremendous mix of children!"

So I turned to the kids. "Hey kids," I said, "I want to tell you about something. "When we first started in the vegetable business out at our place, Italian people came out and they told us about zucchini and *broccoli; they told us how to cook it. It was wonderful!" I said, "And the East Indian people came about and they told us about how to grow hot peppers and how to use them in cooking." And I said, "And the German people came out and told us how to grow big cabbages and then how to make good sauerkraut. And," I said, "the Lebanese people told us about kusa, which is small vegetable marrow—and it's a wonderful dish!"*

And I happened to look down at that moment and there was a little Oriental boy sitting very close to me. I thought to myself, "Oh, this little boy's probably of Chinese descent." So I said, "And the Chinese people told us about stir fry and how wonderful it was." The little boy is not paying any attention. So I thought, "Oh, darn it, he's Japanese."

So I said "And the Japanese told us...." I went through what the Japanese told us about what to grow, how to grow it, and how to cook it.

The little boy looked up at me and put his hand up and said: "Mrs. Hole, what did the Koreans teach you?" After that all the kids started throw out, "Mrs. Hole, what did the Hungarians teach you?" "What did the Yugoslavians teach you?"

Now, by this time I'm clipping along and I can't think fast enough. So I said: "What did you have for supper last night?" They told me. I said, "And that's what they taught me!"

Building Bridges

AFTER I ENJOY MY TIME HERE ON THE STAGE, it's my intention to tackle one of the most important issues facing us today: the welfare of the students. We all know that it's getting more expensive to get a university education. I've often wondered how many Einsteins are toiling in far-off rice paddies or starving in the world's many ghettoes, their potential unrealized. I often wonder how far humanity could go if we made education our top priority. I wonder what the world would be like if, instead of building walls, we built bridges.

I've had the opportunity and the privilege to be in contact with people from all walks of life. With my many different contacts, I will try to foster understanding of the roles all groups—those who are active in the university community, and those who are not. Many do not see the benefits of having large numbers of university graduates in the population. We have to change that. It can be as simple as inviting people to one of the plays at the Timms Centre, or pointing out that important new medical research continues here at the U of A hospital. We are a leading-edge research and teaching university that is becoming more and more internationally recognized. We must show that what we do here is indispensable to the rest of the country and the world; and at the same time, we have to guard against becoming elitist. We have to stop being walls or towers; we must instead become bridges and pathways.

It's important to do this not just to increase understanding and appreciation; it's important because we'll only get financial support from the community if they realize how vital the university is. And that financial support will go a long way towards easing the burden on students.

Our philosophy at our greenhouse has always been to give back to the community; that's our bridge to the people. I know that's helped us to prosper; people recognize goodwill and will return it eagerly when given the chance. This is how relations between the university and the community should work. It's like the ecosystem; you need to replace what you take out of the ground, or you'll pay dearly in the long run.

With that in mind, I hope that after you've gone out and pursued your ambitions, you'll revisit this place. I hope you'll embrace the memories, recognizing that all kinds of experiences were necessary to make you the wonderful and unique person that you are. And I hope that you will endow your alma mater with the gift of your involvement once you're on your feet. Get involved with our fundraising and promotional efforts. We need you to speak well of us to your colleagues, your family, to anyone who shows interest, and even to those who do not. A vital and involved alumni is critical to the university's health.

Conclusion

I FORESEE A DAY when anyone with the ability and the desire can come to this university and earn a degree. I foresee a day when, because of this, Canada becomes a more just, a more caring, and a more prosperous society. I foresee a day when your children and grandchildren will look back upon you with admiration, because you built the bridges for them to cross.

In the words of Ralph Waldo Emerson:

To laugh often and much; to win the respect of intelligent people and the affection of children; to earn the appreciation of honest critics and endure the betrayal of false friends; to appreciate beauty, to find the best in others; to leave the world a bit better, whether by a happy child or a garden patch or a redeemed social condition; to know even one life has breathed easier because you have lived.

That is to have succeeded.

Lois in the greenhouse with
an enthusiastic young reader.
[Hole Family Archives]

2000

Lieutenant-Governor, February 2000—January 2005

Every Parent's Dream
Installation Speech of Lois E. Hole, C.M.
The Legislature, Edmonton

February 10, 2000

HONOURABLE PREMIER, Honourable Chief Justice, Honourable Speaker, Honourable Ministers and Members of the Legislative Assembly, Honourable Member of the Privy Council, Honourable Senators, Honourable Justice, Members of the Clergy, Members of the Consular Corps, Honourable Chief Judge, Deputy Mayor and Alderman, Members of the Aboriginal Community, Senior Government Officials, University Officials, Members of the Police and Military, distinguished guests, and my fellow Albertans.

I stand before you today with great joy and humility. To serve Alberta in this manner is an unexpected but very welcome delight and honour.

As a way of expressing my deepest appreciation and my commitment to this new role, I have a few things I'd like to say about my plans for this new undertaking.

But before I begin, I would like to thank the Honourable H.A. "Bud" Olson for his service to Alberta over the past three years.

Every parent's dream is a better life for his or her children. When Ted and I moved to St. Albert, I was thrilled because it was a French community. I thought that meant that our children would have a chance to learn a second language. But it wasn't long before I discovered that there was no French program in St. Albert.

I was disappointed, to say the least. But a vacancy came up on the Sturgeon school board. Ted urged me to take a shot at the job. "If you want change, Lois, why not run for that position?" Well, why not?

So, over thirty years ago this month, my friend Laura Henry and I packed a Thermos, a few cheese sandwiches, and set out in a shiny red half-ton to visit every home in the riding.

During the campaign, I was touched by the devotion parents showed for their children. It didn't matter which home I visited—as soon as I mentioned the position I was running for, the discussion was always lively. One family that invited me in to talk had an enormous old-fashioned farm kitchen with the biggest kitchen table that you've ever seen!

I was treated to homemade bread, homemade butter, and cream so thick you had to use a spoon to get it into your coffee. "Cut the bread thick," the mother told us, encouraging us to spread generous portions of jam, butter, and cream on top. The hospitality was wonderful, but it was no free lunch—it was obvious that if I were going to be a school trustee, I'd better be dedicated, because these parents wanted to be absolutely sure that their children's education would be a good one.

One young woman greeted me with a baby in her arms—one of seven young children in her family. Though there were two brand new tractors beside the house, there were no modern conveniences or creature comforts in this woman's home. She used a hand pump for water and a coal stove for heat.

All of the family resources were geared towards building a prosperous farm, a sacrifice the mother was more than willing to make for the sake of her children's future.

It was a common theme. None of the people I visited were any less than passionate about education. They knew that a well-educated, well-trained population was the best way to ensure happiness and fulfillment for everyone—especially for their children. The breadth and depth of those parents' conviction has inspired me to this day.

Well, I won the seat and wound up serving on that school board for over 30 years. Though we didn't get those French courses right away, they came eventually. And it turned out that the experience gave me far more than a chance to fight for any one program.

During my time as a school trustee and the U of A chancellor, I've become convinced that learning is the key to personal growth and happiness. That's why I support education and literacy at every level. Besides, it gives me a chance to read storybooks to a lot of adorable little babies, while encouraging their parents to do the same.

As Lieutenant Governor, I will do my best to lend what support I can to those who hope to realize their full potential. I want to let them know that there are educational opportunities for everyone. I hope to visit every community in Alberta, to encourage people from all walks of life to help themselves and their neighbours take advantage of the incredible opportunities that Alberta offers. I want to help make connections between Albertans from one end of the province to the other.

For the heart and soul of Alberta doesn't lay in the rich farmland, the majestic Rockies, the precious oilfields, the bustling cities.

As wondrous and important as these features may be, that heart resides in our people—each and every one of them, from the hard-working community leaders to those on the fringes of our society: the poor, the disenfranchised, the discouraged, the isolated, the different. We are all Albertans, and we are all both teachers and students, every day of our lives.

If I can help people to understand the enormous educational resource each citizen represents, if I can help the parents of today realize the dream of a better life for the children of tomorrow, I feel I will have done my job as Lieutenant Governor.

Thank you so very much for giving me this opportunity to serve the people of Alberta. I will do my best to justify the trust you have placed in me.

Lois had been lieutenant-governor for only two months when she began inserting politically charged comments into her speeches. The most pointed comments here were aimed at the Ontario government led by Premier Mike Harris. However, Harris was often associated with Alberta Premier Ralph Klein. Criticizing the Ontario government came close to criticizing the Alberta government, while leaving room for doubt about Her Honour's intentions. Criticism of the Ontario government appeared infrequently at later dates. The main point—the centrality of the arts to education and life—reappeared constantly throughout the next four years. At the time of this speech she was also still chancellor of the university. While the written speech refers to a degree in music, she had actually earned a certificate.

A Night of Music
University of Alberta
April 2000

GOOD EVENING, EVERYONE, and welcome to a very special night of music. What a pleasure it is to be surrounded by so many talented people—Dr. Pier, Dr. Cook, Concert Choir Director Debra Cairns, our wonderful conductor Malcolm Forsyth, and this magnificent orchestra. I note that the Madrigal Singers are here, too, with their director Leonard Ratzlaff. I'm looking forward to guest-conducting you this year. Don't worry, I'm taking some lessons, so I'll be ready for it! Thank you all so much for being here tonight.

Though I'm certainly not in the same league as any of the players gathered here tonight, I was fortunate enough to have a mother who encouraged me to play music. In a sense, I was a little spoiled; given the choice between having me practise piano or do chores, Mom always urged me to practise. So I did, and eventually I earned a degree in music from the Royal Conservatory. That's always been one of my proudest achievements. It thrills me to no end that my granddaughter Kate is pursuing the piano, too—I've sure had more luck teaching her than I had with my two sons!

Still, there's nothing quite like the musical education you get in a university environment. Unfortunately, there's a completely erroneous school of thought that contends that fine arts are an extra, a pleasant but nonessential component of life and education. Certain Ontario politicians even seem to think that funding should be diverted from Fine Arts programs to other, more "practical" faculties. Nothing could be further from the truth. Fine arts teach us how to think critically, with a keen eye for both the smallest details and the big picture. That's why I spearheaded a campaign of university chancellors from all over the country to protest this misguided Ontario government plan.

The arts enrich us all; they are not a frill, they are an absolute necessity. That's why it's my pleasure to support the Faculty of Arts and the Department of Music. Please join with me in congratulating our artists on the crucial work they do.

Many of her early speeches were short and avoided controversial subjects, although she never totally shied away from speaking her mind. She was still finding both her way and her voice.

Eating Disorder Education Organization Conference
April 28, 2000

GOOD EVENING, EVERYONE, and welcome to this very important conference of the Eating Disorder Education Organization. Given that eating disorders are a serious problem in our province and beyond, I think we are very fortunate to have so many leading educators gathered here for the weekend. Education, after all, is our best tool in the prevention and treatment of eating disorders.

Like most people, I have some experience with the importance of proper nutrition. I've always been a bear for the traditional three square meals a day—and plenty of vegetables are always on the family plates. Of course I'm no expert, but you don't have to be too observant to notice that proper eating habits make people much happier. Years ago, my niece came to work for us and she was irritable as all get-out—until I refused to allow her to start the day without something for breakfast.

Let me tell you how important regular eating habits have been to my family.

People often ask me how we can be in business as a family and still get along. After all, some families have a hard time getting through a holiday dinner without a fight.

I jokingly tell them that it's all thanks to me. If a father and sons are going to work together, they need to have the mother involved as well—to make sure they don't kill each other!

In fact, I think the answer can be found around my kitchen table. It's funny how something so basic can be so much more important than it seems. Over the years, that kitchen table has been our lifeline.

Every day at noon, we leave the office and greenhouse behind and head over to the house for lunch. We catch up with what everybody's doing, chat about the day's events, and subject one another to good-natured ribbing. Although our lunches occasionally include a bit of

yelling, and even a tear or two, you're much more likely to hear
laughter and friendly conversation.

Lunchtime also gives us a chance to settle our differences, because
problems aren't left to simmer day after day. They get worked out
right away, and when this happens over a pleasant meal, things rarely
get out of hand—even when the family is divided on an issue.

Early in my married life, I learned that if I wanted to raise a diffi-
cult topic with Ted, it helped to feed him first. To this day, I don't talk
to him seriously until he has something in his stomach. That rule
continues to serve me well with my entire family.

When Bill finished university, he had to make a choice about what
he wanted to do: join the family business or pursue something else.
Naturally, he brought up the difficult topic at the dinner table. He
would happily stay on the farm, he said, but only if we expanded our
operation significantly. While Ted agreed in principle, he was anxious
that Bill wanted to move too far, too fast. Tempers flared, and Ted
wound up stomping out of the kitchen.

The kitchen at lunchtime is also our informal boardroom, the one
place where everyone knows it's okay to express their opinions. They
also know they won't be distracted by customers, phone calls, and the
like. The table brings focus to anything that needs debating—or good
stories that need sharing.

With the number of strong personalities involved in our business,
the work day invariably generates some significant differences of opinion.
Just when the discussion threatens to become an out-and-out battle,
though, it's time for lunch. Everyone files into the house and eats as
though nothing had happened, at least for a few bites. When the prob-
lems of the day finally arise, they somehow seem much easier to sort
out. Everyone goes back to work with no grudges and no bad feelings.

We often draw other people into the circle as well. One of our
suppliers might make a delivery just before lunchtime, or somebody
from out of town might be inspecting our trial garden. Dave Grice, a
long-time employee and friend, eats with us regularly. When you
bring people to your table and feed them good food, you build a bond.

So that's my secret to ensuring harmony. In any business, and a family business in particular, communication is absolutely crucial. And if good food is involved, so much the better.[2]

Unfortunately, there's so much pressure in our society today to fit unrealistic expectations of beauty and body shape that the nutrition picture becomes distorted. My own granddaughter has experienced this. My daughter-in-law Valerie usually packs Kate a large, well-balanced lunch. But one day Kate was teased by a classmate about her eating habits—she was told that she'd get fat if she kept eating so much. Well, Kate is certainly not fat—she's actually quite an athlete. But the psychological impact was so great that Kate was throwing her lunch in the garbage for a week before Valerie caught on. It took quite a bit of convincing before Kate could get back to her regular lunch routine.

This is just one example of the kinds of pressures that people of all ages face; it's no wonder that eating disorders are such a widespread problem.

Thank goodness for conferences like this, where experts in the field can share their experiences and strategies for dealing with this important health issue. And what more appropriate time to reflect and discuss the problem than with a good meal?

Town of Gibbons Volunteer Awards Event

April 29, 2000

GOOD EVENING, EVERYONE. It's my pleasure to join you in recognizing the wonderful volunteer efforts of the citizens of Gibbons.

Volunteers keep the heart of the community beating—especially rural communities. Without volunteers, many farming communities like this one would lack those essential places of gathering like churches, barns, hockey and curling rinks, town halls, and parks. Something about the rural spirit recognizes that volunteering means a better life for everyone, and there's a good deal of satisfaction to be had in lending a hand in community endeavours.

The people we honour tonight are fine examples of the spirit of rural volunteerism, dedicating their brains, brawn, and time to helping their neighbours.

Like the rest of you, my life has been enriched thanks to the efforts of volunteers. Just off the top of my head, I recall that my granddaughter Kate was able to participate in a school basketball free-throw tournament because there were plenty of volunteers to keep score. A simple job, but without people willing to commit to the task, there would have been no tournament.

Of course, volunteers often dedicate themselves to far weightier efforts. They comfort the elderly in hospitals and rest homes, they build playgrounds for our children, they distribute food and medicine to those suffering the terrible poverty of the Third World—there's an endless list of noble causes, and we mustn't allow ourselves to become jaded or complacent by the success of our volunteer efforts. For every person like the honourees we pay tribute to tonight, there are countless others who would doubtless love to help, but don't know how. Making volunteer opportunities available to potential helpers is a crucial task of any community.

Fortunately, I think the town of Gibbons has done an excellent job of encouraging citizens to pitch in, and I hope that other communities will take your example to heart.

Volunteer of the Decade
Spring 2000

MY DEAR FRIENDS, I can't tell you how honoured I am to be named as Volunteer of the Decade. St. Albert has been very good to me, and it's been my pleasure to try to give something back to the city. But I hope that this recognition will not obscure the fact that St. Albert has had hundreds of equally deserving volunteers, people who have devoted so much time and energy to making this a better place to live for everyone.

Volunteerism is vital to the health of any community, but it can't exist unless the connections are made between willing and able potential volunteers and community needs. I think that St. Albert has done an excellent job of making these connections, but there is always room for improvement, especially as our population ages. There are hundreds of seniors in this city alone who I'm sure would love to devote their priceless accumulated wisdom to worthwhile projects. I'm reminded of my dear friend Mrs. Durocher, a woman who had little formal education but overflowed with decades of hands-on experience. When I think about how little of her wisdom I wrote down for posterity, it nearly makes me cry. We can't afford to waste such precious resources.

Perhaps that's not a bad idea for a volunteer project; we could get some young folks with spare time on their hands to spend some time recording that irreplaceable information.

But young or old, volunteers keep the heart of the city beating. I accept this award not so much for myself, but for everyone who takes a little time to pitch in and do something good for their neighbours. Whether you volunteer five minutes a week or fifty hours, the gesture is eminently worthwhile.

Thank you once again for this wonderful honour. It means a lot to me.

The earlier speech defending the place of the arts was soon expanded. Later it would be expanded still further as Lois settled into her new post and became more convinced she was approaching these issues in an appropriate manner.

Alberta College of Art & Design Convocation
May 3, 2000

STUDENTS OF THE ALBERTA COLLEGE OF ART AND DESIGN, faculty, staff, and board members. First of all, allow me to thank you for inviting me to your convocation. I have a bit of a soft spot for artists, so being here, surrounded by so many talented young people, is a genuine pleasure for me.

For the students of the Alberta College of Art and Design, who will be convocating this afternoon, today marks both an end and a beginning. It marks the end of four years of hard work, four intense years during which, with the help and instruction of your faculty, you have refined and developed that most precious of skills—your creativity and imagination.

But today also marks a new beginning. Because from now on we will all begin to benefit from the role that you will play as artists and designers, and the contributions that you will make with your imaginations, your creativity, and your finely honed skills.

And that is what I want to talk about today—those incalculable benefits which the skills of imagination, creativity, and vision, which we call the creative arts, bring to our daily lives, to our society, and to our understanding of ourselves as human beings and the world in which we live.

It is often said that the arts are good for us, that we cannot do without them, as though the arts were some medicine to be taken at the onset of a headache or to soothe a sore throat. But I think this is the wrong way to look at the arts. The arts are not some pill one takes to ward off the onset of an infection. Nor should we look at our support of the arts as some kind of duty, something we do simply because civilized societies should. The arts are more than this.

To see a great painting, to listen to a wonderful piece of music, or watch a profound play is an exhilarating experience. But why? Why do people all over the world flock to museums, to galleries, to theatres, to concerts?

Because every piece of visual art, every musical score, every well-written text, every well-wrought realization of a brilliant design is a celebration of our humanity. Even in this most practical, utilitarian era, where "efficiency" is the buzzword of the day, we need the arts to celebrate and experience our humanity.

Our creative intelligence, and our capacity to use that intelligence, is what defines us as human beings. It is this that allows us to imagine the impossible—and, having once imagined it, to bring it into the full flower of being. The power of imagination makes our reality one that we can mould and shape for the betterment of humanity. It releases us from the tyranny of poverty and boredom. Creativity is nothing less than our most important instrument of human progress.

When we use our creativity, we are building our future; but creativity does not emerge from a vacuum. It comes from our experience. To create something meaningful, we must observe and understand our present and our past. Examining our current and former reality in anticipation of building the future is how creative intelligence becomes an instrument of insight into our origins, our current behaviour, and a thousand possible destinies.

Unfortunately, recognizing the value of the creative act has become one of the great challenges of our modern society. Today, technology, efficiency, the bottom line, and precise measurements have become the panaceas for our problems.

Let me make it clear that I believe in science as a great positive force for humanity. It is central to our progress and our ability to eventually build a prosperous society that includes everyone on Earth. I couldn't have gardened for so many years without recognizing how vital science is to growing lush and vibrant plants.

But science cannot do it alone. Measuring a thing, defining it with numbers, is not the same as truly understanding a thing. If we are to build a better future, the people gathered in this hall are the ones we need—the visionaries with the creative imaginations that can truly grasp the complexities of human beings and our communities.

Recently the Ontario government has indicated that perhaps government spending should be diverted from the liberal arts to the more "practical" sciences and trades. I strongly disagree with this position, and hope that the notion can be derailed.

Thankfully, there is some hope that others do indeed recognize the importance of the arts. Not long ago, a report from some of this country's top business leaders indicated that more funds were needed to support the liberal arts. The new digital economies, they said, could not be built by technology grads alone. They argued that there is an equal need for broadly educated, culturally literate decision makers who think creatively, reason well, and can write. A liberal arts and science education nurtures skills and talents increasingly valued by modern corporations, according to these business leaders.

My own son often speaks on business issues, and one of the things he tells his peers is that every business should hire two vital people: a writer and a designer. The need to communicate the message of a business is crucial to its success, and every business needs someone with the training and talent to handle the job. As you all know, art and design is about just that: communicating ideas. Businesses are finally recognizing that photographers, sculptors, graphic designers, painters, and all the other artists have an important role to play in their success.

As encouraging as this support from business leaders is, we should keep in mind that the arts aren't just about fostering a healthier economy. Imagine your favourite cities. When people visit Paris, London, New York, Toronto, Moscow, Montreal, New Delhi, Tokyo, Edmonton, or Calgary, they aren't coming for low taxes or roads without potholes. People visit the world's great cities for the depth and breadth of their arts and culture, their history, their storehouses of human knowledge—in other words, they come to experience the soul of the city.

That's why all of you are so important. The contributions that you will make in the years to come will make our cities and our world worth living in.

I want to thank you for your years of effort in coming to this point. The contributions you make will add significance and value to our lives, and I know that all of you are going to make a positive difference in the years to come.

Stay true to your visions and have fun designing the future.

Lois often used family stories to illustrate whatever point she was making and make her speeches more entertaining. This speech was a good example. She also referred here to "year after year of drastic cuts to social programs." Later speeches made the point without the bold and direct reference to provincial government policy.

Alberta Knights of Columbus Ladies Luncheon
May 20, 2000

GOOD AFTERNOON, EVERYONE. It's a special pleasure for me to be with you here today, celebrating this state convention and over 100 years of charitable work by the Knights of Columbus.

What impresses me about the work of the Knights and other Catholic social services is that their goodwill is expressed in so many different ways, and that they are all too willing to help those in need, no matter what their religious persuasion. Charity that extends beyond the boundaries of religious difference is, to me, the highest expression of true virtue, and the Knights have much to be proud of in this regard.

I am particularly grateful to the Knights of Columbus for their steadfast support of women's shelters. Ensuring that women in need have a safe place to stay has been a personal concern of mine for many years, and the presence of the Knights puts my mind a little more at ease in this regard.

Mrs. Durocher, my dear friend and co-worker, gave me my first strong connection with the native community and my first insights into the difficulties native and Métis people face every day. Every time I saw other people dismiss her, it saddened me to think how much they were missing. Once I got to know Mrs. Durocher, I learned to look at all people more carefully.

When Ted and I first started farming, we truly depended on members of the native community to help us. Unfortunately, we quickly discovered that the problems of alcohol and conflicting cultural values meant we couldn't plan on having their help every day.

Mrs. Durocher's nephew, Peter, was one of the hardest working employees we ever hired. He wasn't always available for work, but Ted made it clear that he was welcome to show up whenever he could, no questions asked.

Peter was a handsome young man, lean and athletic, with a neatly groomed moustache. He was strong, but also shared much of his aunt's grace and agility. I remember when the barn was being shingled, he would slip some nails between his lips and criss-cross the roof like an acrobat, hammering away. The others would struggle to keep up, pausing now and then to watch Peter in amazement. He was quick with a joke and got along well with everybody. Ted often said he breathed a little easier whenever Peter was on the farm.

Then suddenly, one day, Peter was gone. They found him alone in a hotel room, where he had choked to death. He wasn't yet 30.

When you read items like this in the paper, stop and think for a minute. When that person was born, he or she should have the same human potential as your own child. But somewhere, somehow, things went terribly, tragically wrong. I believe very strongly in personal accountability, but it would be foolish and unfair to discount society's role in deaths like these.

I wish I had the answers, but I don't. I try, in my own way, to accept people for what they are and help wherever I can. I just know that we can't afford to simply throw our hands in the air and lament that there's nothing we can do.

Every time our world loses a Peter Durocher, it loses a lot. [3]

My own granddaughter, Kate, participates in the Knights of Columbus basketball programs, and I can personally attest to how her life has been enriched by her participation. My son Bill has gotten involved by coaching Kate's team, and I think he's having almost as much fun as she is.

But I don't think the Knights of Columbus could have been as effective as they have been without the people gathered in this room— the wives who have offered their unwavering support to their Knights. My own secretary, Astrid Casavant, just happens to be here, since her husband is one of the Knights attending this convention. Astrid has been so vital to my work as Lieutenant Governor that I have an excellent idea of how much her husband and his charitable work must benefit from her support. The goodwill crusade of the Knights of Columbus is your crusade as well, and on behalf of all Albertans who have benefited from your work, I thank you.

As vital as the role of the Knights of Columbus is, it is my fervent hope that in the coming years governments will realize that charitable organizations like yours are becoming increasingly burdened by the social disruptions caused by year after year of drastic cuts to social programs. In keeping with their good natures, charitable organizations rarely express complaints about the situation. But I think it is every Canadian's responsibility to express how important it is that our taxes be used to support the citizens who need it. Health care, victim services, welfare, employment insurance, developmental assistance to Canada's poorer regions—these, I believe, are all part of our social responsibilities as Canadians. It is unfair to ask the Knights of Columbus to rescue governments from their consciences. We must return to a more equitable division of labour between government and charities; only in this way will we have a chance of ensuring a better quality of life for all. The Knights of Columbus can do the most good if a compassionate citizenry and government stands with them.

In closing, please accept my good wishes for a successful convention and a joyous Jubilee year. Congratulations once again for your dedication to making Alberta a better place to live for all.

A speech at Premier Ralph Klein's prayer breakfast saw a departure from tradition. Lois would not cross certain lines she drew for her own behaviour. It was usual for the lieutenant-governor to say a prayer at this annual event. Lois preferred to let two stories from her own experiences deliver the message she wanted to convey. She also rewrote the entire speech. A staffer had written a much more overtly religious version that Lois told her family she could not deliver. People called the office with accolades later, leaving the staff person who had written the original quite pleased, and blissfully unaware that the lieutenant-governor had delivered an entirely different version of the speech. Note the reference to Tommy Douglas and Mary Robinson—two personal heroes whose names were cited often over the years. In this address and others, she inserted stories from I'll Never Marry a Farmer. *The written text originally had only page numbers to remind her of which stories to tell. Here and in other speeches, the story as it appeared in print is reproduced in italics.*

Klein Prayer Breakfast
Spring 2000

THERE IS NO QUESTION THAT LEADERS ARE VITAL in our civilization. But there's more than one kind of leader. Some provide guidance in a very visible way; they lead from the front, as the old expression goes. We require leaders like this; they can provide much-needed hope and inspiration. Personally, I've always taken great comfort in knowing that people like Tommy Douglas, the father of medicare, Mary Robinson, Irish president and human rights advocate, and other high-profile leaders were giving their all to the cause of a better society.

But equally important are those less famous heroes—the ones that never make the papers. I'm talking about the volunteers, the supportive husbands and wives, friends and relatives, even the Good Samaritans who spend all too brief interludes in our lives.

All my life, I've been surrounded by these quiet leaders—as I'm sure you have, too. I'd like to share with you a couple of stories about the leaders who gave me vital guidance over the years.

People sometimes marvel at my busy schedule and ask me how I find the energy to manage it. I don't think I'm some kind of Superwoman. I pretty much take things as they come and deal with them one at a time. If life starts to get a little crazy, there's no reason to go crazy along with it. Stay calm, keep moving, and you'll always find a way to work things through.

My mother-in-law was a much busier woman than I'll ever be, and I never heard her complain, not once. Grandma Hole knew what it was to work. In an era when child-rearing was largely the job of the mother, she raised nine children—seven boys and two girls—and she was there for each of them. And this was a woman who didn't even have a washing machine until after her fifth child was born!

She always found a way to make every minute of her day count. If a friend dropped by for coffee, Grandma Hole always had her mending bag handy, so she could darn socks while she chatted.

Likewise, she never wasted a single speck of food. She fed nine children on a very limited budget. But nobody cooked a better meal. Nothing fancy, but always very tasty. She prepared the big meal at noon, and in the evening it was always a salad, some cold meat, some nice bread, and lots of tea. She was great at making bread pudding and other puddings with sauces. Those puddings taught me that there's something to be said for English cuisine after all!

From today's perspective, Grandma Hole's life might seem overly traditional and confining. I know she never felt that way, though. She took great pride in running a comfortable, supportive, efficient household. Although she was never involved in her husband's plumbing business, they both recognized the indirect role she played in its success. If she hadn't been able to handle things so well at home, that business wouldn't have stood much of a chance.

She also saw her own success reflected in the lives of her children. She was determined that all of her children would be educated— including her daughters, an attitude not shared by everyone in those days. If she found one of her girls doing housework, she would say, "Don't bother with that. I can do the housework, but I can't do your studying for you."

As a result, all nine of her children graduated from the University of Alberta. At the time, this was an astonishing achievement. The Edmonton Journal published the story, complete with a picture, and that clipping remained a treasured keepsake for the rest of her life.

If I do one thing differently from Grandma Hole, it's that I try to take time to truly relax. I remember her telling me once, "I always felt guilty if I was reading a book, because I thought I should be doing something more productive." If she was reading when her husband came home, she quickly put the book away and got busy doing something else. When she got older and could afford to relax a little, she realized she really didn't know how.

Just the same, she has always remained an inspiration to me. She taught me that by caring for others, and helping them succeed, you can create a truly successful and fulfilling life for yourself. Anytime I feel I'm under too much pressure, or have too much to do, I take a deep breath and ask myself, "How would Grandma Hole have dealt with this?"

Thanks, Grandma Hole.[4]

ক

People often tell me they're amazed by my gardening expertise. Well, it's true I'm a pretty good gardener, but much of my knowledge comes from the advice I have gathered from others. I've had many great teachers, and one of them will always hold a special place in my memory—not just for the knowledge she passed on, but for the inspiration I took from her courage and determination.

Mrs. Durocher was a Métis woman who often worked for the Gervais family, potato farmers who lived on the farm next to us. Mrs. Gervais knew I needed help with my vegetable garden, so she introduced me to Mrs. Durocher. Little did I know the impact this extraordinary woman would have on my family.

The first day she came out to our place, I was struck both by her wisdom and by her generosity of spirit. That week, cucumbers were just starting to appear on our vines. She told me that if I picked them right away, the vines would go on to produce a much heavier crop. I was a little leery of the suggestion, but decided to give it a try. Well, those plants just exploded. I had never seen so many cucumbers.

When I give that tip at gardening talks, people think I'm a genius. But it was Mrs. Durocher who taught me.

During long summer afternoons, as we worked side by side, Mrs. Durocher would tell me about the plants that grew in the area and the many uses she had for them. If you made a tea out of one plant, it would help you get over a cold. You could apply the leaves of another directly to cuts or blisters to help them heal properly. She even knew of a plant that she claimed could prevent baldness!

With the depth of her knowledge, she wasn't always ready to accept the word of "experts." When she gave birth to her first child, the doctors told her that the baby was weak and frail, and might not survive. They said there was nothing they could do. So Mrs. Durocher decided to see what she could do to help her new-born son.

Mrs. Durocher was determined to save him. She filled dozens of discarded bottles with hot water and wrapped the child in blankets, creating an incubator. That heat, warm milk, and love were all she needed to save the child.

Because we thought so highly of Mrs. Durocher, it sometimes came as a shock that she didn't think very highly of herself. I remember how excited she was when she gave birth to a son with light-coloured hair—she was thrilled that his hair wasn't pure black.

Once, Ted asked Mrs. Durocher if he could take her picture. She had the most striking, unforgettable face, Her olive skin seemed smooth, even though it was deeply lined, and her eyes radiated wisdom and character. Ted wanted to capture the image of this important part of our lives forever, and Mrs. Durocher was delighted to be asked.

When Ted visited her with the camera the next day, he discovered, to his dismay, that she had coated her long, white hair with shoe polish, trying to look young for the photo. This story always makes me sad. If only she would believe that we loved who she was and how she looked.

She truly touched the lives of everyone she came in contact with. Our greenhouse manager, Dave Grice, remembers Mrs. Durocher fondly. He started at the farm as a teenager back in the early '70s and often worked in the fields alongside her. He recalls how graceful and quiet her movements were, as if she were walking on air. Although Mrs. Durocher was 65 or 70 years old at the time, she never had a problem keeping up with the rest of the workers.

When Dave talks about Mrs. Ducocher working in the field, I remember how thorough she was. She had a sixth sense about weeds and seemed never to miss a single one.

Mrs. Durocher died a few years later, and we've missed her ever since. Along with her wise, gentle presence and her unfailing good company, we also lost the opportunity to preserve her wisdom. She tended to mix her English with Cree, and I couldn't always understand her. If only I had taken the time to get somebody who could translate, to help me get it all down on paper. All that knowledge died with her. She had many children, but as far as I know, they had never taken an interest in her "old ways."

"You know," Dave told me recently, "I'm amazed at how often the image of Mrs. Durocher comes to my mind. She knew the soil like no one else I've ever known."

In this helter-skelter, technological age, people are desperate to get back to the soil. Gardening continues to boom and every supermarket has a corner devoted to organic fruits and vegetables. Even in the local pharmacy, you can find a wide range of herbal remedies squeezed in among the aspirins and toothpaste.

Mrs. Durocher would have been delighted by all this interest in nature and natural ways. It's such a shame that, in her day, her wisdom wasn't fully appreciated, not even by her.

I like to think that, if she were alive today, Mrs. Durocher's life would be very different. She would be a respected elder in the community and would feel free to take pride in her native ancestry.

After all these years, perhaps the world is finally starting to catch up with her way of thinking. I learned so much from Mrs. Durocher—and not just about gardening. [5]

Some of the most important leaders will forever remain invisible to history, but their legacy will exert a powerful influence on human affairs.

The reference to music lessons speaks to one of Lois's great enthusiasms; she made similar remarks two days later at a University of Lethbridge convocation.

Alberta College Convocation
May 25, 2000

GOOD EVENING, EVERYONE. It is my pleasure to be here tonight to congratulate you all on your tremendous achievements. Congratulations to the students, for successfully completing a challenging program; to the parents, for their unwavering support and love; to the teachers, for their care and commitment to their students; and to the president and the board of directors for their tireless work in preserving this fine institution. You all have much to be proud of.

You know, I took music lessons at Alberta College when I was a girl. It was one of the most satisfying times in my life....

That quality remains undiminished today. Older than even the province itself, the college has a long, rich history to build upon, and its guardians have instituted many improvements over the past few years, making connections with the Edmonton arts community, the downtown core, and other academic institutions. Many of the courses offered here are now transferable to the University of Alberta, making it much easier for students to pursue their education should they desire.

The fact that the first graduates of the new post-secondary career programs are receiving their diplomas today is a sign that Alberta College is continuing to expand its vital role in the academic health of the community. The high academic standards set here and its promotion of the Fine Arts make Alberta College a precious institution that I hope will enjoy a long and fulfilling life in the city.

I would also like to commend all of you on the diversity I see before me. I know that many of you have overcome significant obstacles in your pursuit of learning, but you have risen to the challenge with grace and style. When people of widely varying cultural and economic backgrounds can work and study together as you have, it gives me hope that one day such harmony will be commonplace all over the world. It doesn't really surprise me that Alberta College is a safe harbour for

Lois playing the piano in her home. She earned her Grade 10 piano certificate from the Royal Conservatory of Music. [Hole Family Archives]

diversity; the fine arts and humanities programs offered here foster such compassion and understanding of our common humanity.

Which is not to say that scientific pursuits can't also encourage such feelings. I understand that Cintia Lao, our Governor General's Medal winner, is a whiz at math and science and that she is excelling in English, too. I know that others are going to address Cintia's accomplishments, but I wanted to offer my personal congratulations.

Once again, congratulations to all of the students gathered here on the completion of your various programs. You've all done a fantastic job and I know that you will find success as you move on to the workforce or further studies. Best of luck to you all!

Lois often explained to her American friends what the monarchy meant to Canada. This speech was an example of how she went about that task.

United Empire Loyalists Certificate Presentation
May 29, 2000

GOOD EVENING, EVERYONE. Thank you very much for inviting me to this very important occasion and wonderful dinner. Congratulations to the new inductees, who through their stories have shown that the principles, sacrifices and struggles of their ancestors have not been forgotten.

By their very existence, these inductees serve to remind all Canadians of the importance of keeping history alive in our hearts and minds. Some might suggest that after 200 years, the United Empire Loyalist cause has become a mere historical footnote, not worthy of remembrance. But that will never be the case. No matter how you feel about the American Revolution and the British Empire, the important thing is that history must be preserved. It would be a disservice to humanity if we forgot that not all of the settlers in the 13 colonies were in favour of rebellion. There was dissent, and recognition of the right to dissent is one of the cornerstones of true freedom. The choice to remain loyal to the British crown in the face of overwhelming revolutionary sentiment is a shining example of integrity and steadfastness. I imagine that many Americans of the day respected the choice, even if they didn't agree with it.

To ensure these important historical events are not forgotten is a noble pursuit, and you are to be commended for your efforts. Let us hope that your work will continue, so that the memory of the integrity of the original United Empire Loyalists will be preserved for future generations. The children of tomorrow will need such examples of virtue.

This was her first speech to an aboriginal group; it is also one of the first times that Virginie Durocher appears in a speech, but far from the last. Lois often spoke about the Métis and First Nations. Her family believed she took that on as a challenge because an old Métis friend had denied her heritage. Lois could not understand why and thought her friend should have been proud of her Métis past.

Kihew Asiniy Education Centre
Saddle Lake
June 28, 2000

GRADUATES, teachers, staff, parents, elders, chiefs, and guests—welcome to this very special occasion. Today we honour the young men and women of Saddle Lake, who have worked with steadfast dedication to complete their high school studies.

Graduates, I am especially glad to be here today because to me you represent the possibility of a brighter future for Alberta. I say that because you have learned much about the complexities of the modern world while maintaining the rich cultural traditions of the Cree nation. That's a powerful combination, one that can enrich yourselves, the community of Saddle Lake, and the province as a whole. This isn't the end of your education—you will continue to learn and grow as the years pass—but from this moment on, you will also be teachers, though much of the time you may not even know it.

I'd like to tell you a story about a dear friend of mine named Virginie Durocher. Mrs. Durocher was a Métis, half French, half Cree, who worked with me on the family farm for many years.

If you were to ask me the one time I was angriest at my husband, I wouldn't have to think for a second. I have never, ever been more furious at Ted than I was the day he ploughed under an entire patch of beets.

When I say it that way, it sounds ridiculous. Who would get so upset over a few beets? Well, let me tell you, to this day I can't even think about it without getting a little bit hot under the collar. Vegetable farming was such a struggle that to plough under any vegetables struck me as a horrible act.

To be fair, I have to say that they were pretty pathetic beets. It had been a dry summer, and they hadn't received nearly enough water or attention. Unless you looked closely, it was difficult even to spot the beet greens among the weeds.

Still, they were the only beets we had. I knew that in a few weeks people would start asking for beets, and it would be nice to have at least something to offer them. So one morning, I asked Mrs. Durocher to weed the beet patch. I watched her work for a few minutes, moving through the rows slowly and meticulously as only she could, and knew the crop could be salvaged. I headed off to a School Board meeting feeling greatly relieved.

When I returned, around suppertime, I went up to see how Mrs. Durocher had managed. I stood at the edge of the field, my mouth agape. The entire patch was demolished. There was nothing there but freshly turned soil.

Apparently, Ted had also noticed how badly the beets were doing. Without asking me, he had decided they were more trouble than they were worth and went out to plough them under. When he got to the field, he hadn't even noticed that the beets were newly weeded. He just went ahead and destroyed the crop.

I was livid. What on earth would I say to Mrs. Durocher when she arrived for work the next morning? All that effort wasted without a moment's thought! I suspected her feelings would be hurt, yet she never said a word. She must have trusted that we had a good reason for changing our minds.

Of course, we didn't.

Ted should have consulted me before making that kind of decision. After all, I was the one who dealt with the customers, and I was the one who would have to spend the rest of the summer apologizing because we didn't have any beets.

That evening, we had friends over for supper and the atmosphere was less than convivial. Much later, they told me, "Lois, we had no idea you could be as angry as you were that night."

Of course, our relationship was solid enough to withstand the bitter experience. It made me understand, though, how marriages sometimes break up over the most trivial things.

It also reinforced, for both of us, the importance of communication and trust, because these problems would always happen. We couldn't afford to assume that we each knew what the other was thinking and we needed to know that we could get past our problems.

And finally, it taught me that other people could be much more forgiving than I.[6]

MRS. DUROCHER was able to teach me many valuable lessons about farming and life, with no education other than her own hard-won experience. Just imagine the things you can teach others, with your high school education and your Cree traditions.

When you leave today, you will carry my hopes with you. I hope that you will all have the opportunity to enrich your fellow Albertans and other Canadians with your unique talents and experiences. I hope that you'll share your wisdom with others, like Mrs. Durocher shared her wisdom with me. And finally, I hope that each of you finds a bountiful harvest of success and happiness. Like the eagle, you will soar, because you carry in your hearts both knowledge and valour.

Thank you for inviting me, and best wishes.

Her first Canada Day speech notably reminded the audience of the country's social safety net.

Canada Day Celebrations
Legislative Grounds
July 1, 2000

GREETINGS, EVERYONE, and welcome to these Canada Day celebrations.

During the last few weeks, my new role as Lieutenant Governor has resulted in my meeting a number of foreign dignitaries from all over the world. Each and every one of them has made a point of commenting how wonderful they think Canada is—from its natural beauty to its stable government and healthy economy.

Of course, they all visited during the spring and summer—I think the reactions might change a little when I'm entertaining people in January and February.

I'm grateful to these visitors because they remind me how much I love being Canadian. There's nothing like an outside perspective to help you realize how incredibly fortunate you really are.

Just a few days ago, the United Nations once again ranked Canada at the very top of their Human Development Index. Our very high literacy rate and long life spans, part of the criteria used by the UN to rank nations on the Index, are testament to the success of our educational and healthcare programs—and a reminder, I think, that we should never stop working to ensure that these programs remain properly funded and accessible to all.

Canadians' commitment to the common good, as expressed by our social safety net, is one of the reasons I'm very proud to be a citizen of this country. I think we have managed to strike a unique balance between the importance of individual rights and the needs of the community. We respect individual expression of artistic and political views, while pulling together to create a better life for everyone.

The other reason I'm proud to be Canadian is our growing acceptance of and delight in a multitude of cultures. Immigrants made this country great, and they will continue to do so in the 21st century. It's been my privilege to work with and befriend people from many cultures, and I wouldn't give up any of those experiences for anything in the world.

People often tell me they're amazed by my gardening expertise. Well, it's true I'm a pretty good gardener, but much of my knowledge comes from the advice I have gathered from others. I've had many great teachers, and one of them will always hold a special place in my memory—not just for the knowledge she passed on, but for the inspiration I took from her courage and determination.

Mrs. Durocher was a Métis woman who often worked for the Gervais family, potato farmers who lived on the farm next to us. Mrs. Gervais knew I needed help with my vegetable garden, so she introduced me to Mrs. Durocher. Little did I know the impact this extraordinary woman would have on my family.

The first day she came out to our place, I was struck both by her wisdom and by her generosity of spirit. That week, cucumbers were just starting to appear on our vines. She told me that if I picked them right away, the vines would go on to produce a much heavier crop. I was a little leery of the suggestion, but decided to give it a try. Well, those plants just exploded. I had never seen so many cucumbers.

When I give that tip at gardening talks, people think I'm a genius. But it was Mrs. Durocher who taught me.

During long summer afternoons, as we worked side by side, Mrs. Durocher would tell me about the plants that grew in the area and the many uses she had for them. If you made a tea out of one plant, it would help you get over a cold. You could apply the leaves of another directly to cuts or blisters to help them heal properly. She even knew of a plant that she claimed could prevent baldness!

With the depth of her knowledge, she wasn't always ready to accept the word of "experts." When she gave birth to her first child, the doctors told her that the baby was weak and frail, and might not survive. They said there was nothing they could do. So Mrs. Durocher decided to see what she could do to help her new-born son.

Mrs. Durocher was determined to save him. She filled dozens of discarded bottles with hot water and wrapped the child in blankets, creating an incubator. That heat, warm milk, and love were all she needed to save the child.

Because we thought so highly of Mrs. Durocher, it sometimes came as a shock that she didn't think very highly of herself. I remember how excited she was when she gave birth to a son with light-coloured hair—she was thrilled that his hair wasn't pure black.

Once, Ted asked Mrs. Durocher if he could take her picture. She had the most striking, unforgettable face, Her olive skin seemed smooth, even though it was deeply lined, and her eyes radiated wisdom and character. Ted wanted to capture the image of this important part of our lives forever, and Mrs. Durocher was delighted to be asked.

When Ted visited her with the camera the next day, he discovered, to his dismay, that she had coated her long, white hair with shoe polish, trying to look young for the photo. This story always makes me sad. If only she would believe that we loved who she was and how she looked.

She truly touched the lives of everyone she came in contact with. Our greenhouse manager, Dave Grice, remembers Mrs. Durocher fondly. He started at the farm as a teenager back in the early '70s and often worked in the fields alongside her. He recalls how graceful and quiet her movements were, as if she were walking on air. Although Mrs. Durocher was 65 or 70 years old at the time, she never had a problem keeping up with the rest of the workers.

When Dave talks about Mrs. Durocher working in the field, I remember how thorough she was. She had a sixth sense about weeds and seemed never to miss a single one.

Mrs. Durocher died a few years later, and we've missed her ever since. Along with her wise, gentle presence and her unfailing good company, we also lost the opportunity to preserve her wisdom. She tended to mix her English with Cree, and I couldn't always under-stand her. If only I had taken the time to get somebody who could translate, to help me get it all down on paper. All that knowledge died with her. She had many children, but as far as I know, they had never taken an interest in her "old ways."

"You know," Dave told me recently, "I'm amazed at how often the image of Mrs. Durocher comes to my mind. She knew the soil like no one else I've ever known."

In this helter-skelter, technological age, people are desperate to get back to the soil. Gardening continues to boom and every supermarket

has a corner devoted to organic fruits and vegetables. Even in the local
pharmacy, you can find a wide range of herbal remedies squeezed in
among the aspirins and toothpaste.

Mrs. Durocher would have been delighted by all this interest in
nature and natural ways. It's such a shame that, in her day, her
wisdom wasn't fully appreciated, not even by her.

I like to think that, if she were alive today, Mrs. Durocher's life
would be very different. She would be a respected elder in the commu-
nity and would feel free to take pride in her native ancestry.

After all these years, perhaps the world is finally starting to catch
up with her way of thinking. I learned so much from Mrs.
Durocher—and not just about gardening. [7]

Despite our success in building a generally prosperous, open, and
free society, we should not become complacent. Canada Day is about
celebrating, but there's no reason we shouldn't also spend a little time
considering ways to make this country better. There are still
disturbing—and growing—inequalities between rich and poor. There is
still racism. And we must recognize the fact that Canada, like the other
industrialized nations, consumes a disproportionate amount of the planet's wealth. We are Canadians, but we are also citizens of Earth, and we
should work towards the day when all peoples of the world can enjoy the
freedom and security that Canadians take for granted.

Thank you everyone, and have a wonderful Canada Day.

The following address looks like part of a lieutenant-governor's normal routine. It was anything but. Lois may have seen her address to a support society for sufferers of schizophrenia as normal. However, her son Bill said that after she died, a representative called the family to express appreciation for her efforts; a number of other public figures had declined to be publicly associated with mental illness.

Schizophrenia Convention
July 14, 2000
Lethbridge

HELLO, LADIES AND GENTLEMEN. Thank you so much for inviting me to be a part of this wonderful gathering of minds. As you know, schizophrenia is a complex disorder, with no easy solution in sight. But I firmly believe that by working together, a cure can eventually be found.

I don't think there are many people whose lives are untouched by mental illness of one form or another. My own experience with schizophrenia began about 30 years ago, when a friend was admitted to hospital for her increasingly erratic behaviour. She was initially diagnosed with a nervous breakdown but, even then, I wondered if that could really be what was wrong. Later on, a more thorough analysis revealed that she was schizophrenic, and we've been coping ever since.

In my experience, mental illnesses are, in many ways, more difficult to acknowledge and deal with than even the gravest physical conditions. For some reason, it's easier to discuss cancer or diabetes with your peers than it is to admit that there's a mental disorder in the family. There's a stigma attached to mental problems, a stigma that even today makes it hard for me to mention my friend's problem to you. It's ironic, because of course you are the people most familiar with schizophrenia and most sympathetic to its victims.

It seems to me that this stigma is gradually becoming less severe, though there is still much work to be done. Education is so important— to erase the stigma, to ensure that research can be conducted, and to encourage students to pursue careers in mental health disciplines. If we only had a fuller understanding of the causes of schizophrenia, surely we can do more for the victims.

People like you sustain the hope that allows people like me to offer my heartfelt support to this cause. Thank you for all your hard work, and please accept my fondest wishes for a productive and enlightening conference. I hope you all take many new approaches and ideas for understanding and treating schizophrenia home with you.

Albertans did not tend to think of Lois as a feminist. She never paid attention to the label "feminist." This speech and many others like it suggest she nevertheless had a strong belief in women's abilities and responsibilities. She also believed that women often faced unfair traditional barriers in Canadian society. She was not strident about either belief. Neither did she shrink from them whenever the event at which she was speaking centred on women's roles. She never thought that taking care of children compromised a woman. She was confident of women's ability to achieve success. She said more than once that she resented descriptions of individuals as "self-made men." She knew from observation and experience that farm men could not be successful without farm women and applied that lesson broadly to men in other fields. But she was equally capable both of supporting women and of criticizing those she thought had overstepped certain bounds.

The acronym WISEST stands for Women in Scholarship, Engineering, Science and Technology. The organization, based at the University of Alberta, was founded in 1982 to investigate and remedy the reasons that relatively few women were pursuing degrees in science and engineering.

WISEST

University of Alberta
August 15, 2000

GREETINGS, EVERYONE. I'm very pleased to be with you today as we celebrate the success and the potential of the WISEST initiative.

History has proven that women make vital contributions to science when given the chance to do so. The fact that the list of prominent female scientists seems short is due not to lack of ability, but lack of opportunity. Without being given a fair chance to experience the rewards and wonder of studying science, engineering, and technology, girls and women will inevitably migrate towards "traditional" female occupations. Not that there's anything wrong with such career choices, but everyone should have the chance to explore the sciences while they're young and haven't yet decided how to spend their lives. In a truly free society, there should be no "expected" career path for girls. They should have a full range of career options to choose from.

Thanks to programs like WISEST, girls are discovering how exciting and fulfilling a career in the sciences can be. They are discovering that they can change the world for the better through research, exploration, and critical thinking.

I've been fortunate enough to work with a number of women scientists in my lifetime. They have been an invaluable help in the family business and in my writing. Without their expertise, I couldn't have enjoyed the success I have. I am in debt to the teachers, parents, and professors who encouraged these women to pursue the sciences.

We should all be very grateful to the people and organizations that make WISEST possible—the supervisors who donate time and money, the federal and provincial governments, sponsoring industries, and, of course, the University of Alberta. Getting more girls into science and technology will prove to be of great benefit in the 21st century—the coming decades will be very exciting, as the seeds of inspiration planted today bear the fruits of discovery tomorrow.

Thank you.

Her first specific talk on books took place after she had been lieutenant-governor for eight months. After this event, she rarely went more than a few weeks between speeches focussed on books and literacy, and her description of why literacy was important grew more urgent. Books had been a big part of her life since childhood.

Young Alberta Book Society
Chrysalis 2000 Festival Launch
October 11, 2000

GOOD MORNING, EVERYONE, and welcome to this very special celebration of reading.

Why read? Well, people get different things out of reading—for some it's an escape, an afternoon's worth of entertainment. For others, it's a way to experience different points of view, or to learn about a specific topic. In other words, reading can be a means to an end or the end itself. For me, cracking a book was always a joy for its own sake.

When I was a little girl, I was very fortunate to have parents who encouraged me to read. My mother really wasn't one to nag me about doing chores—if I wanted to read, she was more than happy to let me—as long as it wasn't after bedtime. Many times I would read late into the night, only to hear my mother say, "Lois! Go to sleep!" To get around that one restriction, I often stuffed a blanket into the crack between the door and the floor so that the light from my reading lamp wouldn't spill into the hallway and give away the fact that I was still up. I don't think I really fooled her, but she never said anything after I started using that trick. I'm sure she was happy to have me reading, even if it meant I got a little less sleep than I should have.

Christmas was a very special time of year for me. After we opened our presents—which always included a book or two—I spent the rest of the day sitting in a cosy corner and reading while my parents and relatives tended to things like making Christmas dinner. While the snow piled up outside, I was warm and safe by the heat of the fire, carried away to exotic places thanks to the imagination of a good writer.[8]

Lois with granddaughter Kathryn and grandson Michael (on her left) and their friends, fall 1997.
[Hole Family Archives]

I love to read in bed. I'll bet some of you do, too. On trips out of town, I'll ring for a morning cup of tea and all the newspapers the hotel can muster—and then enjoy tea and news in bed, with a plump pillow between me and the headboard. That's my favourite morning routine on the road, something I never have time for at home. And for the hours spent getting there and back, what better companion than Carol Shields.

When I was young, I would buy books anytime I had even a little spending money—and nothing could compete with snuggling under the covers to read those precious words. One of my longstanding favourites was The Bounty Trilogy by Charles Nordhoff and James Norman Hall. What an adventure that was, retracing the voyage of Fletcher Christian on His Majesty's Ship Bounty under the autocratic Captain Bligh.

While my mother certainly encouraged me to read, she didn't always agree with my timing. So I'd be deep into a story, perhaps transported to Pitcairn Island in the far Pacific with Christian and

his mutinous companions, when I'd hear Mom passing by in the hall.
Then would come the inevitable knock on the wall: "Lights out, Lois.
School tomorrow."

Well. Before long, I figured out a way to outfox her. All it took was
a bath towel, rolled up and shoved against the door so the light
couldn't give me away by shining into the hallway. I may have come to
the table with droopy eyes some mornings, but Mom was never the
wiser—at least as far as I knew.

Today, I still make time to read, despite having much less free time
than I used to, and my tastes now run more towards history and politics—Peter Newman, Pierre Berton, and other authors of that nature.
But no matter what I'm reading or where I'm reading it, the effect is the
same: for a time, I'm transported to a different world. And while I'm in
that world, I learn. I learn a little bit more about human nature, or the
world of plants, or the threads of history and culture that connect all the
peoples of the world.

I'll tell you one thing—if I hadn't been a voracious reader, I doubt I'd
be standing here before you today talking about it! What I learned from
books was a huge help in starting my own business, in writing my own
books, and in serving as Alberta's Lieutenant Governor. Now, reading
alone can't ensure success—but it sure as heck helps your chances.

But don't read to get ahead. Read because it enriches your life. Read
because you enjoy a good story. Read so that you can discuss a great
book with your friends.

Most of all, read because it's fun. That's why I do it.

Thank you.

< *Lois Hole with Peter C. Newman during his book tour in Edmonton, 1998. The Hole family was*
mentioned in Newman's book Titans: How the New Canadian Establishment Seized Power.
[Hole Family Archives]

She addressed many small local groups; her willingness to share personal stories suggests why many of her listeners felt close to her.

Mulhurst Bay Ladies' Day & Quilt Show
October 12, 2000

GOOD AFTERNOON, EVERYONE. Thank you so much for inviting me to this lovely event. I've seen some really impressive quilts today—I just love them, and I'm amazed by the talent and dedication required for what has really become a genuine art form.

You know, it's kind of ironic that I'm here speaking to you today, since as a seamstress I make a pretty good gardener.

It's true, I can't sew worth beans. Years ago, Ted actually got me to sew a button onto a shirt for him and when my son Bill saw me, he stopped in his tracks and said, "Mom, you can sew?!?"

But I think there are some similarities between gardening and sewing. Both require patience, a keen eye, attention to detail, and creativity. With that in mind, I thought I'd share a story about gardening that could just as easily apply to quilt-making.

My husband Ted is a terrific sport and always laughs along whenever I haul out one of my old anecdotes. Good thing, too, because he's a central figure in so many of my funny stories.

But Ted has always been a man of great vision, with an inventive and innovative mind. I saw that the very first day we came out to the farm. There we stood, side by side, two kids from the city, while he told me how we were going to make a wonderful life on this little patch of land, with its aging barn and tiny house. He painted the picture so clearly that I could see it myself.'

Of course, once we got down to the actual business of farming, that picture was clouded by dozens of day-to-day details. People who grow up on farms absorb so much knowledge that it becomes second nature. Ted and I, on the other hand, had to learn as we went along.

In the long run, Ted turned his lack of experience into his greatest advantage. Farmers are creatures of habit: if they grow up doing things a certain way, it can be next to impossible to convince them to change. Ted, on the other hand, had absolutely no preconceived notions. He constantly questioned our methods and looked for ways to improve them.

When we started market gardening, the industry was in its infancy in central Alberta. Very few people here farmed vegetables, and those who did weren't operating on the scale Ted envisioned. As a result, we had a terrible time finding appropriate equipment. As far as the manufactures and suppliers were concerned, we might as well have been growing vegetables at the North Pole.

Ted subscribed to dozens of magazines and catalogues from the United States, where the industry was much better established. He'd go through them page by page, looking for new ideas, methods, and tools. After days of research, he chose a John Deere 1020 because, with its adjustable wheel spacing, it was the most suitable for row-crop work. And if he couldn't find the things he needed, he'd adapt the things he had on hand.

Ted relied a lot on our neighbour Len Adams, a talented welder. He would wander down the road to tell Len his latest idea and Len, always the pessimist, would mutter, "Nope, can't be done. It's not gonna work." Ted would ask, "Well, can you at least give it a try?" He'd go back an hour later, and the tool would be built.

After a few years of digging carrots by hand, which is a terrible job, Ted invented a carrot lifter. He had Len weld two grader blades onto a cross-brace, and hitched it to the 1020. As he drove the tractor along a row, the blades loosened the soil on either side. The carrots just popped right out of the ground, ready to gather.

Ted also loved to experiment with new seed varieties. When we first started market gardening, our neighbours told us not to bother trying to grow corn. Ted shopped for the latest hybrids and kept trying different varieties very year. After several years of experimenting, we grew crop after crop of beautiful corn.

Ted also developed a close relationship with the horticulturists at the Brooks Research Centre, at a time when most farmers were skeptical of scientific approaches to farming. From those gentlemen, we learned to try new technologies, many of which we were able to employ successfully.

Of course, not everything Ted tried worked. But when it did, the rewards could be enormous. For instance, if you could find ways to grow an especially early crop, your profits multiplied. Dill cucumbers, which might fetch fifty cents a pound in August, were worth two or three dollars a pound in July. Ted invested a lot of time and effort in his ideas, and it usually paid off for us.

If people poked fun at his unorthodox thinking, Ted never let it bother him. In the later 1960s, I was on the board of the Rural Safety Council. At the time, we were fighting to have roll-bars installed on tractors and to make their use mandatory. Ted saw it as an issue of simple common sense: by spending a couple of hundred dollars, he might save his life or that of one of his kids. When the neighbours got a look at Ted's tractor, all fitted out with a roll-bar, canopy, and radio, they were beside themselves. One of them even climbed right up and danced on the canopy. Ted just stood there and watched, not saying a word.

Of course, his foresight has since been proven right, as roll-over protection systems (ROPS) are now legally required on all new tractors. Ted was also an early advocate of hearing protection, another development that has substantially reduced injury on farms in the last few decades. (In fact, Ted swears he lost much of his hearing operating our first potato harvester—hearing protection came a little too late for him.)

But not all of our neighbours made fun of Ted. Other families in the market gardening business began to keep a close eye on him and often followed his example. For years we had people stopping by our house to check out our crops or borrow equipment.

Ted still helps shape our business and his bold spirit continues to be reflected. Customers often tell me how much they look forward to the new plant varieties we offer each year, and our garden centre is always well stocked with ingenious gardening tools.

So when you read one of my anecdotes about Ted, don't forget that behind the laughter stands a most remarkable man.[9]

I think Ted would feel quite at home in Mulhurst Bay, a place where creativity seems to flourish.

The MacEwan Campaign
Philanthropy Day
November 14, 2000

HELLO, EVERYONE. Thank you for having me here to day to talk about a subject I feel very passionately about: philanthropy.

Philanthropy is central to the health and well-being of any civilization. By sharing our wealth, our time, and our knowledge rather than hoarding it, we make everyone richer—not just wealthier, but richer in culture, health, knowledge, and spirit.

My own urge to share developed out of what my father taught me. He always said to respect other cultures, to never speak ill of someone just because of their race, religion, or place of origin. I tried very hard to follow my father's advice, and I soon discovered that respect goes hand-in-hand with understanding...and with understanding comes empathy and a desire to help one's neighbours.

So when Ted and I started out on the farm, it was only natural that we gave away things. It was a casual thing, mostly—if people wanted some rhubarb or dill, for example, they could have it—after all, we had more than we could ever use. And when the business took off, we started to make more formal donations to a number of worthwhile causes. Edmonton and St. Albert had been so good to my family that we had to give something back.

But it was really when Ted and I turned over day-to-day operations to our sons Bill and Jim that we organized how we supported different groups. Philanthropy actually requires a lot of work—there are so many genuinely good causes that it's often difficult to decide how much to give, and how often.

We eventually decided that we would try to honour every legitimate request we received, rather than giving large amounts to any single charity. That's what we thought was fair, but of course there are many approaches to philanthropy. If someone wants to make one large donation to a single cause they feel passionately about, that's wonderful.

Of course, sometimes the urge to share isn't enough to spread the wealth around. Let me tell you a story about the time I tried to give something away and had no luck at all...

We're all taught to believe "there's no such thing as a free lunch" and "if it looks too good to be true, it probably is." I generally agree, although every rule has its exceptions. In some people's minds, though, if something's free, there's no way it can be worth anything.

For example: if your household has even been "blessed" with a litter of pups, you know how hard it is to get "unblessed." It seems as if everyone in the world who wants a dog already has one.

Like most people years ago, we never gave much thought to having our dogs spayed or neutered. As a result, our farm was often visited by the pitter-patter of furry little feet.

It should have been easy enough to find homes for the pups. We kept beautiful purebred German Shepherds. The pups were guaranteed to grow into attractive, gentle, intelligent farm dogs. More often than not, though, our ads or the "Free Puppies" sign we displayed drew little or no response.

But one year, we hit upon the solution. We put a little ad in the paper: "German Shepherd pups. No papers. $10." Inside of two days, they were gone.

It just goes to show: if you literally can't give something away, try selling it instead. [10]

I've always been very thankful for the people who helped Ted and I and the boys through the bad years when we were starting out. Those were some tough times, but because of the spirit of philanthropy, we survived and even prospered. I'll never forget people like the Sernowskis, Mrs. Durocher, and the countless others who gave us a helping hand over the years. I am absolutely thrilled that I was fortunate enough to have the chance to do the same for others.

I have three grandchildren now, and I know that they will grow up to help others, too. They'll find their own style of philanthropy, no doubt, one for the 21st century, and they'll find new causes to support. But as long as they share their knowledge and compassion, I'll be happy—they have both in abundance. And I'd say that even if I weren't their grandmother.

Before I leave the stage, I want to thank you all for doing your part. You've made the world a better place. I know that's a cliché, but I mean it with all my heart. Philanthropy is one of the finest expressions of what it means to be human, and I am so very proud to share a room with you all today.

Thank you.

A farmgirl at university calls for a sense of responsibility. Her family knew she regretted never having had the opportunity to attend university.

Honorary Degree Acceptance Speech
University of Alberta
November 15, 2000

EMINENT CHANCELLOR FERGUSON, President Rod Fraser, Vice-Chairman of the Board of Governors, honoured platform guests, honoured guests, friends, and most especially, students:

Thank you so much for this singular honour. One of the few regrets in my life is that I didn't attend university, and now you have truly made me feel a part of this remarkable institution. I could not be more proud and thrilled, and I promise to honourably represent this university for the rest of my life. I may not be chancellor anymore, but I will always think of myself as an alumnus of the University of Alberta.

When I first learned that I was to be granted this honorary degree, I felt a little bit guilty—after all, I've attended no classes, I've written no theses, I've faced no peer review.

But after thinking about it for a bit, I realized that I have done some of these things—in a sense. When I worked in retail at Eaton's and Woodward's, I had to deal with some pretty unusual customers. That experience was probably the equivalent of Psych 101. Raising two very strong-willed boys? Family Studies 210. Serving on the St. Albert school board? Political Science 400, along with a little Marketing, Economics, and Phys. Ed.

As for my theses and peer review, I guess I can count my experience in horticulture and the two very intense interviews I went through before being chosen as chancellor. Now there was a stressful time—but well worth every minute of it!

But of course I am not trying to compare this honour with what you students have achieved. In the end, I'm so envious of you. You've enjoyed instruction from some of the finest professors in the world, and you've learned so very much—about science, about art, and about the amazing diversity of human culture and thought.

I hope that you will give some consideration to your responsibilities as university graduates. You've joined an elite group; only a small percentage of Canadians ever pursue their education as far as you have. Personally, I hope that one day a majority of people have the opportunity to attend university or college; it should be a birthright, not a crippling financial burden or a privilege for the rich. One day, university will be accessible to everyone, regardless of their economic and social background. That day must come, for the sake of this great country and her citizens.

But until that day comes, you university graduates, and even honorary grads like me, have a daunting task: to make a positive difference in the world. This responsibility falls upon your shoulders because you have been given the best tools with which to make that difference. Very few people understand your chosen field as well as you do. Don't be afraid to use that knowledge to build a good life for yourselves; you've earned that right. But at the same time, remember that we must look after each other. Being a part of the human community means, above all, that you need to show compassion.

Sometimes that's easy, and sometimes compassion means being willing to sacrifice. Perhaps it simply means donating time or money to charity, or helping out a stranded motorist or a single mother. Or it might mean helping a new immigrant who doesn't understand our customs or language. Maybe it even means accepting and understanding someone who chooses a lifestyle you might not approve of.

Whatever the issue, I ask you to use those remarkable brains that have served you so well thus far. Consider the issues that shape our world today and use your abilities to bring people together rather than setting them apart.

Engineers, musicians, political scientists, chemists, teachers, nutritionists, economists, writers, actors, dancers—it doesn't matter what your major is. You all have the same potential to make a difference. You have the power to change the world.

All you really need to do is ask yourself one question: how can I make things better? And then—well, then, set out to accomplish whatever answer you came up with. That's not always going to be easy; but then, what worthwhile thing ever is?

So go, and take your rightful place in the world. Be a builder—a builder of both a good life for you and yours, and of a cleaner, safer, more compassionate world for everyone.

Thank you.

This was the first of many strong speeches in support of libraries. Her language was growing stronger when she spoke about libraries and literacy. Her interest in libraries continues to be reflected after her death in the Lois Hole Library Legacy Program, established to help build the collections at libraries around the province. The program evolved from the practice she established for gifts people wanted to give her as she appeared at public events. She would ask people not to give her more, but to give a book to their local library instead.

Coronation Memorial Library
Official Ribbon Cutting
November 30, 2000

Part I: At the Ribbon Cutting

LADIES AND GENTLEMEN, it gives me great pleasure to join with you in celebrating the opening of the Coronation Memorial Library.

Of all the things that humans build, libraries are among the most noble, the most precious. Their vital role in our communities cannot be overestimated. Libraries serve us in many ways: they are repositories of all that we've learned, sources for wonderful, uplifting entertainment, and islands of calm and quiet in a sea of noise and confusion.

But most importantly, libraries provide students and citizens with the necessary tools to learn about our world, its peoples, and the powerful ideas we have generated over the course of human history.

This library will serve its people well, and I urge all of you to make good use of its precious gifts.

Part II: At the Assembly

HELLO, EVERYONE.

I've been asked to say a few words about my role as Lieutenant Governor. You probably all know the basics: that I serve as the Queen's representative to the Province of Alberta, ensuring that the Monarchy is represented at important provincial events and giving royal assent to provincial legislation in the Alberta Legislature.

As proud as I am to carry out those functions, I also feel that part of my role is to enhance the public good and, to me, the best way to do that is to promote the value of a solid education. And nothing contributes to a solid education like a library.

Back when we cut the ribbon, I said that libraries are among humanity's noblest creations. I say that because libraries in this country promote certain universal values that most people cherish. Libraries stand against censorship, encourage thought and learning, and provide their services at virtually no cost to the users. Universal access to libraries is one of the great triumphs of civilization, and we must do all we can to retain that legacy. Support your new library, and support all libraries, all your life. Even if you don't use one more than once a year, libraries still contribute to your health and prosperity by giving others the tools to expand their knowledge.

Would any of the technological wonders we enjoy today be possible if scientists had not had libraries to draw upon? Would any of the great social programs like universal health care and welfare have arisen if politicians and social planners had not had access to the thoughts of the great thinkers, or to the statistics of past governments?

A world without libraries is a world without education, without progress, without justice. Use your library. Cherish it. Love it. Fight for it.

Her first speech on agriculture was full of her enthusiasm for gardens.

Prairie Oat Growers & Canadian Grains
3rd Annual Conference
December 2, 2000

DEAR FRIENDS,

I am so pleased to talk with you tonight. You know, before Ted and I started our market garden business, we tried a number of different farms, grain included.

When I was four or five years old, I would ride with my Dad down to his stockyards on the outskirts of Buchanan, Saskatchewan. My dad was a stock buyer, and I used to enjoy watching the farmers and stockyard workers loading and unloading the livestock. Although I didn't realize it at the time, my young mind absorbed the whole process in surprising detail.

Many years later, Ted and I tried our hand at raising pigs. I'll always remember when it first came time to take them to market. We needed a chute to get them onto the truck, of course, so Ted set to work building one. I assumed he knew what he was doing, so I didn't pay much attention. However, although he had sound carpentry skills, he had never built a pig chute.

When he brought out the chute, I took one look at it and said, "Ted, you can't use a chute that big for pigs." It was as wide as the half-ton. Pigs need a narrow chute so they can't turn around. Not surprisingly, Ted didn't welcome my unsolicited advice. "What the hell do you know about loading pigs?" he grumbled.

He managed to get three or four pigs part way up the chute. Suddenly, the first pig decided he'd rather be down with his buddies in the pen, so he turned around. Ted blocked his path with a sheet of plywood and let out a whoop, just to show the pig who was boss.

Well, utter chaos ensued. All the pigs were upset now. Every time Ted lunged one way, a pig scrambled another. You might think it's impossible for a pig to climb over the wall of a chute, but get one good and agitated and you'll find out differently. Not a single pig made it

Lois watering in the greenhouse, 1982. [Hole Family Archives]

all the way onto the truck. Eventually, we threw up our hands and
deserted the field of battle.

Ted had to dismantle the chute and rebuild it, while I wisely
suppressed the urge to say, "I told you so." When the time came to try
again, I suggested, "You should hold a piece of plywood in front of you
and walk up the chute behind the pigs." Ted set to work, trying his
best, but again the pigs refused to cooperate. Within a minute or two,
Ted was yelling and swearing, and the pigs were squealing, grunting,
and running around madly.

"Ted, calm down!" I shouted. "You're not going to get anywhere
that way!" In his state, that wasn't what he wanted to hear. He
continued pushing away at the pigs and sure enough, we didn't get
them loaded that day either.

Later in the evening, once Ted and the pigs had settled down, I
convinced him to let me give it a try. From what I had seen as a kid, I
knew that you had to be very gentle and quiet when loading pigs.

The next day we assembled the pigs for a third attempt. I walked
slowly out, crept right up to one of them, put my hand down, and
directed a pig up the chute and into the truck, making a gentle

"whooshing" sound the whole time. Anytime the pig felt like pausing for a little look around, I'd wait right beside it. When it was ready to continue, off we'd go together.

I herded the pigs into the truck, one by one, while the others patiently, silently waited their turns. Ted could only stand by and chuckle in amazement. From then on, loading the pigs was my job: Ted never could seem to get the knack.

After a few years, it became clear to both of us that we weren't cut out to be pig farmers. And it may be an awful thing to admit, yet those pigs taught me a thing or two about dealing with excitable people. The quiet approach is often the only one that works. If you speak softly and lay a gentle hand on their shoulder, you can lead them almost anywhere.[11]

This is a cautionary tale for all you men out there.

When you have a particularly bountiful crop, you can spend much of August and September storing and preserving vegetables. If you're lucky enough to have a good friend to keep you company, the chore can actually be quite pleasant. But one year we had a harvest my husband Ted will never forget.

Our daughter-in-law Valerie had put a lot of peppers into the trial garden that summer, and her experiments were a bit too successful. We gave peppers away to customers and friends, and still had two huge baskets full of them.

Ted said, "Lois, why don't you chop them up and freeze them? I'll help you."

We turned on the cbc and set to work, chopping and chatting away. I noticed my hands were feeling hot. I thought, "Oh, for heaven's sake, we've got some hot peppers mixed in." I wasn't too worried, since I was sure that we hadn't picked any really hot peppers like jalapeños and habañeros. Still, my hands were beginning to feel like they were on fire. I asked Ted, "Are your hands hot?"

"No," he shrugged.

We kept chopping and chopping, and from time to time, I'd run to the tap to cool my fingers. I kept asking, "Ted, are you sure your hands *aren't hot? Because mine are really getting painful."*

"No, no," he said.

Finally, just as we were getting to the end, Ted excused himself. Maybe he should have thought to wash his hands first.

A minute later, I heard his mournful wail from the bathroom: "LO-O-O-ISSSS!" I guess his hands had been hot after all!

He walked very gingerly for the rest of the day. [12]

You all know far better than I how grain farming has changed over the years. Since our flirtation with it was so brief, my own firsthand experience of those changes has been fairly minimal, though working with the Farm Credit Corporation for so many years has given me some insight into the changes farming faces. Certainly there seems to be a new diversity in Canadian farming; there's such an amazing wide variety of crops being grown today that Ted and I would never have considered.

And of course we didn't have to deal with the influence of genetic engineering or the counter-trend of organic agriculture. This is a dynamic time for farmers, and it's going to take a lot of thought and work to create farms that can thrive in the 21st century.

But I ran across an intriguing piece of news recently. I'm going to share a quote with you from a book review I read a few days ago:

According to the book Who Will Feed China? Wake-Up Call for a Small Planet, *by Lester R. Brown, most of the rapidly developing countries around the world are spending more of their gross domestic product on food. At the same time, their citizens are demanding an improved diet that includes increasing amounts of protein-rich grains, meat, eggs, etc. Historically, the countries that have gone through this phase go from net exporters of high quality foodstuffs to net importers. Recent examples are Japan, South Korea, and Taiwan.*

Now, it is China's turn. However, with its 1.2 billion people the magnitude of the impact on worldwide demand could easily over-shadow past events. 1.2 billion times anything is a lot. For example, the official goal for egg consumption in China has been set at 200 per capita per year by the year 2000, double the level of 1990 but still less than the average of 235 in the U.S. The number of chickens necessary to generate these eggs would consume the entire grain export volume

of Canada. Two more beers per person in China would take the entire
Norwegian grain harvest.

This is all the result of predictable long-term patterns. As devel-
oping countries' populations increase, land is taken out of agricul-
tural production for urban uses such as roads, factories, parking lots,
etc. Also, agrarian people migrate to urban areas where incomes are
higher, and, perhaps most important, water becomes more scarce and
is given over to more productive industrial uses (this is a particular
problem in China where available water in the agricultural areas is
limited to begin with).

Thus the internal demand for food, and the demand for higher
quality diets increases, while internal supply decreases. In any given
country, increased agricultural productivity will rise, but will only
make up a portion of the increasing gap between supply and demand.
The developed countries, typically, must make up the remainder.

If the author is right, there's real reason to hope that Canadian
farmers can regain some of the ground lost in recent years. I certainly
hope so, since I've always believed that farming is integral to a healthy
society. Farming develops a certain kind of character in people—men
and women who are deeply conscious of the importance of community,
charity, and a healthy environment.

I thought I'd share with you some of the trends in horticulture I've
participated in more directly. I think some of these trends may at least
provide some food for thought as to how gardening trends may affect
larger agricultural trends.

As free time gets scarcer and lives continue to become more and
more hectic, instant gratification becomes more attractive than ever. I've
noticed that gardeners are buying large plants with full blooms right
from the greenhouse, so that they can enjoy an "instant garden."

These days, we sell a lot of tomato plants in big five-gallon pails, and
almost without exception it's men who buy them. With tomatoes, like
many other things, men can be awfully competitive. Whereas a
woman spends a dollar or two on a small plant and usually shops for
the best-tasting varieties, a man wants big tomatoes and he wants
them now. Men love the idea that they can have this big plant in their

garden right away and be the first on their block to slice into a ripe tomato.

This trend stretches right back to our very first (and most faithful) five-gallon tomato customer.

Back when the greenhouse was still new, we had planted a half-dozen or so tomato plants very early, just as a trial. This man came out to buy tomatoes for his garden and spotted the five-gallon pails sitting in the back. The plants were thriving, their branches loaded with fruit. Some of the tomatoes were even beginning to ripen.

Well, once he saw those plants, nothing else would do. He had to have one, no matter what he paid.

So we settled on a fair price, and off he went. The next spring he was back, buying his stock of tomato seedlings plus one huge plant. Every year after that, we'd get a phone call from this fellow, asking us to set aside a five-gallon tomato plant for him.

Curiosity gradually began to take hold. I'd hang up the phone and ask my husband, "Ted, what in the world does he do with that big tomato plant every year?"

"Oh," Ted would say, "he probably gives it away as a birthday or anniversary gift."

Finally, one year when the man came out to pick up his order, I asked him, "Why do you always get only one big one? I mean, you must have plenty of tomato plants."

"Oh yeah," he said, "My back yard's full of them."

"Well, is it a gift for someone?"

"I'll tell you, Mrs. Hole," he said slyly. "I take that tomato plant home. I put it in a special place in my garden. And then I call the neighbours over and say, 'See? That's how to grow tomatoes!'"

"You're going to get caught one of these years," I warned him, smiling.

"Oh no," he laughed. "The neighbours keep changing." [13]

But now gardeners are taking this trick to new extremes. The newest trend is to buy huge hanging baskets full of blooming annuals, pull the whole arrangement, intact, out of the basket, and plant it. In no time at all, a gardener has a huge mound of annuals right in the flowerbed—no fuss, no waiting.

Gardeners are getting more daring with their landscapes, too. Mustard greens and multicoloured Swiss chard are no longer confined to the vegetable garden; people are using them as beautiful foliage plants. They're even mass planting parsley in containers, letting the deep green foliage contrast with their bedding plants.

Thanks to the influence of immigrants, television, the Internet, and books, herbs are enjoying a surge in popularity. While enjoying old standards like basil and mint, we are discovering exotic choices like shiso, epazote, and red orach. These herbs and many others not only add some culinary dash, but also look right at home planted alongside colourful annuals—just make sure not to plant invasive species like mint too close to less competitive plants. This trend is just the continuance of one that I remember from back in my market gardening days; before the Italian and the Lebanese and the Eastern European immigrants visited my farm, I'd never tried to grow hot peppers or kohlrabi or raddichio, to name just a few.

A global gardening culture is developing, one that exchanges the best elements from each national tradition. Whatever happens, the 21st century is going to be a true adventure for gardeners all over the world. Perhaps the same is true of agriculture, as farmers become more important than ever in the ongoing quest to properly feed an increasingly hungry world.

Despite her aversion to war, there were to be many speeches in support of veterans and the Canadian military. Her aides were all military or reservists.

Mewburn Veterans' Centre
Edmonton, December 10, 2000

DEAR FRIENDS,

First of all, let me tell you how pleased I am to be here today. It is always a great pleasure to meet with the noble people who have given so much to ensure that Canada remains strong, free, and committed to its ideals.

I was just a little girl during World War II, living in a small town in northern Saskatchewan. My aunt was a nursing sister and tended to the wounded in Great Britain, and I had an uncle serving as a doctor on the front lines in Italy. The war seemed very far away to me, an abstract, even imaginary thing that didn't seem to have a direct bearing on my life; the only direct effect at the time was that I had to get used to pies made without sugar because of the rationing. I couldn't know how wrong I was, not at that age.

It wasn't until I was older and wiser that I could really appreciate the sacrifices made by Canada's soldiers. They went in good faith to defend the country—from the frontline soldiers to the supply clerks, cooks, war correspondents, chaplains, entertainers, and so many others who believed in a common cause. They fought and bled and sometimes died, so that I and all the other little girls in Canada could grow up free of fear. Without their devotion to duty and country, I wonder what my life would have been like? Certainly not as happy and prosperous as I've enjoyed; like thousands of other Canadians, my life has been drastically improved by soldiers I've never met.

Even today, Canadians continue to serve honourably, protecting the weak all across the globe as members of United Nations peacekeeping forces, stopping wars before they reap their terrible harvest. These brave men and women deserve all the support we can give them and our undying gratitude. And we mustn't forget the men and women who protected us during the other wars of this century, and those who stood guard through the tense years of the Cold War. For decades, the members of the Canadian armed forces have stood sentinel, in times of war and peace alike, and through all those years they have been steadfast in their commitment, even in the face of terrible danger, loneliness, deprivation, and uncertainty. To be a soldier, you have to be made of stern stuff.

Despite all its horrors, war does have, at least, the ability to forge deep ties of love and friendship. I imagine that many of you here have been friends for decades, and that just as many lost friends long ago to the carnage of war—friends you've never forgotten, and never will. Your presence here honours them. It honours their sacrifice, yes, but it also honours the fact that they lived and loved, that they made a difference in the world, that they were more than faceless names on some gravestone.

Like many people, I long for the day when war will be a part of history. But until that day arrives, I am so very glad that people like you have the will, the valour, the honour, and the strength to protect the weak from those who would seek to oppress them.

Thank you for being there for me, for my family, and my country.

A speech to the school board on which she once served became her first really strong talk on education. The reference to kindergarten funding recalls one of the first controversial budget cuts in 1994, rescinded after wide public protest. The school district's name is an anomaly. It's known as St. Albert Protestant because the Catholic school board came first, given the area's origins as a Roman Catholic mission site. The Protestant board was formed as the separate school board.

Lois took great offence to the government's attempt to cut kindergarten funding in half and to its claim that research had not shown conclusive bene-fits from kindergarten. The love of early schooling apparently ran strongly in the family. She had a vivid demonstration from the experience of her son Bill's children. When Bill's son began kindergarten at age five, his daughter Kate, then three, climbed onto the school bus, assuming that she would be heading off to start school as well. She almost had to be hauled physically off the bus.

St. Albert Protestant School District
December 14, 2000

GOOD EVENING, EVERYONE. I'm very glad to be here tonight, discussing something that's obviously close to my heart: the St. Albert Protestant school district. As you know, I served as a trustee for this district for many years, and that is one of my proudest achievements; not so much because of what I did, but because the district has consist-ently performed with excellence.

When I was a trustee, people often told me that they'd moved to St. Albert because of the school system. And no wonder: we have excellent special needs programs, well-stocked libraries, strong music and sports programs, and for years our students have performed magnificently on the Grade 3, 6, 9, and 12 provincial achievement exams. Our teachers regularly win recognition through a number of awards of excellence. And I can't tell you how many students have come back to this district to serve as teachers and administrators—well, of course some of you are here right now. You don't come back to a school district to serve unless you have memories that make you care about that district.

Over the years, I've had the opportunity to help shape district policy; there are quite a few interesting stories that came out of those times:[14]

I've always believed our schools need to be open for community use. When I was growing up in the small town of Buchanan, Saskatchewan, the doors were never locked. Schools were a hub for all sorts of events, evenings as well as daytime. That's the way it should be.

But one afternoon almost thirty years ago, my son Bill and his friend Terry took that thinking a little too far. By the end of the day, they'd been hauled in by the RCMP, finger-printed and severely rebuked by my husband Ted. Which of those scared them the most, I'm not quite sure.

It all started innocently enough, with a Sunday afternoon wander past the new high school being built beside their old school. The two boys were deeply into basketball, so of course they were eager to see the new gymnasium. It had to be quite the contrast from the gym they knew, with its sagging hoops, dim lights and general air of decline. They'd tried to convince the coach to let them into the new building for a look but that hadn't worked, so naturally, they wanted to see for themselves.

Peering in through the windows, they spotted a fine-looking floor, already laid. And the basketball hoops were up, ready for action. Mouth-watering. Then their wander took them past an entrance, and they couldn't help noticing a gap between the doorjamb and the latch. All it took was a comb to push the latch back, and they were in. I know the boys were thrilled beyond belief with the new gym. It was huge. It had bleachers, bright lights and shiny new hardwood floors.

They had a good look around—but as it turned out, they weren't alone in having a good view of things. An entire row of backyards faced the school, and someone across the way had seen them disappear inside. As they left the gym, they walked right into the hands of the RCMP.

The officers were worried about vandalism of course, but soon real-ized these strapping young lads were simply scoping out the gym. Still, they were marched down to the station for a sermon and finger-printing—not for the record, but to maximize the scare factor. Many years later, Bill ended up speaking to one of the officers involved at a civic function. The officer smiled and, in mentioning the incident, said, "We knew at the time you were just two curious kids and your

actions were harmless, but we also knew it was important to scare you
a bit and deliver a message."

One of the stories that stands out in my mind is when the issue of putting condom machines in the schools came about. It was a pretty huge issue during the trustee election of the late '80s, and a divisive one. Many board members who favoured installing the machines received angry phone calls and letters; I myself received a death threat, as well as numerous pledges from people who said they would no longer frequent my business. But in spite of all that, everyone on the board stuck to their guns, and I think we won an important victory for common sense and for the public health. If even one unwanted pregnancy or case of AIDS was prevented, the struggle was worth it.

I also feel good about this district because I think it has been able to resist some of the pressure from extremist business interests to make the system more "efficient." Well, in my experience, making the system more "efficient" usually means keeping the teachers in line, and I think this district has done a pretty good job of resisting the pressure. I really believe that teachers are among the most important members of our community. We entrust them to teach the people who will be our future leaders, our scientists, our doctors, our writers, musicians, and poets, and still certain short-sighted people think they should be paid far less than they are worth. We can't afford to lose our best teachers, so I hope you'll keep fighting the good fight.

I also remember what happened in this district when the government decided to cut full funding for kindergarten. Many school districts in the province dropped kindergarten programs or charged families extra to maintain them—but not this district. Instead, teachers and administrators came together, volunteering their precious time and resources to provide full kindergarten at no extra cost to families. I think that St. Albert's leadership was partially responsible for the government's eventual decision to restore full funding for kindergarten.

Schools work best when they are inclusive, when they throw open their doors for all kinds of students, regardless of culture, religion, disabilities, gender, or economic background. A learning environment made of a wide variety of students gives them the best chance to learn not just math, science, English, and the other regular subjects: it helps them learn about each other, and those lessons are perhaps the most important of all.

This district has much to be proud of, and I know that it will continue to serve future students well. It must, for only by ensuring a steady flow of educated, well-rounded, tolerant, critical thinkers can our society continue to grow and prosper.

The Christmas spirit was tied closely to philanthropy for Lois. But she renewed her appeal for a philanthropic spirit many times during the next four years. Her beliefs on that score were not merely a Christmas-time sentiment.

Christmas Bureau
December 19, 2000

GOOD MORNING, EVERYONE. Thank you for having me here to day to talk about a subject I feel very passionately about: philanthropy.

The Christmas Bureau has been enriching our citizens for 60 years now, providing Christmas dinner for thousands of families. This is such important work—I love Christmas, but expectations are raised so high at this time of year that for many poor families, the holidays are not a season of joy but a crushing financial and emotional burden. The Christmas Bureau helps relieve that pressure.

Such giving is central to the health and well-being of any civilization. By sharing our wealth, our time, and our knowledge rather than hoarding it, we make everyone richer—not just wealthier, but richer in culture, health, knowledge, and spirit.

My own urge to share developed out of what my father taught me. He always said to respect other cultures, to never speak ill of someone just because of their race, religion, or place of origin. I tried very hard to follow my father's advice, and I soon discovered that respect goes hand-in-hand with understanding...and with understanding comes empathy and a desire to help one's neighbours.

So when Ted and I started out on the farm, it was only natural that we gave away things. It was a casual thing, mostly—if people wanted some rhubarb or dill, for example, they could have it—after all, we had more than we could ever use. And when the business took off, we started to make more formal donations to a number of worthwhile causes. Edmonton and St. Albert had been so good to my family that we had to give something back.

But it was really when Ted and I turned over day-to-day operations to our sons Bill and Jim that we organized how we supported different groups. Philanthropy actually requires a lot of work—there are so many genuinely good causes that it's often difficult to decide how much to give, and how often.

We eventually decided that we would try to honour every legitimate request we received, rather than giving large amounts to any single charity. That's what we thought was fair, but of course there are many approaches to philanthropy. If someone wants to make one large donation to a single cause they feel passionately about, that's wonderful.

Of course, sometimes the urge to share isn't enough to spread the wealth around. Let me tell you a story about the time I tried to give something away and had no luck at all....

I have three grandchildren now, and I know that they will grow up to help others, too. They'll find their own style of philanthropy, no doubt, one for the 21st century, and they'll find new causes to support. But as long as they share their knowledge and compassion, I'll be happy—they have both in abundance. And I'd say that even if I weren't their grandmother.

The line between those who have and those who do not is often drawn not so much by skill or hard work, but by simple luck. Now, I know several successful business people who would strongly disagree with that statement, but I stand by it. Yes, hard work is crucial for financial success—but anyone who thinks they got rich all on their own, without any help from others, is kidding themselves. Without the help and support of their neighbours and a lot of luck, they could just as easily have wound up on the other side of the charitable donations.

That's why I've always liked the statement, "There but for the grace of God go I." The world would be a better place if people would just keep this simple phrase in mind.

Before I leave the stage, I want to thank you all for doing your part. You've made the world a better place. I know that's a cliché, but I mean it with all my heart. Philanthropy is one of the finest expressions of what it means to be human, and I am so very proud to share a room with you all today.

Thank you.

Lois Hole and Moe Wolff, Aide-de-camp at Canada Day citizenship ceremony, Alberta Legislature grounds, July 1, 2004. [Hole Family Archives]

2001

Lois spoke at many events honouring police and firefighters. This speech refers to one of her own close contacts with police, during an attempt to extort money from her family in 1998.

RCMP Wall of Honour Dedication

January 5, 2001

DEAR FRIENDS,

For over one hundred twenty-five years, officers of the North-West Mounted Police, the Royal Northwest Mounted Police, and today's Royal Canadian Mounted Police have upheld the law and protected the citizens of Canada. They have been steadfast in their pursuit of order and decency, from helping lost travellers to volunteering at charitable events to apprehending dangerous criminals. To make a commitment to such a life requires an abundance of courage, compassion, intelligence, and a host of other vital qualities.

The work of the RCMP makes a profound difference to the lives of all Canadians. They certainly helped my family enormously in 1998, when we faced the terror of an extortion attempt. In the face of such emotionally devastating events, the professionalism of the RCMP officers working on the case was welcome comfort. We felt safe in their hands.

The men and women of the RCMP are truly the best and the brightest, and none more so than the 38 members on this Wall of Honour. They died as they lived, in the pursuit of justice. Thanks to the RCMP Veterans Association and the Alberta March West re-enactment Committee, these names will stand forevermore as testament to the courage, dedication, and selflessness of the members of our national police force. I hope the families of these fallen members can take some comfort that their loved ones died so very honourably, while protecting the welfare of their fellow citizens.

I thank our officers, both those who have fallen and those who still serve us today, for their kindness, their courage, their loyalty, and their devotion to duty. Canada could not stand without you.

One of her chief strengths was an ability to bring lofty ideas down to earth but still retain a sense of occasion and explain their importance. Compare this speech to the way that other officials may handle the subject of cultural exchange.

Sherwood Heights Japan Day

January 24, 2001

GOOD MORNING, EVERYONE. Thank you so much for inviting me to this very special event. I'd like to share with you a little story that I think shows how important it is for cultures to share their values and experience.

A couple of years ago I had the opportunity to speak to students at Tokyo's Meiji University. Given how much Japanese culture has influenced Canadian gardening, it was an opportunity I wasn't about to turn down.

When I reached Japan, I couldn't help but notice the striking difference in landscaping style. As we whizzed along the highway from the airport to the hotel, I admired the long hedges of azaleas that divided the north and southbound lanes. They were tall and thick and absolutely immaculate, with gorgeous pink flowers in full bloom. I noted that interspersed with the azaleas were rows of orange marigolds, also in full bloom.

I also took note of the homes along the highway. The front yard vegetable gardens were incredibly efficient—pole beans ran up fences and exterior walls, cole crops flourished where Canadians would put grass, and there were even potatoes, more densely planted than I've ever seen. These vegetable gardens were incredibly clean—not a single weed dared intrude upon these sacred spaces.

When the time came to address the students at Meiji, I told them that the most striking difference I'd noticed between the Canadian way of gardening and the Japanese approach to gardening is the utilization of space. In a typical Canadian garden, every patch of soil is filled up with plants. When I wander through a Japanese garden, I notice the open spaces, the mass plantings, the sand and rock. It's a more holistic and spiritual approach to gardening that evokes feelings of peace, serenity—and often wonder.

The most striking reaction to my talk came when I showed the students a few slides, including one of a Tumbler tomato heavy with ripe red fruit. They all leaned forward in their seats when I told them about this amazing variety, which produces hundreds of juicy, delicious tomatoes on each plant. I wouldn't be surprised if pots full of Tumblers were already springing up on Japanese balconies. Given food prices in Japan, the Tumbler should be a big hit. After the talk, I spoke to several of the students individually—and nearly everyone had questions about container gardening and the Tumbler in particular.

Years ago, the number of Japanese plants people grew in their gardens could be counted on the fingers of one hand. Today, there are hundreds of Japanese imports gracing Canadian gardens. Double hepaticas, jack-in-the-pulpits, ornamental ginger, peonies, woodland perennials, rhododendrons, hostas, evergreens, Floral Showers snapdragons, Pageant primulas, Big Smile sunflowers, Imperial pansies—those are just a few examples. Then there's the flowering kale and cabbage and bonsai.

That trip really reinforced my belief that cultural exchange is a powerful progressive force. Our countries would be much poorer without continuous exchange of ideas and values.

A simple summary of a theme she would later explore many times, and often at greater length. She was greatly concerned that people like Mrs. Durocher and others with an aboriginal background had little or no opportunity to pass on their culture.

Lansdowne School Multicultural Event
Edmonton, January 26, 2001

HELLO, EVERYONE. Welcome, and thank you so much for inviting me to this celebration of multiculturalism.

My family and I have benefited tremendously from the cultural mosaic of Canada. My dear, late friend Mrs. Durocher is just one example; she was Métis, and she was one of the wisest people I've ever known. I learned more about gardening from her than from any other single source, and I will always be grateful for her kindness and friendship. And then there are the many immigrants, like the Italians and the Pakistanis, East Indians, and Lebanese who introduced me, so many years ago, to vegetables like broccoli and hot peppers, eggplant and patty pan squash. These vegetables are commonplace now, but forty years ago they were as exotic as edamame, an Asian vegetable I just tried out this Christmas, is today.

Canada's greatness comes from its people, and its people come from all parts of the world. We are great because we recognize and foster the contributions of people from all cultures, races, and religions. From the First Nations peoples to the early European settlers to today's arrivals from Asia, Africa, and all other points of the globe, Canada has a history of welcoming newcomers for the benefit of all.

However, our conduct has not always been perfect in this regard, and there is still much to do to ensure that Canadians, whatever their origins, remember to treat each other with respect and dignity. There is still racism, and there is still fear of unfamiliar cultures.

Fortunately, children do not share this fear. They have the advantage of innocence; they can only learn to hate from adults. Our most sacred responsibility, then, is to teach our children not just to tolerate the differences in their friends, but to love and cherish those differences. Because when it comes right down to it, there are no majorities or

Archbishop Desmond Tutu meets with university president Rod Fraser and Lois Hole during his visit to the University of Alberta, November 29, 1998. [Hole Family Archives]

minorities; we are all simply human, with the same basic desires for security, health, intellectual stimulation, and love.

The ideal Canada, the one that I hope to someday see, will be one where love and acceptance of our brothers and sisters isn't something to strive for, but something we accept as part of our daily lives. Those are the days worth fighting for, and I thank you for doing your part today. The people of tomorrow—red, white, yellow, and black—will thank you for starting down the path that leads to a better, more forgiving, more accepting, more loving world.

Rocky View is a municipal district in the rural—but rapidly urbanizing—area
north of Calgary. It was solidly in the camp of the Klein Conservatives. It was
to Rocky View school support staff attending a professional development day
in Calgary that Lois made her first extended speech on the virtues of educa-
tion, and of public education in particular. She also stepped close to the line
separating her office from politics—some might have said over the line. She
made virtually the same speech, a few paragraphs shorter, the same day in
Calgary to a convention of teachers from the Palliser school district, in south-
eastern Alberta. These speeches set the tone for many similar ones to follow.
Her pointed comments did not become the subject of a news story until more
than two years later, when she said the loss of public education would be a
"catastrophe." By then, however, she had been giving speeches similar to this
one many times and did not pull back.

Rocky View School Division
Professional Development Day
Calgary, February 22, 2001

GOOD MORNING. Thank you very much for inviting me here; I'm always
glad to share a room with the people who keep our schools running.
Without you, quality public education would be impossible.

Whenever talk of education comes up, people tend to focus on
teachers. Make no mistake; I love and respect teachers. But I think it's
crucial to acknowledge the vital contributions made by people like you.
Without secretaries, library technicians, assistants, caretakers, and
school board members, our schools would be a shambles. Not only do
you carry out critical functions, you all serve other, just as important
roles: as friends, counsellors, and guardians. I recall very well from my
own school days the caretakers who took the time to talk to troubled
students down in the furnace room, or the librarians who helped shy
children find a book to give them company.

By the way, I'd like to make a small digression just to mention how
glad I am that immigrants continue to play a role in our schools.
Whether they be teachers, caretakers, administrators, or trustees, they
contribute to our schools by providing students with the opportunity to
appreciate and learn from other cultures. Over the years I've learned

much from immigrants of every culture, and I'm gratified that today's young people have the same chance.

Now I'd like to talk a little about public education in general. These days, it's more important than ever to speak out about public education; here are my feelings, which I hope will prompt you to examine your own role in the effort to keep public education healthy.

British author H.G. Wells once wrote: "Human history becomes more and more a race between education and catastrophe." It's clear that the race begun so long ago continues to this day. All of the people at this convention are like members of a relay team, passing the baton from runner to runner as we strive towards the goal of creating a populace that has the tools to prevent catastrophe and bring about a smart, healthy, compassionate society.

My mother carried the baton for many years. Like many others, she taught under less than ideal conditions, conducting classes for children in Grades 1–9 within the confines of a tiny one-room schoolhouse about 17 miles away from the nearest community, my hometown of Buchanan, Saskatchewan. The schoolhouse was generously equipped with chalk, a chalkboard, and a stove that never seemed quite adequate to heat the place in the winter. It had a well-stocked library of seven books—all of which, if I remember correctly, were supplied by Mother. And, naturally, there wasn't enough money to pay her, so the school board gave her an old piano in lieu of money. She had no support staff; what she would have given for a secretary or a caretaker!

My mother wasn't the only member of the family to be involved in education. I've had cousins, a brother-in-law, and a sister-in-law that have all taught. And my husband's parents made darn sure that every one of their children got a university degree. But it was really my mother who showed me how important education is to our well being. It's because of her that I decided back in the '60s to get involved in public education.

> When I was a little girl, raiding gardens was simply part of growing up. Although we never took more than a stalk of rhubarb or a carrot, and were always careful not to cause damage, the risk of capture made our young hearts pound.
>
> That's why, as an adult, I've never been worried about kids sneaking into my garden now and then. For heaven's sake, if that's

the worst mischief they get into, we should count ourselves lucky. And if nothing else, it's one way to get them to eat their vegetables!

A lot of people aren't as easy-going, unfortunately. One day back in the 1970s, when we were selling u-pick vegetables, a woman came huffing and puffing down to the house. She had spotted a group of little boys raiding the pea patch and had run all the way from the field to report them. She wanted to see these "hooligans" punished.

Now, normally, I would have shrugged it off. But because this customer was so upset by the incident, I felt compelled at least to investigate the situation. I asked my son Bill to drive the truck up to the pea patch and sort things out.

As the truck approached, four little faces dropped suddenly out of sight between the rows. Bill just sat and waited. When the kids finally poked their heads up for a peek, they discovered all six-plus feet of Bill motioning at them to come over to the truck. "Get in," he told them ominously. "My MOTHER wants to talk to you."

The boys climbed reluctantly into the back of the truck, hanging their heads. I'm sure they thought they were in real trouble. I was waiting for them in the yard.

"So, you boys like to pick peas, do you?" I asked them. They nodded their heads sheepishly.

"Well," I said, "it just so happens that we need some help picking peas. Give me your names and addresses, and come back tomorrow at 7:00 a.m."

For the rest of the week, they obediently showed up to pick peas, a couple of hours before lunch and a couple of hours after. On Friday afternoon, Bill brought the boys down to the house, along with all our other farm workers. I started passing out cheques, including one for each of the four boys.

For a moment they just stood there, dumbfounded. They looked down at the cheques and then up at each other, down at the cheques, then up at each other. One of them asked timidly, "You mean, you're actually paying us?"

"Of course I am," I replied. "You've worked hard!"

He cleared his throat. "Mrs. Hole," he said fervently, "you are the nicest person in the world." I had to fight to keep from laughing. It finally dawned on me that those boys had thought they were being punished, and that if they didn't come out to work, I would phone *their parents. Instead, they were all going home with money in their pockets, to tell their folks about the job they found.*

I've always felt that, in the long run, punishment often does more harm than good. If kids behave in a certain way simply to avoid being punished, they're not learning a darned thing. Kids need to be taught the value of behaving responsibly.

Instead of coming down hard on those boys, and getting them into trouble at home, I gave them a job to do and paid them for it. As a result, they ended up learning a much more valuable lesson.

And I ended up with a pretty good story to tell. [15]

In this province there's an awful lot of talk about the Alberta Advantage. Let me tell you what I think the real Alberta Advantage is: a well-educated population. We have that advantage today because years ago there was an understanding that investment in education had positive long-term effects on the country. We must not let that advantage slip away because of short-term difficulties and shortsightedness. Why isn't education at the top of the list for investment? Public education benefits everyone: it benefits you, it benefits me, it benefits the children, it benefits the elderly, it even benefits the banks, large corporations, and politicians. I can't think of a single reason why everyone in this province shouldn't be solidly supporting our public schools. They're the cornerstone of a strong, intelligent democracy. They're the source of our future prosperity. They're what holds back catastrophe and encourages invention, thought, debate, creativity, and wisdom.

I think one of the things we need to do is be more assertive about the importance of public schools. We need to be better at promoting ourselves, of telling people about what we get out of public education.

A while back, Gordon Thomas, over at the ATA's Public Education Action Centre, sent me some very interesting articles on the benefits of public education. One article struck me in particular. It describes a study in which the progress of 60,000 students from private and public schools was tracked. The study found that of students entering university with identical A-level grades, those who attended public schools were 20 per cent more likely to get better grades in university than those from private schools. When public school graduates and private school graduates get together on a level playing field—the university—the public school grads come out on top. I think it's pretty obvious that our public school system is working, and will continue to work should the government make a real commitment to it. It's not that I have anything against private schools—just as long as they don't drain a single cent from the public system.

Public schools built the Canadian political culture that most of us are so proud of. So let your MLA and the minister of education know how you feel about public schools. Let them know that you support a system that provides every child with a quality education, regardless of ethnicity, religion, income, or ability. Let them know you support a system that has accountable, elected representatives. Write a letter to the paper. Ask a reporter to cover a special event or a typical day at your school. Just letting people know you care about the system can make a difference.

Education transcends the fault lines that divide political parties. No matter who is in power, we must make sure they have a genuine commitment to an ideal: that every student in Alberta have an equal opportunity to rise to his or her full potential. To me, that means fully funded public schools, smaller class sizes, private schools that are funded only by the private sector, lower university tuition fees, and well compensated teachers, administrators, and support staff. It means devoting time, effort, and money to ensure that our facilities and curriculum remain relevant as we progress through the 21st century. It means respect for all disciplines; music, drama, and physical education programs are not frills, but essential to helping our students become fully rounded, well-balanced individuals. And it means not having to go to corporate sponsors to fund our programs. We need to foster creative thought, not create another generation of passive consumers.

That, at any rate, is what proper respect for the process of education means to me. You may have a different approach, and that's fine; all I ask is that we all continue to think hard about the future of education in this province.

The race that Wells talks about is one that we all need to participate in. When the baton is passed, I know your hand will be open and ready to accept it.

A talk on women and their role in health care featured not only Virginie Durocher but Lois's uninhibited Auntie Anne, whose adventures served as the basis for many of the stories that enlivened Lois's speeches. Virginie Durocher literally applies warmth and love in the story told in this speech, but also had a working knowledge of medicinal herbs.

Grace Women's Health Centre
International Women's Week Celebrations
March 9, 2001

GOOD EVENING, EVERYONE.

[Reminder to thank other speakers; it looks like Laurie Blahitka, Director of Women's Health and Pregnancy Services of the Calgary Regional Health Authority is giving a welcome right before your speech.]

This is, as you know, International Women's Week, and the theme is "Canadian Women: Raising Our Diverse Voices for Positive Change." It's an excellent message, especially when it's related to the field of women's health.

There are a number of stereotypes surrounding women and health care. Traditionally, women have been assigned the role of caregiver; it's a role we play at home all the time, and I'm sure many of you have cared for sick children or husbands while fighting off illness yourself—and at the same time continuing to cook and clean. It's part of the maternal mystique, I think—moms don't have time to get sick.

Well, of course, women do have a wide range of health concerns, and thankfully those concerns are finally starting to get real attention from doctors, legislators, the media, and even women themselves, who, I certainly hope, at least, are now more willing to admit when they're sick and ask for help.

That being said, I do believe, quite firmly, that women do make excellent caregivers. My aunt, after all, served as a nurse for decades—never marrying, never having children, devoting her life to the care of others. She died at age 92 just a couple of years ago, and I can't even begin to count the number of lives she touched, helping soldiers recover in World War II at her station in England and after the war at the veteran's hospital in Edmonton. Auntie was an excellent nurse, and let me tell you, she was never afraid to raise her voice for positive change in the hospitals![16]

Doctors really liked Auntie Anne. When she was on the floor, things got done—on schedule, efficiently and with no extra fuss. But when doctors started sounding too high-handed or refused to consider improvement that clearly made good sense, they could be sure she'd set them straight. A mere five feet, four inches tall, Auntie Anne may have come no higher than their armpits, but she had no worries about challenging the way things were "always done."

Looking back on her war service, Auntie Anne would often lament about one key practice that nobody knew enough to challenge. Time after time, she'd help soldiers heal from catastrophic injury only to see them die of pneumonia. Back then, the best medical journals said "Keep them still and off their feet." It wasn't until later that people realized that complete bed rest was inviting pneumonia to settle in for a fatal visit.

Once back on Canadian soil, Auntie Anne was predictably efficient in applying everything she knew. Of course sanitation was a huge issue in wartime hospitals, so whenever she helped us out with laundry, she'd pour in the bleach. Our clothes suffered for it, but at least we knew they were clean. I remember a new pair of Ted's jeans that Auntie washed in too much bleach. Most of the threads had disintegrated.

After retiring, Auntie Anne came almost every day. She mended, baked, made preserves and of course prepared lunch for the family every noon hour. And in true Auntie style, she wouldn't sit still for latecomers. We either arrived on time, or she'd come hunt us down.

When I think of all Auntie Anne contributed in the many phases of her life, I can't help but be thankful for all those years—especially because they almost didn't come to be. When she was very young, her parents took her to the hospital in acute pain. "Appendicitis," the doctor said. He prescribed removal, but the family couldn't afford to pay for the operation. It was fifteen dollars, precious money they didn't have. So little Anne was taken home to die. Miraculously, the *appendix shrivelled rather than bursting and filling her with poison, and she not only survived, but thrived. No wonder Auntie Anne became a nurse with attitude.*

What a shame it would have been if Auntie Anne had died. She modelled many things in life—as a nurse, a strong independent woman and a loving caregiver. But the first lesson she taught our family was the importance of making health care freely available—to everyone, no matter what they can or cannot pay. I always say, "There but for the grace of God go I."

Speaking of diverse voices, I'm reminded of another remarkable caregiver, my longtime friend Mrs. Durocher, a Métis woman with no formal education who nonetheless taught me a great deal about compassion. Many, many decades ago, she gave birth to her first child— but the boy was very frail, very weak, and the doctors told her that the child had little hope of surviving; there was nothing they could do.

In that kind of situation, I think many people would have given in to despair, but not Mrs. Durocher. You won't believe it, but she made herself an incubator for that baby, filling up empty bottles with hot water and wrapping the child in blankets and showering that baby with all the love she had in her heart. And the child lived.

Mrs. Durocher was a supernaturally quiet woman; even the smoke from her cigarettes seemed to move with slow, deliberate grace—but she was passionate. She didn't need to raise her voice for positive change; she created change by example. I have enormous respect for the people who speak out for health care—in fact, I think it's crucial these days to be very, very vocal about it—but I don't think we should forget the quieter people, like Mrs. Durocher, who work so hard to care for others in their own way. They, too, have voices, but softer ones....

One of the premier annual charitable fundraising events in Edmonton gave
Lois an opportunity to talk about poverty to some of the wealthiest and most
socially active people in the city. It was a subject she took to heart. She knew
that Virginie Durocher's son-in-law, John Ward, had sometimes been refused
access to city buses because he was carrying food and drink to work. Other
people, more visibly affluent, were not getting the same treatment. She always
gave money to panhandlers and made a point of looking them in the eye as
she approached them.

Inner City Agencies Foundation
Mac & Cheese Luncheon
March 21, 2001

GOOD AFTERNOON, EVERYONE, and welcome to today's fundraiser. I
think that Bruce Saville and the Inner City Agencies Foundation deserve
enormous praise for coming up with the Mac & Cheese Luncheon; not
only is it a good way to raise funds for several vital inner city agencies,
but it also raises the profile of our often forgotten poor. That's especially
important now, when the economy is thriving; in good times, it becomes
far easier to forget or simply ignore the fact that not everyone has benefited from the Alberta boom.

Today, we gather together as members of a privileged class before an
atypically humble meal, in the hopes that by doing so we recognize both
our own extraordinary good fortune and the appalling circumstances of
far too many of our fellow citizens. What seems like rather pedestrian
fare to us—a simple plate of macaroni and cheese—is a staple food or
even a luxury to the poor.

And then there's that phrase, "the poor." "The underprivileged." I'm
always a little wary when I use such phrases, because then a large group
of people gets lumped together as a class, and that makes them distant
and a little less human. I'd like to try to put a human face back on some
of the people we're trying to help today, and I think a couple of stories
might do that.

A few years back, my son Bill and his wife Valerie went to dinner at
the Westin. After the meal, an obviously destitute fellow approached

them and asked for five dollars for bus fare so that he could visit his sick mother in Saskatoon. Well, Bill gave him the money, and the man thanked him.

About a week later, Bill and Valerie bumped into this man again, right in the same part of town. And the man gave them the same story—he needed bus fare to visit his sick mother in Saskatoon. Bill recognized the man and the story immediately, and blurted out, "Didn't you ask me the same thing last week?" At that point, the man recognized Bill and realized that he'd blown it; it was obvious his story wasn't true. Now, Bill didn't care, and he tried to give the guy another five bucks anyway, but nothing Bill could say would convince the man to take the money once his story was revealed as being untrue. He just held his hands up, backing away, saying, "No, no, I'm sorry," and not meeting Bill's eyes.

That story sticks with me, because I think it shows that this man had a sense of pride, or integrity, or some kind of code of honour that wouldn't allow him to take advantage of the same person with the same story twice. Now, when I say "take advantage of," I'm referring not to the reality of the situation, but to what the man might have thought in his own mind. Bill and Valerie certainly didn't feel taken advantage of, and I know that Bill still feels bad about pointing out the man's lie rather than just letting it slide. The point is, the man had enough dignity and a strong enough sense of self-worth that he absolutely refused to take that second five dollars. Or maybe he was simply too embarrassed to take it; we'll never know. Either way, he reacted in undeniably human fashion, with all the same fear, pride, and shame that you and I feel from time to time. When you get right down to the nitty-gritty, all that separates us is a few dollars in the bank.

Here's another story I'll never forget; it happened to a friend of a friend, a very poor Métis woman who received a summons to appear in court for some minor infraction; I forget what. The appointed hour arrived, and the judge was incensed when he called the woman's name and she wasn't there. She did turn up eventually, but days later. Well, the judge ripped her up one side and down the other. "Don't you have any respect for this court? How can you treat this matter so casually?"

The woman endured this harsh upbraiding, head down, never saying a word until the judge was finished. And then she said, "I tried to get here on time, but I had to walk, and I live out of town. I was hoping someone would give me a ride, but no one stopped, and so I had to walk all the way here. No one would pick me up, Your Honour."

And then she looked up at the judge, and she asked, quite respectfully, "Would you have picked me up?"

And the judge dismissed the case.

I hope I'm not romanticizing the poor, because that's not my intent. Like everyone else, the man or woman or child in desperate circumstances has both noble and selfish qualities. Like us, he or she is capable of great compassion or wilful disregard for their fellows. They might be polite and humble in their requests for help, or they might be demanding and ungrateful. *But it doesn't matter which.* The point is, they need help, and as compassionate human beings, it is our solemn duty to provide that aid. To paraphrase Hemingway, the poverty of another is my own poverty. The destitution of one diminishes us all.

By being here, you recognize that important truth, and I apologize if I'm preaching to the converted. But if there is a danger to events like these, it is to congratulate oneself for participating and then become complacent. Make no mistake—you've done a wonderful thing by coming here today. But really dealing with the problems of the inner city requires a constant effort. Perhaps you could start a small endowment to provide inner-city residents with a good set of clothes for job interviews, or write your MLA to see if some of that surplus could be poured back into mental hospitals or low-income housing or shelters. Talk to the administration at your alma mater to see about starting some kind of scholarship program for the underprivileged; education, as many of us know from direct experience, is one of the keys to escaping poverty. Contact the Boyle Street Co-op and see what kind of help they need; they do a lot of excellent work, and are always looking for volunteers or fiscal support. And of course, continue to support Bruce and the Inner City Agencies Foundation—their work continues year-round.

I'd like to close with a poem by John Wesley:

Do all the good you can,
By all the means you can,
In all the ways you can,
In all the places you can,
At all the times you can,

To all the people you can,
As long as ever you can.

Thank you so much for coming today. You've really helped make a concrete difference in the lives of underprivileged Edmontonians, and I know that Bruce and Shelley and all their colleagues are profoundly grateful for your support.

She claimed "a pretty traditional career as a farm wife." It was traditional only in the sense that other strong women from the Prairies had also become involved in public life over the last century. She was inspired by the work and dedication of farm women and believed they did not get nearly enough credit for what they did.

National Conference on Women in Trades & Technology
March 23, 2001

GREETINGS, EVERYONE. I'm very pleased to be with you today as we celebrate the success and the potential of the Women in Trades & Technology National Network.

History has proven that women make vital contributions to the trades, technology, and blue-collar sectors when given the chance to do so; we need only remember the experience of the Second World War and the decades that followed to know that. Women have made great strides, but as we all know, there is still much to do. Without being given a fair chance to experience the rewards and wonder of studying trades and technology, girls and women will inevitably migrate towards "traditional" female occupations. Not that there's anything wrong with such career choices—up until relatively recently, I had a pretty traditional career as a farm wife—but everyone should have the chance to explore a variety of fields while they're young and haven't yet decided how to spend their lives. In a truly free society, there should be no "expected" career path for girls. They should have a full range of career options to choose from.

I think we should also try to educate people that blue-collar work is just as important and challenging as some jobs that society currently gives more prestige to.

I've always said that in a greenhouse or garden, watering is the most important job. To a plant, water is everything. If you water it too much, too little, or inconsistently, you'll have real problems. You'd better do it right.

In the beginning, I did most of the watering myself. Later, as the job became too big for me to handle alone, I always made sure that I had confidence in the people helping me.

People have this strange idea that just because a job appears menial, it doesn't require any brains. In my experience, though, intelligence can express itself in almost any task. We used to hire teachers during the summer to help thin and weed the crops. I'd explain the basic principles once, and they'd grasp them right away. After a couple of days, you'd swear they'd grown up on the farm.

Watering is much the same. Anybody can point the business end of a hose, but it takes real skill to do the job right. I have employees who can look along a row of flowers, sense the temperature and humidity, and know just how much water the plants need. They can tell at a glance when a plant needs moisture, long before it actually begins to wilt.

I was once at a bedding-plant conference and had signed up for a special luncheon. The keynote speaker was Nancy Austin, who had co-written the motivational bestseller In Search of Excellence. *She told us that as greenhouse managers, we should ensure we put our time to its most productive use. "You people shouldn't be out there watering. That's the kind of job anybody can do. You've got better ways to spend your time."*

At the end of her talk, she asked if there were any questions. I just couldn't stand it any longer. I put my hand up and said, "I'm afraid I have to make a small criticism. You may be an expert on time management, but I'm afraid you don't know a lot about greenhouses or plants. You made it sound as if watering were a menial job, one that doesn't take any skill. That's just not true. Watering is the most important job in the greenhouse." Well, the audience practically gave me a standing ovation. They knew that it needed to be said.

I'm surprised at how often I have to set people straight on this issue. I remember a friend of mine who called me one afternoon with an extra ticket for a theatre matinee. I said, "Oh crum, I can't go. I have all this watering to do." She said, "Why don't I get Susan to come out and do it for you?" Susan was her twelve-year-old daughter!

If your plants aren't properly watered, they simply won't thrive. They'll grow unevenly, they won't produce very good blooms or fruit, or they could very well die altogether.

In fact, some plants die before they even break the surface of the soil. People put seeds into dry earth, sprinkle on a little bit of water, and wait. The seeds germinate, dry out, and die. A few times each year, somebody will tell me, "I planted a whole patch of carrots, and not a single one came up." In almost every case, poor watering is the reason.

For goodness' sake, plant your seeds early in the season, while the ground's still moist, then hope for rain. If it doesn't rain, you're going to have to get out there and water thoroughly, every single day.

In fact, that may mean watering even after a rain. Unless you're hit with a real soaker, the rain won't penetrate more than an inch or so beneath the surface. If you just leave it at that, the rain actually causes more harm than good. The roots will grow where the moisture is: near the surface. Without deep roots, your plants will be much more vulnerable to drought later.

Water regularly and water thoroughly. Nothing is more essential to growing a beautiful garden. And if you drop by our greenhouse one of these days, don't be surprised if I'm busy watering. [17]

Thanks to conferences like this, women are discovering a whole world of new choices. They are discovering that they can lead more fulfilling lives through careers that match their talents and interests.

We should all be very grateful to the people and organizations that make this conference and the work of the WITT National Network possible. Getting more women into trades and technology will prove to be of great benefit in the 21st century—the coming decades will be very exciting, as the seeds of inspiration planted today bear the fruits of discovery tomorrow.

You women, by choosing to pursue careers in the trades and technology, are not simply enriching your own lives—you are providing inspiration for young girls and influencing the way that companies operate. A female voice in research or construction can provide insights remarkably different than those provided by men. And let's remember, too, that for every man or woman opposed to the idea of women working in non-traditional jobs, there are many more who are genuinely thrilled to have women working alongside them, from the sensitive guy working on the oil rigs who can drop a little of his macho façade to the female research scientist glad to finally have another woman in the lab to talk to. You're making workplaces more comfortable for men and women alike, and that can only lead to more productivity, more comfortable working conditions, and more happiness overall.

You are to be congratulated, then, for choosing to strike out in this direction. I hope that all of the convention delegates bring home many new insights, new career ideas, and most importantly, new friends, new contacts, and new doorways to opportunity.

Thank you.

Food banks were well established in Alberta by 2001 and were still spreading despite a resumption of strong economic growth after a downturn in the early 1990s. Lois paid more attention to them than most provincial politicians. She had often packed extra cinnamon toast or other food into her children's school lunch packages to provide for friends whose parents were sending them to school without enough to eat.

Edmonton Gleaners 20th Anniversary
March 28, 2001

HELLO, EVERYONE.

Like many of you, I feel conflicted over this, the 20th anniversary of the Edmonton Gleaners. On the one hand, you deserve the highest honours for twenty years of meritorious public service to our most desperate citizens. On the other hand, it's saddening that in spite of Alberta's prosperity, the need for the food bank hasn't abated; in fact, I understand the demands upon it grow year by year.

Do we celebrate this anniversary, then, or mark it as a solemn occasion?

I had to think about that for a while before I came up with the answer. I'd like to share a story with you that I hope will lead you to the same conclusion I came to.

About eight years ago, while I was serving on the Quality of Life commission, I visited an elementary school in the inner city. They had been running a school lunch program for a short time and were hoping to keep the program running with the help of some extra sponsors.

During my visit with the school's principal, he looked up at the clock on his office wall, noted that it was almost lunchtime, and took a glance out the window, into the hallway. "Look there," he pointed, and I looked and saw a little girl, about nine years old. She was a thin little thing, wearing clothing that was obviously handed down. The principal said, "She's going to run straight home as soon as the bell rings."

Well, the bell rang, and sure enough the little girl was off like a shot. "Is she off to tell her parents about her report card?" I asked. "Or to watch the Flintstones on her lunch hour?"

"No," the principal said, "Just wait a few minutes and see."

So we waited a few minutes, and the little girl came back, but with her brother and sister in tow, running as fast as they could for the cafeteria.

"She brings her brother and sister in every day so that they can have something to eat," he explained, "Goodness knows they're not getting fed at home. Sometimes I worry this might be the only meal they get all day."

Today I still wonder about those children, who will be teenagers now, and I wonder if they got enough to eat to stay healthy and able to learn. Because that's what I think is the most important service the food bank provides: they help to ensure that children get fed. And that gives children a chance to focus on their schoolwork instead of worrying about if their brothers and sisters are going to get any lunch. By providing families in need with food, the Edmonton Food Bank is giving children a chance to learn, and therefore also a chance to break the cycle of poverty.

I hope that the need for the food bank will gradually become less urgent. But the reality is, we will always need a food bank; after all, any one of us could find ourselves out of work, or without a spouse or the victim of a disability. When bad times hit, it's crucial to have the food bank to turn to. For that reason, I encourage donors, volunteers, and supporters to continue their efforts, and all levels of government to recognize that they, too, must pay their dues to the food bank. It's very sad that Edmonton must have a food bank, but it would be an even greater shame if we didn't support it. No, it would be more than a shame—it would be a crime.

Thank you for giving deserving Edmontonians 20 years of goodwill and aid. I tell you that your work has not been and shall not be in vain, and that history will look upon your efforts with an approving eye.

No community was too small to visit. No audience was treated with anything less than complete respect. This speech was made at a school gathering at Waskatenau (pronounced Wa-SET-Na), about 50 kilometres northeast of Edmonton. The village was founded in 1919 when a rail line was built through the area. In 2001 it had a population of about 250, of whom about 40 were school age. Lois spoke at the school and gave the local audience both her usual personal stories and a serious talk on libraries. The village was already putting a lot of effort into its library service. For Lois, this was a chance to lend moral support to the local volunteers who kept libraries and other public serv-ices running in Waskatenau, as in countless small communities. Her famili-arity with local personalities and institutions was not casual. She insisted all communities deserved respect, and routinely had her staff look up information about them before she visited. That respect was reciprocated. A visit by Lois Hole was always a highlight in local life.

Waskatenau School

April 20, 2001

GOOD AFTERNOON, EVERYONE.

First of all, allow me to congratulate you on the 30th anniversary of the Anne Chorney Public Library and 30 years of exemplary volunteer service. Without people like Irma Lunn, George Shapka, Cathy Zon, Grace Flaska, and Lucy Chaba, and so many other volunteers, the people of Waskatenau would be deprived of a vital resource.

Speaking of volunteers, I must also, of course, congratulate Leonard Scott once again, whose dedication to the community has touched the lives of all of Waskatenau's citizens. I must tell you, I was reading some of the stories about Leonard that Bernice and Gail sent my office, and my goodness, I don't know how he does it. Leonard, as I'm sure you all know better than I, has kept busy serving as a baseball umpire, he's been active with the United Church, he's worked on the rural electrifica-tion board and even helped set up the phone system here in Waskatenau. And that's just the tip of the iceberg! In this International Year of the Volunteer, Leonard's dedication to the community is an inspiring example that I hope will encourage others to try their own hand at volunteering.

Leonard's concern for the happiness and welfare of children is particularly moving, and I think it's quite appropriate that we should celebrate Leonard's efforts today at the same time we celebrate the library's anniversary, since libraries, too, are so important to the welfare of our youngsters.

To me, a library is the highest architectural expression of human civilization. It represents all the best parts of the human soul—our desire to learn, to explore, to question, to ponder, to dream. Within a library you can find the most compelling ideas of our greatest thinkers, and, just as importantly, the darkest and most terrifying notions of our cruelest tyrants. History, with all its shadings of good, evil, and indifferent, is there for the curious mind to explore.

Furthermore, a library holds works that fire the imagination, that bring peace to a troubled heart, or the fire for change in one that's grown too complacent. The library can show you how to build a birdhouse, or how the Space Shuttle works.

I used to take my sons Bill and Jim to the library all the time when they were boys—Bill was particularly fascinated by go-carts, and he took out all the books the old Westmount library had on the subject. Where else could he have found all that information? We certainly couldn't afford to buy all those books, I can tell you, and that's why libraries are so important; anyone, rich or poor, can use them and take advantage of all the knowledge within.

I read a little bit about the history of the Anne Chorney Public Library before I came, and I must say, it's a good model for other communities that hope to effectively combine facilities and services for everyone's benefit. When resources are limited, it's crucial for government, townspeople, and small business to get together and build something that will bring a real benefit to everyone's lives. You've done that here, and you've kept those partnerships alive for three decades now. I can't think of an endeavour more noble than getting together to build a library.

Within a library can be found the seeds of a better tomorrow. If planted in the right fertile minds, these seeds, properly nurtured, can grow into the ideas that will make the world of the future more just and more compassionate than the one we live in today.

Her Excellency the Governor General recently gave a speech about libraries, and she quoted George Locke, who back in 1934 was the chief librarian of the Toronto Public Libraries. Locke said, "The pride of a library is not the mere possession of books, but rather the explanation of the significance of those treasures and the development of interest and pleasure among those who may have the taste, but not the material means of satisfying it."

I love that quote, because it sums up what librarians do: they make all the knowledge of the past available to those who could not otherwise afford to learn. Thank you for giving all the children of Waskatenau the chance to learn, to grow, and to discover all the wonders that can be found between the covers of a good book.

A national conference on children afforded a platform to talk about the impor-
tance of bringing up children well. A few pointed comments about the Alberta
Advantage set her remarks in the Alberta political context and suggested the
province should consider new priorities.

Canadian Association for Young Children
National Conference
April 27, 2001

GOOD MORNING, DELEGATES. I am honoured to officially open the
National Conference of the Canadian Association for Young Children.
Whether you have travelled just a few blocks to this conference or from
thousands of kilometres away, welcome. Your commitment to the
welfare and happiness of young children is cause for profound joy and
celebration.

"The best way to make children good is to make them happy." Oscar
Wilde said that, and I firmly believe that he was correct. There seems to
be a growing current of thought today that leans more towards that tired
old saying, "spare the rod and spoil the child." As if that were the solution to any problem—beating it into submission.

I think Wilde's philosophy is vastly preferable, and that's why I
appreciate how the Canadian Association for Young Children focusses
on the importance of play in a child's life. As so many studies have
shown, play increases a child's ability to think, to learn, to develop the
cognitive skills that will be so important to he or she's future happiness
and development as an intelligent being.

Here in Alberta, we like to talk about the Alberta Advantage. When
politicians and businessmen use that phrase, it usually refers to tax
breaks and energy resources. But I think the real Alberta Advantage—
and the real Canadian Advantage—is our children. And the thing about
an advantage is this: it can either be employed, or ignored. It's with the
children that our future lies, and it is they who will determine the shape
of things to come. Ignore the children, and you're ignoring our best
resource, and our best hope for a better tomorrow.

Thank you for treating our children like a precious resource; not just
in the sense of something to be mined or harvested, but in the sense of

Lois and her granddaughter Kathryn, summer 1992. [Hole Family Archives]

something that needs to be nurtured for its own sake as much as for its usefulness to us.

I hope that you enjoy a successful conference, and that the children of Canada will reap the rewards of your efforts here. Thank you for devoting yourselves to this most noble cause.

Lois backed up her words with action. The young woman she talked about in this speech was only one of a number of young people who lived with the Hole family for a time while dealing with a variety of personal problems. Her name was Cecile Ethier; she later died of breast cancer. Women's shelters were one of a number of women's issues that drew Lois's attention. Alberta continued to have relatively high rates of spousal abuse through the early 2000s, however. It also had one of the country's highest rates of spousal homicide and a chronic shortage of shelter space that resulted in hundreds of women being turned away from shelters each year.

7th Annual Passport to Hope Gala in Support of Lurana Shelter

Edmonton, April 27, 2001

GOOD EVENING, ALL, and thank you for inviting me to the 7th Annual Passport to Hope Gala. I'm going to share one quick story with you, because it bears directly on tonight's event.

Some years ago, I had occasion to take in a young woman who was being physically and emotionally abused by her family. It's no surprise that this was a very moody young woman, and I have to admit that she nearly drove me mad. She was a rough and tumble girl, never taking any nonsense from anyone. I remember she used to bathe my sons Bill and Jim, and she scrubbed them so hard it's like she thought she was peeling potatoes.

In fact, at one point, I reluctantly told her that it just wasn't working out, and that perhaps she should start looking for another place to stay. Well, she nodded and agreed, but somehow she never did get around to leaving; she didn't really have anyplace to go. I'm glad now that she stayed; her mood was improving, especially after I forced her to start eating a little more; I realized later that she hardly ate anything for fear of costing us too much money.

She expressed interest in nursing, and so I told her that she should pursue a degree in that; and so she did. She attended nursing school at the Misericordia here in Edmonton, and she did fairly well—but one day, she phoned me up in tears.

"They kicked me out," she told me. "But why?" I asked her.

Well, she told me that one of the instructors, a priest, had started badmouthing Protestants. Well, of course I'm a Protestant, and out of an outraged sense of loyalty, my young friend stood up and told the priest exactly what she thought of him. "A Protestant family took me in when I had nowhere to go, so you can just—" and then she told him to—well, I'll leave it to your imagination. But it certainly wasn't the kind of thing anyone should say to a priest!

I can laugh about it now, of course, but at the time this was a serious matter. Of course she shouldn't have directed such language at a priest, but I have to admit I was touched by her loyalty and affection. So I told her, "Look—don't worry. Let me make a couple of phone calls."

I phoned the matron and told her, "Look, you've got to take her back. You've got to understand that she felt very close to us and she was upset. And if you refuse, I'm going to fly to Ottawa and sit on the steps until the prime minister agrees to talk to me. And then I'm going to tell HIM what happened."

Well, I don't know if the prime minister would have done anything, but they took her back.

Back then, there were no shelters to provide refuge for people like the young woman I just described. Today things are different, and the existence of the Lurana shelter is ample proof that the Catholic Church cares deeply for the plight of women and girls in situations like the one my friend had to endure. Lurana shelter truly is issuing a Passport to Hope to victims of domestic abuse. You are providing shelter from a storm more terrible than anything Mother Nature could possibly inflict—the storm of hate, fear, and anger unleashed by an abusive spouse or parent. With your help, abused women can stand against the tempest to rediscover their strength, pride, and hope.

Speaking to students afforded an opportunity to remind them of a few tradi-
tions they likely weren't learning elsewhere. Lois depicted her short spelling
and pronunciation lesson as a short course in political skills; it was really an
attempt to preserve Canadian traditions, one young person at a time. The
speech closely resembles a generic speech for high school students worked up
in her office the preceding October. She used this format on occasion, but was
just as likely to try other ideas. The key to all her speeches to students was
careful attention to stories they might find both entertaining and instructive.

Lilian Schick School
Career Day
Bon Accord, May 1, 2001

HELLO, EVERYONE. Thank you so much for having me here today; I'm
delighted to have the chance to meet with you.

You've heard from many different experts today about all kinds of
interesting careers. Some of you may even be interested in a career in
Canadian politics. If that's the case, I have just a few short tips:

Remember that the last letter of the alphabet is "Zed," not "Zee."

Remember to spell honour, colour, valour, neighbour, and harbour
with a "u."

And finally, it's "Left-tenant," not "Loo-tenant," Governor.

Naturally I'm kidding. If you really want to go into politics—and
remember there's a big difference between elected office and an
appointed position like mine—you need two things: a commitment to
help people and a willingness to learn. Well, there are other things you
need to know if you're thinking about entering politics, but I think those
can wait until you're a little older. Just keep those two things in mind:
helping people and being willing to learn, because those will help in any
career.

Well, my career, of course, has mostly involved gardening. I got pretty
good at it by the time I changed jobs just last year, but it didn't always
come easy:

> *When I was four or five years old, I would ride with my Dad down*
> *to his stockyards on the outskirts of Buchanan, Saskatchewan. My dad*
> *was a stock buyer, and I used to enjoy watching the farmers and*

stockyard workers loading and unloading the livestock. Although I didn't realize it at the time, my young mind absorbed the whole process in surprising detail.

Many years later, Ted and I tried our hand at raising pigs. I'll always remember when it first came time to take them to market. We needed a chute to get them onto the truck, of course, so Ted set to work building one. I assumed he knew what he was doing, so I didn't pay much attention. However, although he had sound carpentry skills, he had never built a pig chute.

When he brought out the chute, I took one look at it and said, "Ted, you can't use a chute that big for pigs." It was as wide as the half-ton. Pigs need a narrow chute so they can't turn around. Not surprisingly, Ted didn't welcome my unsolicited advice. "What the hell do you know about loading pigs?" he grumbled.

He managed to get three or four pigs part way up the chute. Suddenly, the first pig decided he'd rather be down with his buddies in the pen, so he turned around. Ted blocked his path with a sheet of plywood and let out a whoop, just to show the pig who was boss.

Well, utter chaos ensued. All the pigs were upset now. Every time Ted lunged one way, a pig scrambled another. You might think it's impossible for a pig to climb over the wall of a chute, but get one good and agitated and you'll find out differently. Not a single pig made it all the way onto the truck. Eventually, we threw up our hands and deserted the field of battle.

Ted had to dismantle the chute and rebuild it, while I wisely suppressed the urge to say, "I told you so." When the time came to try again, I suggested, "You should hold a piece of plywood in front of you and walk up the chute behind the pigs." Ted set to work, trying his best, but again the pigs refused to cooperate. Within a minute or two, Ted was yelling and swearing, and the pigs were squealing, grunting, and running around madly.

"Ted, calm down!" I shouted. "You're not going to get anywhere that way!" In his state, that wasn't what he wanted to hear. He continued pushing away at the pigs and sure enough, we didn't get them loaded that day either.

Later in the evening, once Ted and the pigs had settled down, I convinced him to let me give it a try. From what I had seen as a kid, I knew that you had to be very gentle and quiet when loading pigs.

The next day we assembled the pigs for a third attempt. I walked slowly out, crept right up to one of them, put my hand down, and directed a pig up the chute and into the truck, making a gentle "whooshing" sound the whole time. Anytime the pig felt like pausing for a little look around, I'd wait right beside it. When it was ready to continue, off we'd go together.

I herded the pigs into the truck, one by one, while the others patiently, silently waited their turns. Ted could only stand by and chuckle in amazement. From then on, loading the pigs was my job: Ted never could seem to get the knack.

After a few years, it became clear to both of us that we weren't cut out to be pig farmers. And it may be an awful thing to admit, yet those pigs taught me a thing or two about dealing with excitable people. The quiet approach is often the only one that works. If you speak softly and lay a gentle hand on their shoulder, you can lead them almost anywhere.[18]

Now, Ted and I didn't raise pigs for very long, which was probably good, all things considered. We switched to market gardening and then we started the greenhouse, because these businesses suited our talents and our education better. The most important thing is to understand that to find the perfect career and enjoy the fullest, happiest life possible, you have to keep your mind open to learning.

I know that some of you have enjoyed school more than others. Some probably can't wait for summer holidays. But look back for a moment, across the years, and really think about all that you've learned and experienced. Perhaps your list includes the following:

- The power of a good book.
- Standing up to a bully—and then making him a friend.
- The pride in craftsmanship of a well-constructed bit of woodwork.
- Working up the nerve to ask someone you really care about to dance.
- Learning how to manage time.
- Writing a really great essay.
- Breaking a school record.

- The adrenaline rush of a really close ball game.
- Being exposed to the amazing world of history, full of stories wilder than any fantasy.
- Struggling with teachers—and then discovering sometimes they need help, too.
- Discovering your talent for music.
- The satisfaction of finally getting that really tough equation.
- Finding out in drama class that you can act.
- The challenge of really being yourself.
- Laughing at those hopelessly outdated educational films you still see from time to time—only to discover that some of them still contain a kernel of truth and wisdom.
- The haunting beauty of poetry.
- The delight in discovering that yes, you can cook—and you're not bad, either.
- Being exposed to different cultures for the first time.
- The value of friendship.
- And finally, the great feeling you get when you can actually answer a question correctly—when you can help someone with your knowledge. There's a power and joy in that feeling that's unlike any other.

You've experienced so much in such a small window of time. Your experiences at school have played a huge role in shaping who you are and what you might become. But it's not going to suddenly stop when you graduate a few years from now. You have many years ahead of you, with experiences even more varied and intense than those you've enjoyed—or endured—so far.

Some say the world is getting smaller every year. In a way, that's true; but it's also far bigger than any one person can experience in its entirety. The world is huge and full of wonders, and those who keep their hearts and minds open to new knowledge will be best equipped to enjoy it—or even to make it a better world for everyone.

You have that capacity, that potential, and if you hang on to what means the most to you, you'll find the perfect career and be helping people at the same time. And that's the best job in the world.

The message is delivered with a light touch. It was important to Lois. She felt she witnessed surprising amounts of prejudice in both public and private life. The effect was heightened by the tendency of many people to confide in her in ways they would not do with others.

Didsbury Mayor's Prayer Breakfast

Didsbury, May 4, 2001

GOOD MORNING, EVERYONE, and welcome to this solemn but joyous occasion.

Solemn, because in the face of the complex problems of today's society, it is important to reflect, to be humble, and to recognize that there are greater forces at work in the world than us.

Joyous, because though we do face difficult choices every day, we can take comfort in our faith, whatever that faith may be—in the Judeo-Christian god, in one of the Asian or Arabic religions, or even simple secular faith in the notion that people are inherently good and will do their best to be kind to each other.

When my son Bill was eight years old, he came up and asked me "What religion am I?"

"Well, you're Protestant," I told him.

"Oh, darn," he said. "I wanted to be Catholic."

"Why's that?" I asked him.

"Because Larry Kozachuk is Catholic, and he says God is Catholic, too."

I laughed and told him, "Well, don't worry about that. The Protestants think that God is Protestant, too, and the Mormons think God is Mormon, and the Muslims think God is Muslim. Just because you and Larry have different ideas about God doesn't mean you can't still be friends."

And that was that; Bill learned that it didn't matter that he and Larry had different religions; as long as they treated each other well, they'd get along just fine.

One of the greatest philosophies in the Christian tradition is the notion that you should do unto others as you would have them do unto you. If I were to offer a prayer, then, it would be that people of all faiths or even no faith could learn to respect each other's choices. I would pray to see the day when preachers and the scientists, regular churchgoers and the atheists, teenage Goths and Salvation Army volunteers, orthodox Jews and fundamentalist Muslims can share a cup of coffee and some friendly conversation, without prejudice on either side. And I would pray that our leaders recognize the value of each and every person in our great country, and that the people recognize that their leaders carry heavy burdens each and every day, many of which never grace the pages of the daily newspapers.

We are none of us perfect, nor in possession of any great universal truths. As humans, we are fallible, often spiteful, and too little generous. But we do try to do the right thing; we try, by and large, to be kind.

So with a touch of humility, I hope you will join me in genuine thanks for our prosperity, our fellowship, and the promise of a better tomorrow.

This speech was brief, but unusual for its time. The political upheaval that led to the selection of Ralph Klein as Progressive Conservative leader and Alberta premier in December 1992 had included an outbreak of antipathy to government workers at all levels. Some of Klein's cabinet ministers frequently played to those emotions during the 1990s. Lois was an early voice leaning in the direction of praise for public service.

Institute of Public Administration of Canada "Exploring the E-Frontier" Conference
May 7, 2001

IT IS MY GREAT PLEASURE to be with you this morning to participate in opening this conference. A conference like this is a huge undertaking, but one that is eminently worthwhile, especially given the rapidly changing nature of public service in an increasingly technological world.

Public service is done anonymously, and with little fanfare. It is such an important part of a democratic society that is often taken for granted by our citizens. Citizens in every municipality, province and territory in our country owe a debt of gratitude to all those who choose the public service as a career. It is among the most honourable of pursuits and, on behalf of Albertans and Canadians everywhere, I thank you.

I will not take a lot of your time this morning, and I will look forward to meeting many of you at our morning refreshment break. You have a very exciting conference in front of you, and I wish you all the best in having a successful and enjoyable experience.

Gardening—for Lois it was a world of earthly delights, lessons for living, recreation, and sources of good nutrition. It was also the signature pursuit that most people inside and outside Alberta associated with her. For all her other interests and accomplishments, she was always the lady with plants or a trowel in her hand. That was fine with her. She understood that gardening had transformed from something people needed to do to something they wanted to do, for sheer enjoyment.

Seniors Wellness Conference

Breton, Alberta, May 10, 2001

HELLO, EVERYONE, and welcome to the Seniors Wellness Conference. I hope that you'll take home many new ideas for keeping your mind and body active during this event. For my part, I'd like to share some gardening experiences with you.

A business associate of mine retired a couple of years ago. On the day he left behind his high-stakes, high-stress corporate job, he looked absolutely exhausted by the years of constant pressure. Even so, he was worried about retirement. What would he do all day?

Naturally, I gently suggested he give gardening a try. He took it up, building an arbour to grow some hops on. Gradually, he filled his yard with plants of all kinds, and today, that man looks ten years younger. He's full of energy, and he's smiling every time I see him.

I see this kind of thing all the time. In my experience, gardeners tend to be more robust and much more relaxed than most people are.

But don't take my word for it. During a recent study in Japan, ten students were placed in rooms and were surrounded with different combinations of decorative plants. Their brainwaves were measured, and the researchers discovered evidence of mental satisfaction among all of the students. Even a few plants placed on a windowsill had a beneficial effect. And gardening keeps you fit—as an exercise, it's roughly equivalent to volleyball, baseball, or brisk walking.

Gardening also provides a common ground for people of different attitudes, philosophies, and cultures to gather at. Over the years, I've spoken to thousands of people, many from different ethnic groups, some of whom had reason to distrust each other. But all of that negative emotion seems to fade into the background when they start talking about gardening. At worst, there have been a few good-natured disagreements over which plant has the most spectacular blooms, or the best way to grow a really huge tomato. A few months ago I spoke to a group of young people in Japan. Now, I don't speak a word of Japanese, but everyone there knew what I was talking about when I showed them how beautiful the spectacular new peonies were.

Of course, gardening isn't all a bed of roses, so to speak; an unseasonable frost or insect invasion that wipes out your entire garden can create loads of stress. And just ask my husband Ted how I reacted when he plowed under a whole row of perfectly good beets! But then, sometimes a good release of rage can be therapeutic, too.

Even if you're not into gardening per se, there are still many gardening-related activities that can promote relaxation and a sense of accomplishment. Some of my friends enjoy experimenting in their workshops to invent better tools, like one fellow I know who invented a tomato cart to roll his plants into the garage if a frost was looming. Or even my husband Ted, who made a hand seeder out of scrap metal and a barber's hair trimmer. Another senior couple I know have turned their love of making glass mosaics into a successful business; they now make garden furniture and birdbaths out of stained glass and dyed cement, and it looks great. Gardening isn't just about weeding and shovelling; it can be as large or as small an endeavour as you want. If all you'd like to do is grow the biggest tomato on the block, then that's all you have to do.

Despite the occasional frustrating moment, gardening remains one of the best therapies I know. It's the perfect escape from a world that is becoming increasingly stressful. It soothes the mind, hones the body, and eases the heart. Let me amend that—gardening isn't an escape, it's a refuge, a temporary sanctuary, from which you emerge revitalized and ready to face the world again. The energy I get from a good couple of hours in the garden is more than enough to prepare me for whatever curve balls life decides to throw.

The scent of a rose, the whisper of the wind through the trees, the feel of dirt on my hands, the brilliant colours of salpiglossis and pansies, the deep and meditative solitude—all of this and more is why I love to garden. It's the ultimate therapy.

Thank you for asking me to join you today, and enjoy the conference!

Lois began speaking about cancer before her husband Ted was hospitalized with prostate cancer as well as Alzheimer's disease, and before she was diagnosed with peritoneal cancer. Another example of how she made big subjects meaningful by relating them to personal stories that anyone could identify with, and that opened her life to others.

Cross Cancer Institute
Volunteer Association Annual General Meeting

May 15, 2001

GOOD AFTERNOON.

One way or another, every Canadian is touched by cancer. Even if we ourselves are never afflicted, odds are a family member, friend, or mentor will fall victim to this disease. Everyone here knows that, and everyone here knows what a terrible scourge cancer is; the betrayal of our own cells, the corruption of our own bodies.

I suspect that many of the volunteers here have had experiences with cancer in their family. I have, too, a few times, but the one I want to tell you about today concerns my husband's father, Harry. Harry was a plumbing contractor, a tough, no-nonsense kind of guy; but he was an unrepentant practical joker, too, and had an introspective side that came out on rare occasions. During the winter of 1954, Grandpa Hole, as we called him after our son Bill was born, became desperately ill. It was cancer, and there was nothing to be done.

A few months later, in the early spring of 1955, my mother-in-law called to say that she was going to cook Grandpa Hole a piece of lamb, his favourite meal. Even though it was awfully early in the season, she wondered if I might be able to find some fresh peas in my garden, since they were Grandpa Hole's favourite vegetable.

That, I think, was the signal that the end was approaching, the admission that Grandpa Hole's last days had arrived. I told Grandma Hole that I would do my best. I pulled on a sweater, picked up a basket, and went out into the garden to look.

It was a cool, misty morning, with the tiniest bit of drizzle. The scents and sounds of the dawn brought back powerful memories of Grandpa Hole; I remembered his visits to our farm, when he would wander into the fields, alone, find a spot, and just stand there, becoming a part of the landscape. As I entered the garden, I could almost see him standing there, in his favourite suit, bathed in orange and yellow light as the sun emerged from the horizon.

I checked the first vine I found and caught a glimpse of several pods glistening with dew, barely ready to be picked. I took one of the pods, popped a few peas into my mouth, and I was elated to discover that they were perfect. I still remember how they tasted—fresh and cold, sweet and juicy. The garden was lush with peas, and I realized that it was giving me an extraordinary, priceless gift.

Ted's dad got his dinner, roast lamb with fresh peas and mint sauce. He ate every bite, exclaiming what a treat it was to have a home-cooked meal complete with garden vegetables. In his eyes I could see the memories of happier days; I like to imagine he was thinking about those quiet times in our field, enjoying being one with the land.

Three weeks later, he died peacefully.

Compared with everything that Grandpa Hole did for me and my family, that last meal seems like a tiny gesture. But I know it brought him some joy, some comfort.

The reason I mention this story is because I remember how hard it was to gather those peas, knowing that it would be one of the last things I could do for someone I loved. It was terribly hard to see him suffering, but you do the same thing all the time....

A speech on the twinning of municipalities from Alberta and Japan was an official event likely to end up on the agenda of any lieutenant-governor. For Lois, being open to other cultures was an important part of modern Canadian life. Here she told the story of her adventure trying to make a pie for the prince of Japan. It became one of her staple tales at multicultural events.

Alberta/Japan Twinned Municipalities Association
Twin Town Conference
June 8, 2001

GOOD EVENING, EVERYONE, and welcome to the Twin Town conference. I am very pleased to welcome our guests from all across Japan and
Alberta, who gather together in the spirit of co-operation and friendship.

Our cultures have much to learn from each other; and indeed, we are
already enjoying the fruits of cultural exchange. A couple of years ago I
was asked to make a presentation at a Meiji university in Tokyo, and
before the lecture I had the opportunity to examine some Japanese
gardening techniques. The most striking thing I noticed was that while
Canadian gardeners tend to fill up every patch of soil with plants, the
Japanese have a different way of approaching space in the garden. In the
Japanese gardens I saw, there were small plantings of flowers and vegetables, but there were also small open spaces of sand or rock; it was a
beautiful effect, and invoked in me feelings of peace and serenity.
Canadians are starting to emulate this approach, and they're using
Japanese motifs in garden decorations, too—stepping stones, statues,
fountains, lanterns, and the like. Back when I started gardening as a
business, the number of Japanese plants we carried could be counted on
the fingers of one hand. Today, there are hundreds of Japanese imports
lining the shelves, from double hepaticas, jack-in-the-pulpits, ornamental ginger, peonies, woodland perennials—I could go on and on.

When I gave my talk at the university, the biggest reaction came
when students saw the slide of a large basket of Tumbler tomatoes.
They all leaned forward in their seats when I told them about this
amazing variety, which produces hundreds of juicy, delicious tomatoes
on each plant. And I told them they could grow strawberries or beans or
almost any vegetable in containers to conserve space. Since many

Japanese don't have a lot of space to grow vegetables, the idea of a container plant that produces such an abundant harvest was a big hit.

A few months later, Prince and Princess Takamado visited Alberta; since I was serving at the university chancellor at the time, I was asked to represent the university at a reception for the royal couple. I found out that the Prince had developed a love for rhubarb pie during his days as a student in Canada, so I decided to bake him one. I'd present it at the official reception at Government House in Edmonton.

Of course, my husband Ted had to sample a piece before I took it away—he had to give it a taste test, he said, to be sure that the Prince would like it. So after Ted gave the pie his approval, I was off. After a bit of haggling with the provincial protocol office, I managed, with the help of Mayor Bill Smith, to get permission to present the pie, and the Prince was delighted. His eyes just lit up when he saw the pie, though of course I had to explain that Ted had "tried a little piece" before the reception.

"Not such a small piece," the Prince joked. Though when dessert time came, I noticed that the Prince took a pretty big piece of his own!

Obviously, Canadians and Japanese have already enjoyed great benefits from cultural exchange. As our ties grow stronger, so too will our understanding, our friendship, and our prosperity. Families are families, people are people, whatever their cultural and geographic origin. By coming together today, you have shown that what draws people together is far stronger than what keeps them apart. East may be East, and West may be West, but today you have proved that the twain—or the twins— shall indeed meet, and live in harmony because of it.

When Lois spoke to university students, she always called on them to take on the responsibilities of leadership in Canadian society—responsibilities as she understood them. She usually included tolerance in that list. The written record of her speeches suggests some uncertainty about how strongly to put that message. This address to a convocation at the University of Calgary generally follows a model speech for university students that was worked up in her office in October 2000. Both refer to accepting immigrants. But where the "generic speech" speech asks "if it's really that big a deal if a police officer chooses to wear a turban, or if two consenting adults of the same sex want to enjoy the benefits of marriage," the Calgary speech refers only to accepting "a lifestyle you may not approve of." This phrasing appeared in later convocation speeches, as well. Same-sex marriage was not upheld as a constitutional right in Canadian courts for another few years. Even then it became a hot political issue in Alberta, with the provincial government unsuccessfully spending months looking for ways to avoid being swept up in the court decisions.

University of Calgary Convocation

June 11, 2001

CHANCELLOR PERRATON, President White, honoured guests, family members, and students: welcome.

Before I begin, I'd like to note that this week will include the final convocation ceremonies overseen by your current President, Dr. Terry White. I would like to offer my thanks to Dr. White for his work, and I hope he enjoys whatever comes next in his life. University presidents don't have an easy time of it these days, so I think we should all give Dr. White a hand for his excellent work.

Students, I must, of course, congratulate you on your achievements. Getting this far in life is no easy task, and you have surmounted amazing obstacles to get to this point. A university degree is something to be very proud of, and I applaud you all for sticking it out, applying yourselves, and proving you've got what it takes.

Doubtless many of you have put a lot of thought into considering what comes next. Some of you will begin to build families and careers; others will continue your studies; still others may follow a more iconoclastic path.

Whichever route you choose, I hope that you will give some thought to your responsibilities as university graduates. You've joined an elite group; only a small percentage of Canadians ever pursue their education as far as you have. Personally, I hope that one day a majority of people have the opportunity to attend university or college; it should be a birthright, not a crippling financial burden or a privilege for the rich.

But until that day comes, university graduates have a daunting task: to make a positive difference in the world. This responsibility falls upon your shoulders because you have been given the best tools with which to make that difference. Very few people understand your chosen field as well as you do. Don't be afraid to use that knowledge to build a good life for yourselves; you've earned that right. But at the same time, remember that we have to look after each other. Being a part of the human community means, above all, that you need to show compassion.

Sometimes that's easy; perhaps it means donating time or money to charity, or helping out a stranded motorist.

But sometimes it's hard, especially when you have to overcome your own prejudices—and we all have them. Offering compassion might mean helping a new immigrant who doesn't understand our customs or language. Maybe it even means accepting and understanding someone who chooses a lifestyle you might not approve of.

Whatever the issue, I ask you to use those remarkable brains that have served you so well thus far. Consider the issues that shape our world today and use your abilities to bring people together rather than setting them apart.

Engineers, musicians, political scientists, chemists, teachers, nutritionists, economists, writers, actors, dancers—I don't care what your major is. You all have the same potential to make a difference. You have the power to change the world.

All you really need to do is ask yourself one question: how can I make things better? And then—well, then, set out to accomplish whatever answer you came up with. That's not always going to be easy; but then, what worthwhile thing ever is?

You *should* make a difference. You *must* make a difference. And you *will* make a difference.

So go, and take your rightful place in the world. Be a builder—a builder of both a good life for you and *yours*.

Thank you.

Art in a small town. Viking was already known as the home of the hockey-playing Sutter brothers. Lois believed art had a place there, too. She tried to nurture the arts in many small communities. Like-minded people who lived in them appreciated her support. She may even have had some effect on the less like-minded. In the arts, too, she preached what she practised. She bought a number of works by Charles Hilton, a little-known abstract painter and sculptor who had a difficult time socializing with potential buyers. Her interest in art was also piqued by a print of a medieval painting her husband Ted much enjoyed; he had it hanging prominently in their house, and she could see that visitors also appreciated seeing it.

Viking Station and Art Centre Guild
Choo Choo Luncheon
June 12, 2001

HELLO, EVERYONE, and thank you so much for inviting me today. I have to tell you, I've always loved art, so I am especially thrilled to be here; my home would be so drab and lifeless if I didn't have art to spruce it up.[19]

My husband Ted shares my love of art. In fact, he probably has a better eye than me for a fine piece of work. His favourite Inuit sculpture of a polar bear sits in the centre of our coffee table where he can readily enjoy it, and I've seen that bear give pleasure to others as well. It immediately catches people's eye when they step into our home and draws them over to touch it and run their hands over its smooth surface.

Myself, I'm often drawn to art because of the people who made it. When I see a piece of work that says a lot about the artist's vision and personality, I can't help opening my wallet. That's how I've come to own several pieces by Charles Hilton, who honed his craft during earlier years in Edmonton—and has since gone to warmer climates in B.C.

Being an artist has got to be a tough way to make a living. Imagine all the hours and days Charles Hilton spends in the studio to create just one piece—a piece that may sell for less than a dinner for two at a really nice restaurant.

It's up to us to support the artists in this room—and all across Alberta. We can do that by buying their work, but also by making sure there is public support for artists' ability to create. When budgets are tight, support for the arts is so often the first to be cut. But without the Charles Hiltons of this province, the world would be a poorer place.

We need roads to drive on and hockey arenas to exercise our love of sport, but we also need art to nourish our souls and expand our minds.

And you know, being here, I can't imagine a more appropriate spot to showcase beautiful artwork. That's because art and the railway share an important trait: they bring people together.

Art transcends borders. Like the rail lines stretching across Canada that link Halifax to Vancouver, art reminds us that while we may disagree on many issues, we all belong to one great country, with a common love of the skill and inspiration that leads to great art. The legacy of Emily Carr, the Group of Seven, and all the great Canadian artists since has shown that Canada has a vital contribution to make to the world's artistic heritage. And it's here, in towns like Viking, that some of the finest work has been and will be created, by Canadians living in the thick of the culture, Canadians who have a strong connection to our land and our people.

This gallery will bring people together, too. The citizens of Viking and the surrounding communities will be well-served by having a place to showcase and sell local works, and I expect that artists young and old, novice and advanced, will find it an invaluable resource. Viking should be very proud to have this facility available for its people, and I hope that it will be well funded by the government and by private and corporate donors. Art is always a good investment, and I know our MLAs and business leaders will agree—we should do a good job of showcasing the economic and cultural benefits that this centre will provide.

To the members of the Guild, I congratulate you on your efforts in creating this gallery. I hope that you will continue to work towards a strong societal commitment to the arts; as a country we need to recognize, as you have, that the arts are not a frill, but a vital component in our economy, our culture, and even our mental and spiritual health. Art produces joy; one could argue that the creation of art validates our existence as human beings. What are we here for, if not to create beauty, if not to explore the connections between people and nature, between men and women, between philosophy and day-to-day life?

Naturally, art is about fun, too, and I hope that the seniors and children of Viking, as well as the dabblers and the hobbyists, will be able to use this place just to have a good time experimenting. And sometimes the crude brushstrokes of a child can contain as much truth and beauty as the more insightful, experienced hand of a master. It's exploring the possibilities that really brings art alive.

Just as the railway helped build a great country, art will ensure that Canada endures as a vibrant, sophisticated, cultured nation with something to say about life. Our artists are our ambassadors. We should treat them as such.

Just plain fun. An expansion of the story repertoire she delighted in bringing to the job.

Cowgirl Cattle Company
2nd Annual Stockholders Meeting and Cowgirl Rendezvous
June 9, 2001

Hello, everyone, and thank you so much for inviting me to your 2nd Annual Cowgirl Rendezvous.

You know, my father was in the livestock business—he was a buyer, and I'll never forget how angry he got when ranchers would whip their cattle. "You must treat them with great gentleness," he told me. Much later, when my husband Ted and I had our own farm, we had a Jersey cow named Charlotte. Well, unfortunately, we couldn't breed or milk Charlotte, and we had to have her butchered. I felt just terrible about it, but Ted wasn't quite as upset. In fact, he used to sing the song "Hush... Hush, Sweet Charlotte," when we sat down to eat the steaks, and let me tell you, that completely killed my appetite.

But my father's lessons and my own experiences with Charlotte did prove quite valuable a little later on, when Ted and I tried raising pigs.

When I was four or five years old, I would ride with my Dad down to his stockyards on the outskirts of Buchanan, Saskatchewan. My dad was a stock buyer, and I used to enjoy watching the farmers and stock-yard workers loading and unloading the livestock. Although I didn't realize it at the time, my young mind absorbed the whole process in surprising detail.

Many years later, Ted and I tried our hand at raising pigs. I'll always remember when it first came time to take them to market. We needed a chute to get them onto the truck, of course, so Ted set to work building one. I assumed he knew what he was doing, so I didn't pay much attention. However, although he had sound carpentry skills, he had never built a pig chute.

When he brought out the chute, I took one look at it and said, "Ted, you can't use a chute that big for pigs." It was as wide as the half-ton. Pigs need a narrow chute so they can't turn around. Not surprisingly, Ted didn't welcome my unsolicited advice. "What the hell do you know about loading pigs?" he grumbled.

He managed to get three or four pigs part way up the chute. Suddenly, the first pig decided he'd rather be down with his buddies in the pen, so he turned around. Ted blocked his path with a sheet of plywood and let out a whoop, just to show the pig who was boss.

Well, utter chaos ensued. All the pigs were upset now. Every time Ted lunged one way, a pig scrambled another. You might think it's impossible for a pig to climb over the wall of a chute, but get one good and agitated and you'll find out differently. Not a single pig made it all the way onto the truck. Eventually, we threw up our hands and deserted the field of battle.

Ted had to dismantle the chute and rebuild it, while I wisely suppressed the urge to say, "I told you so." When the time came to try again, I suggested, "You should hold a piece of plywood in front of you and walk up the chute behind the pigs." Ted set to work, trying his best, but again the pigs refused to cooperate. Within a minute or two, Ted was yelling and swearing, and the pigs were squealing, grunting, and running around madly.

"Ted, calm down!" I shouted. "You're not going to get anywhere that way!" In his state, that wasn't what he wanted to hear. He continued pushing away at the pigs and sure enough, we didn't get them loaded that day either.

Later in the evening, once Ted and the pigs had settled down, I convinced him to let me give it a try. From what I had seen as a kid, I knew that you had to be very gentle and quiet when loading pigs.

The next day we assembled the pigs for a third attempt. I walked slowly out, crept right up to one of them, put my hand down, and directed a pig up the chute and into the truck, making a gentle "whooshing" sound the whole time. Anytime the pig felt like pausing for a little look around, I'd wait right beside it. When it was ready to continue, off we'd go together.

I herded the pigs into the truck, one by one, while the others patiently, silently waited their turns. Ted could only stand by and chuckle in amazement. From then on, loading the pigs was my job: Ted never could seem to get the knack.

After a few years, it became clear to both of us that we weren't cut out to be pig farmers. And it may be an awful thing to admit, yet those pigs taught me a thing or two about dealing with excitable people. The quiet approach is often the only one that works. If you speak softly and lay a gentle hand on their shoulder, you can lead them almost anywhere.[20]

It's been ages since our experiences with cattle, but I'll always remember them fondly. Thank you so much for having me here today, and I hope that the Cowgirl Cattle Company enjoys many more years of success. Women have played a crucial role in the development of the West, and thanks to organizations like yours, you will continue to do so.

Being Canadian had clear meanings for Lois. Canada Day was a perfect occasion to share them.

Citizenship Ceremony
Canada Day
July 1, 2001

HELLO, EVERYONE, and please accept my warmest congratulations on becoming Canadian citizens. It is my pleasure to note that the new Canadians here today came from many different countries; your different heritages, rich in cultural diversity, will be of tremendous benefit to all Canadians, but especially to your neighbours here in northern Alberta.

A few months ago, His Highness, the Prince of Wales, made some remarks about Canada that I thought I'd share, since they fit so well with today's celebration:

"Canada is famous, quite rightly, as a tolerant country, and should be particularly proud of its record of integration and of togetherness. The first thing a Canadian does when setting off for overseas is to place a maple leaf pin in his lapel—and the maple leaf, the world over, is one of the most recognizable of global symbols of democratic values."

I believe the Prince is quite right; one of the reasons I'm most proud of being Canadian is our growing acceptance of and delight in a multitude of cultures. Immigrants made this country great, and they will continue to do so in the 21st century. It's been my privilege to work with and befriend people from many cultures, and I wouldn't give up any of those experiences for anything in the world.

Our Governor General, Adrienne Clarkson, recognized the contribution that immigrants make to citizenship earlier this year. In the Speech from the Throne to open Parliament she said, "Immigrants have enriched Canada with their ideas and talents," and "Our Canadian citizenship has been built over time through the experiences we have shared, when every year thousands of new Canadians stand proudly with their families to take on the responsibilities of Canadian citizenship."

There's another reason I'm very proud to be a citizen of this country: Canadians share a firm commitment to the common good. I think we have managed to strike a unique balance between the importance of

Governor General Adrienne Clarkson and Lois Hole at the greenhouse, 2001. [Hole Family Archives]

individual rights and the needs of the community. We respect individual expression of artistic and political views, while pulling together to create a better life for everyone. Our prime minister calls this the Canadian Way. The Canadian Way is about acceptance, understanding, openness, and neighbourliness. It is about caring and compassion. Equality and fairness. Sharing and respect. These values transcend the differences among peoples. They speak to something fundamental in all of us, no matter where we come from or who we are.

That's really what citizenship is all about: pulling together for a better Canada....

For all her commitment to literacy and social justice, Lois remained an enthu-
siastic and naturally savvy entrepreneur. She did not speak as often on the
subject of business as on some of her favourite other topics, but when she did,
there was no doubting her interest and expertise. This is an early example.

Celebration of the Signing of the Memorandum of Understanding on Scientific and Technological Co-operation between Alberta and the People's Republic of China
July 13, 2001

GOOD EVENING. I am truly honoured to join you tonight to celebrate
the signing of the Memorandum of Understanding between the province
of Alberta and the Chinese Ministry of Science and Technology.

Back in 1965, my family was selling fresh vegetables for a living. The
business was really starting to take off, so we decided to get ourselves a
new technological wonder called an answering machine. We were one of
the first, if not the very first, farms in Alberta to have one. Of course, this
was a huge, expensive piece of technology, with big reels of magnetic
tape and a bulky microphone—not exactly the computerized, miniatur-
ized answering machines we have today.

Whenever something significant was happening on the farm, I would
record it on the answering machine: "Hello, you've reached Hole's Farm.
Our cucumbers are mature and ready for you to enjoy," or "Just a few
days left before the corn harvest." This was just a way to let people know
when the best time to shop was. But of course, it took our customers a
while to get used to the new technology, and often we would hear people
yelling into the phone after the end of the message. "Hello? Hello?
Lois?" And then there would be some choice curse words. Hardly
anyone had even heard of an answering machine back in those days, and
there was even some resentment. Heck, even today, there are still people
who hate answering machines.

But you know, it didn't take long for our customers to really appreciate the service, and soon enough they started to call even at four in the
morning just to hear the message. The first few times those early-
morning calls came in, I used to think something terrible had happened;
after all, who calls at four in the morning? But whenever I rushed over to

pick up the phone, some puzzled person would just say, "Oh, I only wanted to hear if the tomatoes were ready." That was certainly a relief, I can tell you!

Eventually, that answering machine became a very important tool to our business, and it also helped to show us how vital communication was between us and our customers. Today, my sons, who run the business now, have set up an entire communications centre at the greenhouse, with computerized controls and 25 lines coming in. They have half a dozen gardening experts operating the phones all day to answer gardening questions and take orders.

Of course, technology is more than just a tool for generating business. It is also useful in fighting poverty, helping the sick, understanding our natural world, and even building better lines of communication between the peoples of the world.

I hope that this Memorandum of Understanding will build those lines between Alberta and China, and that as a consequence, our peoples will enjoy a better understanding of each other's values, goals, and philosophies. Because I believe that when it comes right down to it, we all want the same things: better schools for our children, better care for our elders, food for the hungry, shelter for the homeless, and a more harmonious, peaceful world, where we can all share in the wonders of nature and work together to explore the human condition.

That is my wish for today's agreement, and in closing I would like to thank all of those, in both China and Alberta, who have worked so hard to make this historic moment a reality. May your efforts be blessed.

An RCMP awards ceremony made a suitable setting for her first speech after the Sept. 11, 2001, terrorist attacks on the United States.

RCMP Long Service Awards
September 13, 2001

GOOD AFTERNOON, EVERYONE.
Like many of you, I'm still in shock over Tuesday's events in the United States. This is a catastrophe that will live in our hearts and minds for the rest of our lives. Like you, I watched the terrible events unfold on the news, and I can take comfort in at least one thing:

The people of New York, like the people of Canada, can be very, very proud of their police officers. I shall never forget how they raced through the rubble, desperate to save as many people as they could from the very gates of Hell itself.

If the tragic events of the last few days have taught us anything, it's to heighten our appreciation of the public servants who put their lives on the line every day in order to protect their neighbours. "Putting their lives on the line": it's such a cliché, but how else can you possibly describe what police officers do? I think we all realize now, if we didn't before, that the world is a dangerous place, and the men and women of the RCMP have answered a very special call that not everyone hears: they have chosen to make our dangerous world as safe as they possibly can.

Today, we honour Constables Peter Brunelle and Stewart Angus, Corporal Jean Cormier, Constables Myles Marshak and Murray Dyck, Constables Arthur Pittman and Wade Lavoie, and finally Constable Nancy Roberge, for a variety of acts of heroism carried out in the course of their duties. Though the circumstances of their stories differ, all of these officers share the noble heart, swollen with courage, that we associate with the heroes of legend.

These officers, I know, will shy away from the word "heroism," but I shall not. Under very difficult and stressful circumstances, these members found the inner strength and courage not just to carry out their duties, but to accomplish them in a manner commensurate with the heroic reputation of the RCMP.

We also honour the day to day heroism of the recipients of the Long Service Medal and the Canadian Peacekeeping Service Medal. For a police officer to maintain his or her integrity, dedication, optimism, and respect for humanity in desperate circumstances, such as our peace-keepers do, or over a period of decades, as our long-serving members have, is truly remarkable. The strength of spirit of these officers is humbling, and they deserve every honour that we can bestow upon them.

Today, more than ever, we need heroes, and it is a great comfort to know that they walk among us.

One of Lois's most important and personal statements on the importance of books and libraries. This was an old theme but she found new ways to express her thoughts here, reaching back into memories of her own days as a beginning reader. Miss Jobb was to reappear in dozens of later speeches.

Peace Library System
Rural Libraries Conference
September 27, 2001

GOOD MORNING, EVERYONE, and thank you for inviting me today to talk about a subject that's very close to my heart: libraries.

I grew up in a little town in northern Saskatchewan called Buchanan. When I was in Grade One, the closest thing we had to a library was two shelves in our teacher's room, with a total of about 15 books. Our teacher was Miss Jobb. She was a beautiful young woman, very trim and petite, with very dark hair, and she was always perfectly dressed.

She was a delightful teacher; she never played favourites, and it was always obvious that she loved children and wanted us to do well. I remember Miss Jobb was very fussy about our schoolwork, and we all wanted her to be proud of us. For a Grade One class, there was an awful lot of competition!

One day, Miss Jobb brought five brand-new books to school for her shelves. One of them caught my eye right away, a book called *The Little Red Hen.* The cover was beautifully illustrated with a picture of the title character. It was such a wonderful drawing, I felt like the little red hen was almost a real creature, one you would love to pick up and carry around with you like a pet cat.

Miss Jobb told us that we would all have a chance to borrow the new books, but since there were 18 of us in the class, we would all have to take turns. To decide which of us would get first crack at the books, she gave us an assignment; I believe it was to write out the numbers one to twenty, very neatly, of course.

It was so hard for me not to rush through the job in an effort to be first, but I knew that for Miss Jobb, getting it done properly was more important than getting it done quickly. So I tried my hardest to carefully write out the neatest set of numbers from one to twenty anyone had ever seen.

Well, wouldn't you know it, Miss Jobb thought I did a very good job, and so I was lucky enough to be one of the first to choose from the new books. I snatched up *The Little Red Hen* right away.

I don't remember much about the story, to be honest, though I do remember the general theme.

It was about helping others, and this little red hen was kind of the leader of all the chickens on the farm and tried to guide and care for them. It was really the illustrations I remember best; I opened the book, and the pictures just came alive.

Miss Jobb's makeshift library brought me a lot of joy, and it helped me develop a love of reading and learning that remains to this very day. Miss Jobb wasn't just a great teacher; she was also, in a sense, the first librarian in my life.

Over the years, many librarians have introduced me to so many different worlds of imagination; the Wizard of Oz was just one of countless favourites. And I was always in awe of librarians; they seemed so knowledgeable. They always knew just where everything was, and they always knew just which books were the best for whatever purpose you were looking for.

But like so many worthwhile institutions, libraries continually face the threats of reduced funding and benign neglect. It's unfortunate and wrong, but libraries must constantly struggle for proper support. But we can turn that around. A few years ago, the Westmount branch of the Edmonton public library system was threatened with closure.

It was old, too expensive to renovate, and there were other branches that people could use; that's how the thinking went, anyway. Well, it was the seniors of the Westmount area who came out full force to throw their support behind that library, and not only did they manage to halt plans for its destruction, they were so well organized that the city decided to refurbish and renovate the branch.

Today it's a small but modern library that the citizens of north Edmonton value highly.

When it comes to libraries, it's the users and librarians that make all the difference.

If the challenges facing rural libraries are to be addressed, we need to mobilize citizens in exactly the same way, cementing the bond between librarians and library patrons. This conference is an excellent way to do so, and I hope it helps raise the profile of the vital work of rural libraries, especially considering the fact that the Peace library system must serve such a huge area.

Delivering public services to remote locations has always been one of the great challenges in Canadian history—but I believe that it can also be a strength. Our commitment to ensuring that all Canadians, regardless of where they live, receive excellent government services, is a very important part of our national character.

It's a reflection of our culture, and I think that to remain truly Canadian, we must remain committed to the principle of equal access. And that principle is nowhere more important than it is when applied to libraries, since so many people, especially those with limited income, depend on them. ...

Libraries are, I believe, the most important institution in our country, because everything else that's good in our society must flow from knowledge. Librarians are the guardians of wisdom and progress, but they don't hoard their treasure; they do their best to see that it is distributed far and wide.

Thank you for giving all the people of Alberta, especially those in rural areas, the chance to learn, to grow, and to discover all the wonders that can be found between the covers of a good book.

Whenever you stack shelves, catalogue books, make recommendations to readers, or help someone find a statistic, you are helping to strengthen the very foundations of Canadian culture and democracy.

Thank you for inviting me here this morning, and please enjoy a productive, fun, and educational conference.

A reworked call to action for defenders of public education. Lois paid close attention to the makeup of her audiences. She used the opportunity to instil in them the importance of their role. As a group, they could have extensive influence.

Western Canada Educational Administrators Conference
October 19, 2001

GOOD AFTERNOON, EVERYONE.

Public education is nothing less than the cornerstone of culture, peace, and prosperity. Henry Adams said, "A teacher affects eternity; he can never tell where his influence stops." That's the absolute truth.

Let me give you an example. People like to look at big companies and gauge their success by saying, "Wow, look at how much money they made this year."

But where would those companies be without their employees, from their CEO right down to the people in the mailroom, the vast majority of whom were educated by the public school system?

We all know exactly where they'd be, and it wouldn't be on the Fortune 500 list.

The staggering truth is, almost everything that we've accomplished in the 20th century can be attributed to our public education system. And I'm not just talking about our great advancements in science, medicine, engineering, and so on.

I'm talking about the vast wealth of great new literature and film, art and dance, music and sculpture and photography and all the rest of it. I firmly believe that the historians of the future will look back and consider the concept of public education the most important instrument of social progress the human race has yet produced.

That is, if we make sure that concept remains true to its roots. Public education has a bit of an image problem these days, and it's up to us to make sure that the public realizes how important public education is to our continued peace and prosperity.

Listen, you people—in a perfect world, teachers and school administrators would have all the resources they need to ensure that each and every student gets the education they deserve. In a perfect world, all you would have to focus on is the students.

But we live in an imperfect world, and that means that you need to be more outspoken about the work you do. Take some of the credit for the success of those big companies, because you *deserve* a large percentage of that credit.

Take every opportunity you can to show business and political leaders the statistics that prove that where public education is properly supported, crime rates go down and more income tax flows into government coffers. Be obnoxious about it if you have to, but get the message out!...

If we are to maintain a high rate of literacy, if we are to continue to expand the depth and breadth of our cultural knowledge, we must ensure that libraries are given at least as much funding, care, and atten-tion as our sports stadiums. Frankly, I dream of a day when teachers and librarians are paid as much as hockey players.

So listen, everyone: I want to make it clear that you people are my heroes. You should take enormous pride in your work. You are the shep-herds of our destiny, and I cannot thank you enough for educating me, my children, my grandchildren, and countless others. Teachers *do* affect eternity, for the better, I believe, and the influence of public educators will be felt through the ages.

It is an awesome duty, and I am glad that you people are the ones who have taken it up.

An appearance at a literacy project at Cremona, a small community northwest of Calgary, produced the opportunity for a rare commentary on writing.

Cremona School
Literacy Project
October 30, 2001

Part One: The Importance of Literacy

WHY IS LITERACY SO IMPORTANT? Why read? Well, people get different things out of reading—for some it's an escape, an afternoon's worth of entertainment. For others, it's a way to experience different points of view, or to learn about a specific topic.

In other words, reading can be a means to an end or the end itself. For me, cracking a book was always a joy for its own sake....

I'll tell you one thing—if I hadn't been a voracious reader, I doubt I'd be standing here before you today talking about it!

What I learned from books was a huge help in starting my own business, in writing my own books, and in serving as Alberta's Lieutenant Governor. Now, reading alone can't ensure success—but it sure as heck helps your chances.

But don't read just to get ahead. Read because it enriches your life. Read because there's nothing more joyous than enjoying a good story. Read so that you can discuss a great book with your friends. Most of all, read because it's fun. That's why I do it.

While we're on the subject of literacy, I hope that you'll use every opportunity to take advantage of our wonderful public libraries; they are a precious resource that can help you take advantage of the wisdom and experience of people from all over the world.

Literacy is the key to not just the economy of our world, but also to developing understanding between the many cultures on our planet. If we are ever to escape the cycle of violence and ignorance that plagues us, we must all not only learn to read, but to read carefully, and to read as much as we can, by a wide range of different authors.

Read some romance, read some science fiction, some history, some adventure, some fantasy, some politics, some drama, but most importantly, read up on the subjects you're passionate about.

Literacy isn't just a way to get ahead, and it isn't just about entertainment. Being literate means being able to really participate in shaping the world, work for peace, and reach understanding with our fellow human beings. Being literate means that you're in control of your own destiny. Being literate means you're one very large step closer to realizing your true potential. Thank you.

Part Two: What it Means to be a Writer

HELLO, EVERYONE. Your teachers have asked me to talk about what it means to be a writer. I had to think about that for a while, but after careful consideration, here are my thoughts on what it means to be a writer.

To me, being a writer means, first and foremost, being truthful, no matter what your subject. When I write about gardening, of course I tell the truth; otherwise, my books would be useless. But it's just as important to tell the truth when telling stories.

Sometimes this won't mean the literal truth, but more universal or personal truths about life, learning, relationships, and the problems that trouble us all. Most importantly, being a writer means being true to yourself and true to your readers.

When you write, whether it's a novel, a story, or an essay, it's important to write what you want and not what you think people want to read. Readers are smart, and they'll see through that kind of deception right away. Of course, you also have to take care to know and understand your subject; otherwise, your readers will be disappointed.

The most important thing to me is to make sure that the reader gets something valuable from the reading experience, whether that means a useful bit of practical information, some new concept to think about, or even just a smile from an entertaining story.

There's really no greater compliment than having one of your readers tell you that they enjoyed your book or your story. Being a good writer means always being faithful and true to yourself and your audience, and that's a lesson that's true of any job, when you think about it, whether you're a carpenter or a painter or a politician.

Not everyone is interested in becoming a full-time writer, and that's just fine; it would be a pretty boring world if we were all interested in the same thing. But if you do want to write, then read everything you can get your hands on. If you really want to be a writer, you should try to read outside your normal interests, just to learn more about the world around you.

And you should also go out and do more in the real world, perhaps by volunteering for a charity or participating in one or two of your school clubs. Not only will you be helping out other people, you'll be learning at the same time, and getting the experience you need to be a writer who has something to say.

In closing, if you want to write, please don't by shy about it. The world needs new ideas and new voices, and I know that you people have some important things to share. Whether your writing touches the lives of thousands of people or just a few friends, the important thing is that you've given your readers something new to think about. And that's what writing is all about.

A provincial literacy conference worked as the setting for an elaboration of ideas broached a few days earlier at Cremona. Her speeches from this date forward linked literacy to some of the most important goals of society and of individual development. She also about this time began speaking about subjects like literacy with a greater sense of urgency.

2001: A Literacy Odyssey
Provincial Literacy Conference
November 2, 2001

GOOD EVENING, EVERYONE, and thank you for asking me to join you tonight.

I must begin by telling you about a wonderful commercial I saw just a few days ago. In the ad, we see a man learning how to read. We watch his progress, and at the end of the commercial, we see an old woman with bad eyesight trying to read a sign.

The man approaches her, and she stops him, asking, "Can you read that?" Hoping, of course, that he'll tell her what the sign says. So he looks at the sign, and then he looks back at the old woman, and of course he misunderstands the question and proudly replies, "Yes, I can!" And then he leaves, and the poor old woman is left in the lurch.

I'll come back to that commercial soon, but for now, I'll ask a question: why is literacy so important? Well, obviously a literate culture is a richer culture, both in economic and social terms. Literate people require less social assistance, they get better jobs and thus pay higher taxes, and they are more likely to contribute to our cultural and artistic legacy.

In other words, it's in our collective interest to maintain a high rate of literacy. Literacy simply makes good sense; it's practical.

But those are a businessman's reasons to encourage literacy. Literacy is more than a simple economic stimulus. Literacy offers the human race hope.

Hope of escaping our violent past and attaining something better. For ignorance is the great villain of history, and literacy is our best weapon against it.

Once upon a time, reading was a skill reserved only for the upper classes. Allowing the masses to read was dangerous. On this very continent, it wasn't so long ago that the law forbade minorities from learning the skill. And it wasn't so long ago, in the great scheme of things, that women who read were called "uppity."

But literacy and education liberated women, minorities, and the working poor; it gave them tremendous power.

The commercial I told you about earlier showed how learning to read empowers people, and how literacy gives us a measure of control over our own lives.

Being literate gives us the capability to form our own opinions and create our own ethical standards. Literacy is a tremendous power, an incredible force for good. Now, it's true that all too often we don't use this power to its full potential, but at least knowing how to read gives each of us the capacity to learn and grow and affect our world.

We know, then, that literacy is more than important; it's vital. Knowing that, we as a society must decide the best means of maintaining and even raising the standard of literacy in our country.

I believe that literacy can only be built upon three important pillars.

The first pillar is made up of the various adult and family literacy organizations, such as the ones this conference serves. The second is public libraries. And the third is public education. These three institutions share two traits: their primary goal is to make people literate, and they are free and open to all citizens.

I cannot stress how important that openness is to the survival of our culture. The most dangerous problem facing our country, and for that matter, our world, is one hardly anyone recognizes: the division of our population into two classes, the literate and the illiterate.

Now, don't get me wrong; I think we've done a pretty good job of gradually raising our level of literacy since Canada's founding. But if we want to maintain and improve upon that record, we can't take our public institutions for granted. The price of literacy, you might say, is eternal vigilance.

Do you ever wonder why we never hear about it in the media when library budgets get cut? I sure do. And yet, you could argue that library budgets are as important as health care budgets or defence budgets. In fact, library budgets are *more* important, since you can't have

Lois signing copies of her bestselling book Perennial Favorites at the Regina city greenhouse, March 1997. [Hole Family Archives]

professional health care or well-trained soldiers without the resources libraries provide.

Here's why you don't hear about library budget cuts: because too many Canadians have taken literacy for granted. According to statistics, Canada is one of those countries that has a literacy rate of something like 98 per cent. With numbers that high, you tend not to worry too much about library budgets.

It took generations to create a literate populace, and we all know how much easier it is to destroy than to create, how easy it is to rest on our laurels and let our best institutions slide into disrepair, on both the physical and the metaphorical plane. The three pillars of literacy must never be allowed to crumble, and it is our responsibility to see that they stand.

Those who promote literacy—the people in this very room—are nothing less than the guardians of democratic civilization, and for that matter, of human existence itself. Why is literacy more important than ever? Because human beings have gotten so advanced, and our problems so complex and so threatening, that it will take the collective brainpower of millions of people to find solutions.

We can't afford to be illiterate anymore; the world is too complex to leave in the hands of a privileged few. Being literate means having the ability to exercise political power, to have a voice in how human beings manage our environment and our dealings with each other.

Literacy is the key to not just the economy of our world, but also to developing understanding between the many cultures on our planet. If we are ever to escape the cycle of violence and ignorance that plagues us, we must all not only learn to read, but to read carefully, and to read as much as we can, by a wide range of different authors.

Literacy isn't just a way to get ahead, and it isn't just about entertainment. Being literate means being able to really participate in shaping the world, work for peace, and reach understanding with our fellow human beings. Being literate means that you're in control of your own destiny. At the individual level, being literate means you're one very large step closer to realizing your true potential.

At the global level...well, imagine what humanity could accomplish if everyone in the world were literate, if every single living soul could read and write and had free access to libraries and public schools. That's not just a pipe dream, not just a vision of utopia: I'm telling you now, it's an absolute necessity.

Because a healthy world depends absolutely upon the literacy of its population. Without literacy, we stumble in the dark, blind to the wonders of the written word, helpless before those who would take advantage of our ignorance.

Literacy is our only hope of finding the path to true peace, true justice, and true equality in our troubled world. We must not fail to spread it far and wide.

Practical matters, especially practical matters dealing with farming, were never far from Lois's heart, despite the much more frequent number of speeches she gave on education, philanthropy, volunteerism, and multicultur- alism. For years she was on the board and very active with the Alberta Rural Safety Council because of the concern she felt whenever she visited a farm and saw children in potential danger. Once again, a story from the farm illustrated what she wanted to say.

Injury Prevention & Control 2001: Partnerships & Practice
November 5, 2001

GOOD MORNING, EVERYONE, and welcome to the conference. Thank you so much for coming together here in Edmonton to continue the fight to build a safer Alberta and a safer Canada.

When I think of all the human potential we lose to senseless acci- dents each year, when I think of all the heartbreak that families go through—well, I'll be honest. It makes me angry.

Have you ever noticed that there are certain people who will try to stonewall and block every single safety measure the government tries to introduce? Remember when seat belt laws first came around? I distinctly remember some people calling it "communism."

Heck, some people still see it that way—"what right does anyone have to tell me that I have to put on this stupid seat belt? I'd be safer if I were flung free of the car."

Yeah, sure. We all know that such objections are almost always without merit, but the truth is, fighting for safety has always been an uphill battle.

In the late 1960s, I was a member of the board of the Rural Safety Council. We were fighting a huge battle to have roll bars installed on tractors, and to make their use mandatory. My husband Ted put it this way: a couple of hundred dollars is a pretty small investment to safe- guard a life.

Ted was never afraid to try something new, especially if it improved safety on the farm, so he installed a set of roll bars on our tractor before it became mandatory. But instead of imitating the idea, some of the neighbours actually mocked him.

One even climbed right up on the canopy and danced on it, the fool, completely oblivious that he could have easily slipped and fallen and maybe broken his neck performing such a stunt. Ted just stood there and watched, never saying a word. He knew he was right.

Not everyone was as skeptical as the man who danced on Ted's canopy. Shortly after we won that fight and roll bars became mandatory, another farmer in the area sent his son off on the family tractor to get one installed at the local dealership. But on the way there, the tractor flipped, and the young man was killed.

I tell you, that story is still a bitter, bitter pill to swallow, all these years later; it was so horribly ironic. My only consolation is that the regulation has doubtlessly saved dozens of lives over the years. And who knows? If we'd managed to get the law passed earlier, that boy might still be alive today.

People who complain about safety regulations usually have two major beefs: it's an infringement of rights, or it costs too much.

Well, I ask you; does it really infringe your rights to have a roof over your head on a tractor? Or to snap a seat belt in place?

Death is the ultimate infringement of your rights, so it seems crazy to me to complain about the "inconvenience" of seat belts....

An address to and about farm women saw a rare recollection of Lois's
maternal grandmother. The story suggests ways in which "Grandma Norsten"
may have influenced Alberta's future lieutenant-governor.

Fall Focus
County of Camrose Farm Women
November 14, 2001

GOOD MORNING, EVERYONE, and thank you for asking me to join you
today.

When I think about the differences between the farm women of today
and those you read about in the history books, it's their tools that come
to mind.

My Grandma Norsten was a farm wife, and she had a wide range of
tools that were never far from her side. One of them was a huge, five-
gallon, cast-iron cooking pot. To me, that pot symbolizes Grandma
Norsten's role on the farm: she was the provider.

Grandma not only prepared three huge meals a day for the family, she
also churned her own butter, baked her own bread and buns, slaugh-
tered the chickens, canned and pickled everything in sight, and sometimes she even baked 15 pies in a single day. And don't forget that she
had to plan all those meals well in advance.

She had to know when the vegetable and fruit crops were ready for
picking, what time of year was right for slaughtering the animals, how
long vegetables would last in storage—it was quite a juggling act.

And on top of all that, she had to take care of all the other little
matters a farm woman must: seeing the kids off to school, mending
clothes, helping in the field, and so much more. Even listing all these
jobs makes me tired!

The mother of a close family friend was a farm woman, and I
remember how she used to slaughter the pigs and steers and wrap them
up for freezing in the grain bins over the winter. Well, one year the
weather warmed up early, and this poor woman was canning day and
night so that the thawing meat wouldn't spoil.

But she put her nose to the grindstone and finished the job, because
the family depended on her to provide.

We've heard all kinds of stories like this, and they're wonderful examples to us all. This generation can never repay the debt we owe to our farming ancestors.

But neither should we fail to pay tribute to the farm women of today. Because I really feel that in some ways, the job of farm women has gotten not easier, but harder.

Yes, it's true that modern technology has saved farm women a lot of time and effort. And not many of us still bake 15 pies a day.

But there's a reason for that: who's got the time? If we're not baking those 15 pies, it's because we're making 15 trips into town—for PTA meetings, or to pick up food, or to stamp out one of the dozens of little fires farm women deal with every day.

For farm women today aren't just providers, though they almost always fill that role; they're also active partners in the business of farming, if they aren't, in fact, running it themselves.

Today's farm women are using computers to keep track of the futures markets, they're handling the bank accounts, they know the loans officer, the salesmen at the tractor dealership, the mechanics at the workshop, the parts suppliers, the buyers, the kids' schoolteachers—the list goes on.

Not only do today's farm women have to deal with dozens of important people, they have to get to know them and stay on their good side. Today's farm women are go-getters who have to have a lot of charm and a little bit of an ability to sweet-talk to really help the farm run smoothly.

The fax machine, e-mail, and the cell phone have become the tools of choice in the modern farm woman's hands.

Today, you might find farm women who still use some of the tools of the last generation or two. But these days, if they've mastered some of those old tools, it's just as likely that they've also picked up some 21st-century skills.

Grandma had the root cellar; we've got the food processor. She had a pickup; we've got a minivan. She spent hours bent over the sewing machine; modern farm women spend hours bent over a computer.

Our mothers or grandmothers may have spent their weekends weeding a vegetable garden with a garden fork or her bare hands; we're just as likely to spend those hours watering and fertilizing those beautiful flower gardens you see at the entrances to modern farms.

To top it all off, I know many farm women who are also pursuing a second career or an advanced degree. You've got to be adaptable, dedicated, and strong-willed to make it as a farm woman these days—just as our grandmothers had to be....

Perseverance carried our pioneer ancestors through numberless trials and tribulations, and that same spirit still burns brightly in the hearts of farm women today. The family farm is in very capable hands, because you've learned to use the tools of the trade, just like those who farmed before you.

Thank you.

A speech to the Family and Community Support Services Association of Alberta produced new explorations of familiar themes. It also introduced ideas that would be repeated many times in later speeches. Foremost was the insistence that the lives of all people on the planet were inexorably intertwined, and making the lives of poor Africans and Asians better would improve security and happiness for all.

Family and Community Support Services Association of Alberta, 2001 Conference
November 16, 2001

GOOD MORNING, EVERYONE, and thank you for asking me to join you today.

I feel very privileged to speak with you, because I am so very proud of the work you do. I have had firsthand experience with the good the FCSSAA has accomplished over the years.

You see, from time to time I visit shelters for abused and battered women, shelters supported in part by this organization. I've heard some pretty terrible stories in those shelters, where the women don't even use their last names because they still live in fear. I wanted to send them some poinsettias as gifts, but I couldn't, because their names were such a closely-guarded secret.

(I wound up sending them to the shelter, where the ladies could come to pick them up.)

Where would these women have been without your help? Out on the street? Or worse? All I know is, you people have changed thousands of lives for the better. You were there to help in times of desperate need.

This organization has done an excellent job of promoting the good work it does, but I think it's still on the fringes of the consciousness of many Albertans. The trouble is, hardly anyone hears about you until they need help.

Now of course that's why the FCSSAA exists, but as you're all aware, we must do our best to show all Albertans, even the ones who never need your help, how they benefit from your presence. Otherwise, we run the risk of falling by the wayside....

Canada is still one of the best places in the world to live, and we still have a chance to speak out for public schools and the balanced programs and educational philosophies they offer.

All we can do, I think, is continue to spread the word that in the long term, it makes more sense to give our children a liberal education and to support our social programs than it does to build more jails.

The reason I support organizations like this one is because I believe in the principle of preventative medicine.

Why do we have mammograms? Why do we get vaccinations? Because catching a problem early is a lot less expensive than treating it later. It's just common sense.

Which is why I'm so puzzled by the number of people that just don't get it.

Let me tell you a couple of short stories from my childhood in Saskatchewan. When I was a little girl, there was a scandal about a young woman who had a child out of wedlock, a little girl. Now, this was quite unusual in those days, at least in my little corner of the world, and I'm ashamed to say that this woman was not treated very well. She was shunned by many members of the community, and there was nowhere to turn for help.

But I think the little girl had it even worse; she was made fun of by the other children when she started school, and many of the teachers, sadly, treated her like she wasn't quite as good as the other kids.

I moved to Edmonton when I was a teenager, so I don't know whatever happened to that young woman and her little girl. But I know that they both must have had to struggle terribly; there were no organizations like yours to provide any kind of comfort or support.

In that same small town, a new widow was faced with a struggle for survival. She had no marketable skills; her husband had been the breadwinner, she the homemaker. With no community support available, she did the only thing she could: she turned to making moonshine. And the townspeople came knocking. Why not? Her booze was pretty good, and it was cheaper than what you could get at the bar.

In fact, when the RCMP started an investigation, her customers protected her, making sure that she never got caught. This went on for years, and who knows how many dollars the police invested to try and catch this woman in the act? It would have been a lot cheaper to provide her with some job training.

Both of these women had to make it on their own. There was no social safety net in those days, at least not to today's extent. I suppose some people would say that suffering builds character, that what doesn't kill you makes you stronger, and all those other clichés. But in my experience, suffering is more likely to build depression, shame, and even resentment and hate.

Nip suffering in the bud, and maybe you can nip violence and crime in the bud, too....

Reminiscences of Swedish immigrant life were spiced with more tales of Auntie Anne.

Scandinavian Businessmen's Club: Ladies Night
November 21, 2001

GOOD EVENING, EVERYONE, and thank you for asking me to join you tonight. I'm especially pleased to be invited to this particular event; after all, I'm of Scandinavian descent, too. You see, my mother's side of the family was originally from Sweden.

When my mother and Auntie Anne were two years old, the family left Sweden to emigrate to Canada. But on the way, my mother and Auntie Anne both caught the whooping cough, so Grandma and the twins had to be dropped off in England while Granddad and my Uncle Harvey continued on the journey to Canada.

Well, there was my poor grandmother, stranded in England with two sick babies, not knowing a single word of English.

But you know, she was a fast learner, and by the time mom and Auntie Anne were well, she'd picked up enough English to resume her journey and rendezvous with Granddad and Uncle Harvey in Saskatchewan.

Thanks to Grandma's perseverance, the family settled successfully in Canada, and eventually my mother and aunt grew up and built lives of their own. And though their lives took different paths, their mother country influenced them equally.

My mother became a homemaker; my aunt, a nursing sister who never married.

My mother's Scandinavian heritage showed up often in the wonderful meals she used to create, including lutefisk, and hardtack slathered in butter, heavily laden with salty pork. But more importantly, in keeping with her Swedish character, Mother had a great respect for education, reading, and the fine arts.

She always encouraged me to read or practise at the piano; in fact, an outside observer might think that I was spoiled, because mother always gave me a choice between doing chores or studying. To her, it was always more important that I be well-read. The weeding in the garden could wait, or she'd just do it herself rather than distract me from my studies.

I inherited mother's respect for arts and literature, and I've always agreed with her passionately held philosophy that learning is the most important thing.

My aunt, on the other hand, embodied the Scandinavian traits of caring for the sick.

She worked her whole life as a nurse, serving all over Europe and North America; she even served in England during World War II. She was a great supporter of public health care and believed that no one should be denied access to medical services for any reason.

But Auntie Anne had a fun side, too. For one thing, she really appreciated her gin. Like many Scandinavians, she liked a nip or two from time to time. You know how when you make Swedish meatballs, you add a little beer to it? Well, with Auntie, the amount of beer she added to the meatballs always seemed to increase according to the amount of gin she was having.

Once, Auntie Anne attended the wedding of a family friend. We were all having a pretty good time, and late in the evening, Auntie Anne tried to get a drink from the bar. Unfortunately, last call had come long before, and poor Auntie had to do without. "Can you believe they closed the bar? What kind of wedding is this?"

She went on in that vein for quite some time, and the rest of us got a real kick out of her antics.

Now of course you realize that I'm exaggerating a little; Auntie was by no means an alcoholic, she just liked to have a little fun, and the gin helped her loosen up a little.

That's what I like about Scandinavian culture; it's relaxed, easygoing, live-and-let-live. The world could use a lot more of that kind of attitude.

I'm very proud of my Scandinavian heritage. The Scandinavian peoples have really set the standard for building just societies, coming very close to a perfect balance between individual rights and community needs. Their respect for public education, for social assistance to those who need it, and for public support of libraries and the fine arts is a trait I hope Canadians will continue to emulate.

Indeed, the Scandinavian culture has had a profound influence on Canada, and I am so very proud of the contributions Canadians of

Scandinavian descent have made to this country. Thank you so much for being such an important part of the Canadian mosaic.

Lois giving her Canada Day speech at the Alberta Legislature, 2004. [Hole Family Archives]

2002

A speech on literacy offered more insights into how Lois tried to recruit people to her causes. Instead of preaching to them about what they should be doing, she shared her ideas and suggested they were already well on the way to taking part in improving the world as she thought it should be improved. This speech also saw one of her first uses of a statement from U.S. scientist Carl Sagan on libraries. It became one of her most frequently cited quotations through the next three years.

Westlock Rotary Club
Charter Night Celebration
January 18, 2002

GOOD EVENING, EVERYONE, and thank you for asking me to join you in celebrating 34 years of Rotary in Westlock.

Rotary's remarkable success since its inception in 1905 can be attributed to one simple truth: that people, by and large, want to do the right thing.

Rotary's motto, "Service Above Self," condenses this truth into one simple phrase. The entire point of this club is to improve quality of life all over the world and to promote understanding, acceptance, and even love among all her diverse peoples. There can be no nobler mission.

The truth is, I admire the work of the Rotary Club so much that it was difficult to decide what I could say to you; as far as I'm concerned, you're already doing the right thing, and doing it remarkably well.

But then I remembered the important work the Rotary Club has done to promote literacy, and I thought I'd share some of my thoughts on reading and the importance of public libraries, not just because they help build stronger minds, but because they may be the key to ending war and poverty....

Crime, poverty, and despair cannot be fought by building bigger, better jails, but by building bigger, better schools and libraries. My greatest fear is that sometime in the future, Canadians will see their neighbours trapped by poverty and ignorance and say to themselves, "How could we have allowed this to happen?"

We haven't reached that time yet. Canada is still one of the best places in the world to live, and we still have a chance to speak out for public schools and the balanced programs and educational philosophies they offer.

All we can do, I think, is continue to spread the word that in the long term, it makes more sense to give our children a liberal education and to support our social programs than it does to build more jails....

These are troubling times. In the past few weeks, we've been faced with images of tragedy on a catastrophic scale, and everyone is saying, "Things will never be the same again." There's a lot of sentiment to increase military spending and cut back on social programs. In times of trouble, in times of fiscal restraint, it always seems like preventative medicine is the first concept we decide to abandon.

Well, I'd never suggest that our soldiers deserve anything less than our full support. But I think there's a better way to prevent terrorism, save lives, and improve living conditions all over the world than trading welfare for warfare. And that way is simply to work towards a world where everyone can read and write.

Can you imagine what a different world it would be if everyone—not just a few folks, like Rotary Club members—finally recognized that the health and welfare of the impoverished in Bangladesh or Nigeria or Indonesia is just as important to our security and prosperity as the state of our automotive or logging industries, or the worth of our dollar?

The work that Rotary Club members are doing to improve literacy all over the world will, I have no doubt, prevent any number of catastrophes. I really believe that you're doing more to protect lives than all the tanks and planes in the Western world's arsenal.

A healthy world depends absolutely upon the literacy of its population. To create the great thinkers and leaders that will help build a better world, we must first create great readers. So I would like to commend the Rotary Club on its efforts to raise the standard of literacy, right here at home and across the planet.

I'd like to leave you tonight with a quote from Carl Sagan, the American scientist:

The library connects us with the insight and knowledge, painfully extracted from Nature, of the greatest minds that ever were, with the best teachers, drawn from the entire planet and from all our history, to instruct us without tiring, and to inspire us to make our own contribution to the collective knowledge of the human species. I think the health of our civilization, the depth of our awareness about the underpinnings of our culture and our concern for the future can all be tested by how well we support our libraries.

Thank you.

Lois strongly supported the military and made many speeches to military audiences or on military themes. Even a military event, however, could serve as a forum for instilling in the audience an appreciation of the importance of education.

Edmonton Garrison Officers' Mess (EGOM) Business Lunch
February 1, 2002

GOOD AFTERNOON, EVERYONE.

For many, many years, it's been a tradition in my family to drop everything at precisely noon and gather together in the kitchen for lunch. And for forty-five minutes or so, we'll talk, laugh, or even argue as we replenish our minds and bodies.

Our daily lunches have kept our family unit functioning smoothly, and while we don't have the same esprit de corps that a military unit does, I think the general idea is the same. I understand how important it is for officers to gather and break bread in a safe, comfortable environment, because I know how important it has been to my own family and business.

So as we gather for lunch today, I'd like to share some thoughts about the pride Canadians have in their soldiers, and why I think our armed forces will play a more important role in the days to come than many might suspect.

Canadians are paying more attention to their armed forces these days, for obvious reasons.

The current effort to safeguard citizens from terrorism has focussed the public eye upon you more directly than it has been in years.

This is a good thing, because I think Canadians need to know that our soldiers set a remarkably high standard for professionalism and capability, even with limited resources.

And I attribute the excellence of our armed forces in large part to our public education system.

An excellent public education system is the necessary foundation for an excellent military.

Canadian soldiers may be called upon to make life and death decisions at any moment. In those moments, a lifetime of learning and

Lois Hole at her installation as lieutenant-governor, February 10, 2000. Lois was recovering from a broken heel. [Hole Family Archives]

experience is brought to bear, and making a correct decision all depends on the judgement of the soldier, informed by his or her education.

Those decisions are always better when the soldier in question has the advantage of a well-rounded education, supported by lots of extra reading. I think a well-stocked library is a great investment for any military unit.

I think it's fair to say that the men and women of our armed forces are among the best-educated in the world, and that's why I'm glad that our soldiers, some of whom are right here in this room, are going to Afghanistan.

Because of our long history of peacekeeping around the world and the solid, liberal education our soldiers enjoy as Canadians, I believe that our troops can serve as a voice of reason in a terribly emotional conflict.

Canadian troops are disciplined, dedicated, and ethical, and in a war as complex as the one we face today, the world needs our well-educated, compassionate, professional soldiers. Canadian soldiers have always been dedicated to ending wars, not to making them worse, and I believe that's the part we are destined to play in Afghanistan.

Not in a huge, dramatic way—we must be realistic, given our relatively small military—but person by person, influencing our allies and enemies alike, doing our best to bring peace, order, and good government to the places where these qualities are most desperately needed.

That is why I am so pleased to be inducted as an Honorary Member of this Mess. It's an honour I will carry in my heart with pride, the same pride I know Canadians have in you. To those of you who will be heading to Afghanistan as part of Operation Apollo—good luck, be careful, and know that the thoughts of all of us are with you.

Thank you.

Another library appearance, this time with the addition of a story of how an appointment with the dentist set a young Lois off on a never-ending journey through libraries and the world of books. The original speech ended with a brief recap of Carl Sagan's comment on libraries.

Bookstock Campaign
Edmonton Public Library
February 1, 2002

GOOD MORNING, EVERYONE.

I was a teenager when I first moved to Edmonton, and I remember well what happened the first time I was exposed to Edmonton's library system. You see, I was in high school at the time, and I had to go downtown to visit the dentist.

Well, I had a little bit of time to kill after the dental appointment, so on the way back to school I stopped in at the public library. I was amazed by the size of it—after using the tiny little library in my hometown in Saskatchewan for years, the rows and rows of books in the downtown Edmonton branch completely overwhelmed me with delight.

Well, I got so excited I spent the rest of the day reading and browsing and exploring, and I missed all of my afternoon classes. But I certainly didn't regret it!

After that, I spent many long afternoons at the Edmonton Public Library, and the books I discovered there brought me so much knowledge and sheer fun that I don't know what I'd be doing today if the library hadn't been there. I certainly doubt I'd have become Lieutenant Governor!

A well-stocked library is essential to the health of any community. Libraries provide us with knowledge, with inspiration, with entertainment—all the tools we need to grow as human beings....

I urge all Albertans to contribute to the Bookstock campaign. Any donation is an investment in a brighter, smarter future for the people of this province.

The Royal Purple is a venerable Prairie institution. Anyone who grew up in rural Saskatchewan would have had memories of it. A speech to the Edmonton lodge included a pointed comment on one of the provincial government cuts of the mid-1990s, as well as a full airing of the "beet incident" story.

Royal Purple Edmonton Lodge #22
75th Anniversary
February 23, 2002

GOOD EVENING, EVERYONE, and thank you for asking me to join you tonight to celebrate the 75th anniversary of this fine lodge.

When I learned that the Royal Purple was so active in helping children with speech and hearing problems, it reminded me of my days as a school trustee.

Back then, there was a government program that provided speech pathology services to children in need, and the families who received that help were so grateful that their children were getting the help they so desperately required.

But then the cutbacks came, and the program was eliminated, and let me tell you, I had parents coming to me in tears, absolutely devastated. What was going to happen to their children now?

Fortunately, the Royal Purple has been able to take some of that load, providing aid to countless children—though I hope that one day government funding will be restored. It's in everyone's interest to support these children, and it's not fair to ask non-profit groups to shoulder all of the responsibility when the entire province benefits.

After all, communication is the most important skill we can teach, whether it's through speech, hand signals, or the written word. If a child doesn't learn that basic ability, he or she is at a huge disadvantage for life. And when children are disadvantaged, they sometimes lose their way in life, turning to crime or succumbing to despair.

Each child you rescue from this fate is a gift, a gift to the child, to the child's family, and to all Albertans.

I have a little story about communication that I'd like to share with you. I call it "The Beet Incident."

Back when my husband Ted and I were vegetable farming for a living, we worked very hard to bring each crop to harvest. Well, one particularly dry summer, our beets weren't doing very well. They hadn't gotten nearly enough attention, and in fact, it was tough to spot the beet greens among the weeds.

But they were the only beets we had, and I knew that in a few weeks customers would be asking for them. At least we'd have something to offer them. So one morning I asked Mrs. Durocher, a dear friend and employee, to weed the beet patch. She started work, moving through the rows slowly but methodically, and I knew that she could salvage the crop.

I headed off to a school board meeting, feeling greatly relieved.

I returned to the farm around suppertime, and I went out to the field to see how the crop looked. Well, I stood there with my mouth open, because the entire patch was demolished. There was nothing there but freshly turned soil.

Apparently, Ted had also noticed how badly the beets were doing. Without asking me, he had decided that the beets where more trouble than they were worth and went out to plough them under. He didn't even notice that the beets were newly weeded. He just went ahead and destroyed the crop.

I was livid. What on earth would I say to Mrs. Durocher when she arrived for work the next morning? All that effort wasted, without a moment's thought! But she didn't say a word about it, even though I knew her feelings must have been hurt. She must have thought we had a good reason for changing our minds.

I have to tell you, I've never been angrier at Ted. He should have consulted me. After all, I was the one who dealt with the customers, and I was the one who would have to spend the rest of the summer apologizing because we didn't have any beets.

But of course our relationship was strong enough to withstand that bitter experience. It's funny how such a trivial thing can upset you so much, isn't it?

Both of us learned, though, how important it was to keep the lines of communication open. We couldn't afford to assume that each of us knew what the other was thinking.

If either of us had communicated our intentions regarding the beet patch to the other, a huge fight could have been avoided.

And just think—even between two people who are normally pretty good communicators, misunderstandings like this can still happen.

I can only imagine how much harder it is for children who struggle to speak or hear.

You've helped children with communication problems avoid far more serious struggles than the one Ted and I had to contend with.

You have helped open up the whole world to such children; you've given them the chance to enjoy a rich, full life, the chance to prosper and to make their own contributions to the community.

That's why I'm so proud of the members of this lodge. Thank you for stepping in to help children find their voices.

The occasion was International Women's Day. Literacy seemed relevant to any event or audience. On this late winter day in Edson, women and words became natural partners.

International Women's Day
Edson, Alberta, March 7, 2002

GOOD EVENING, EVERYONE, and thank you for inviting me to join you in celebration of International Women's Day.

This day is important to women because it gives us a chance to measure our progress. We can see how far we've come, while recognizing how far we have yet to go.

The women of western societies have more power than any women in history, and yet we are still underrepresented in a wide variety of fields. And women in less affluent nations often face lives too terrible to contemplate.

Improving the lives of women all over the world is the work of decades, if not centuries.

The best place to start building a better world is to begin with education and libraries, to improve literacy around the globe.

Why is literacy so important to women? Well, obviously a literate culture is a richer culture, both in economic and social terms.

Literate women require less social assistance, they get better jobs and thus pay higher taxes, and they are more likely to contribute to our cultural and artistic legacy. In other words, it's in our collective interest to maintain a high rate of literacy. Literacy simply makes good sense; it's practical.

But those are a businessman's reasons to encourage literacy. Literacy is more than a simple economic stimulus. Literacy offers the human race, and women in particular, hope. Hope of escaping our violent past and attaining something better. For ignorance is the great villain of history and of women's liberation, and literacy is our best weapon against it.

Once upon a time, reading was a skill reserved only for the upper classes, and that usually meant rich white men. Allowing the masses to read was dangerous to those who cherished the status quo. On this very continent, it wasn't so long ago that the law forbade minorities from learning the skill.

And it wasn't so long ago, in the great scheme of things, that women who read were called "uppity." But literacy and education liberated women, minorities, and the working poor; it gave them tremendous power.

The ability to read empowers people, and literacy gives us a measure of control over our own lives.

Being literate gives us the capability to form our own opinions and create our own ethical standards. Reading good books opens our minds to new opportunities, and gives us the ability to ask the right questions. Literacy is a tremendous power, an incredible force for good. It gives each of us the capacity to learn and grow and affect our world.

We know, then, that literacy is more than important; it's vital. Knowing that, we as a society must decide the best means of maintaining and even raising the standard of literacy in our country.

I believe that literacy can only be built upon three important pillars. One pillar is made up of the various adult and family literacy organizations.

Another is public libraries. And the third is public education. These three institutions share two traits: their primary goal is to make people literate, and they are free and open to all citizens.

I cannot stress how important that openness is to the survival of our culture.

The most dangerous problem facing our country, and for that matter, our world, is one hardly anyone recognizes: the division of our population into two classes, the literate and the illiterate.

Now, don't get me wrong; I think we've done a pretty good job of gradually raising our level of literacy since Canada's founding.

But if we want to maintain and improve upon that record, we can't take our public institutions for granted. The price of literacy, you might say, is eternal vigilance.

Do you ever wonder why we never hear about it in the media when library budgets get cut? I sure do.

And yet, you could argue that library budgets are as important as health care budgets or defence budgets. In fact, library budgets are *more* important, since you can't have professional health care or well-trained soldiers without the resources libraries provide.

Here's why you don't hear about library budget cuts: because too many Canadians have taken literacy for granted. According to statistics, Canada is one of those countries that has a literacy rate of something like 98 per cent. With numbers that high, you tend not to worry too much about library budgets.

It took generations to create a literate populace, and we all know how much easier it is to destroy than to create, how easy it is to rest on our laurels and let our best institutions slide into disrepair, on both the physical and the metaphorical plane. The three pillars of literacy must never be allowed to crumble, and it is our responsibility to see that they stand.

Those who promote literacy—authors, librarians, teachers, professors—are nothing less than the guardians of democratic civilization, and for that matter, of human existence itself....

Literacy is our only hope of finding the path to true peace, true justice, and true equality in our troubled world. We must not fail to spread it far and wide.

A short commentary on leadership showed how Lois could applaud and work with business executives, despite her occasional reference to "businessmen's reasons" for supporting education. But two minutes of speaking time at the University of Alberta still afforded an opportunity to send a message on tuition rates to an influential audience.

University of Alberta School of Business
2002 Canadian Business Leader Award Dinner
March 19, 2002

GOOD EVENING. On behalf of the Crown and the people of Alberta, welcome to tonight's celebration of business leadership.

Tonight we honour Brian MacNeill, chair of Petro-Canada and former CEO of Enbridge, for his remarkable feats of leadership, both in business and in the community.

And in honouring Mr. MacNeill, I'd like to say a few words about leadership.

True leadership is the ability to blaze new trails without destroying the forest. True leaders have an awareness of the larger community that surrounds them; they know that their work does not exist in isolation.

True leaders understand that every innovation, every deal, must be considered in a wider context than the numbers on a balance sheet.

This university is a good example. On paper, it's a pretty expensive place to run, and I can understand why there's some pressure to raise tuition year after year.

But think of the true cost to society if we close the doors to more and more students. And imagine the benefits if we did away with tuition altogether—the best young minds in the country would flock here, and many of them would stay to help make Alberta even more prosperous.

I suspect that's the kind of long-term planning and risk-taking that helped Brian MacNeill lead Enbridge's explosive growth. It takes vision to achieve greatness, and Mr. MacNeill has it.

Through his pioneering work in the energy industry, and his devotion to the community as a director of the United Way, Brian MacNeill has shown us that you can create a lot of wealth at the same time as you improve the lives of thousands of people.

Brian, thank you for providing an example for the students of the School of Business, tomorrow's leaders in the making. I know that many of the young people here tonight will follow in your footsteps, even as they blaze trails of their own.

The Alberta Library Conference in the spring of 2002 made an excellent plat-
form for the launch of the Lois Hole Library Legacy Program. The conference
also offered a chance for a brief comment on library fees, which had appeared
in a number of Alberta communities several years earlier during the first Klein
government's spending cuts. The fees were often in the range of $1 a month or
less, but had been followed by a drop in library memberships; many people
were also offended by the principle of charging fees for library membership.

Lois reprised the stories of Miss Jobb and of the trip to the dentist that
launched her into the world of books. Both appeared in earlier speeches and
are omitted here. Lois's introduction of Miss Jobb reflects the warmth of her
memories.

Alberta Library Conference
Launch of the Lois Hole Library Legacy Program
April 25, 2002

GOOD EVENING, EVERYONE, and thank you so much. I don't think I
can possibly convey how overwhelmed I am by this remarkable honour.

Libraries have been so important to me all my life, and I am
profoundly grateful to have the chance to help our libraries in a substan-
tial way.

Our lives are richer when they are touched by books. I was lucky
enough to have parents who always encouraged me to read; from a very
early age, I discovered how magical books were, with their power to take
you to strange and beautiful places and expose you to new ideas. My
favourite Christmas gifts were books. I'd curl up in the big comfy chair
and read all day long.

When I was in Grade One, the closest thing we had to a library at the
little school in Buchanan consisted of two shelves in our teacher's room,
with a total of about 15 books. Our teacher was Miss Jobb, a beautiful
young woman, always impeccably dressed, very trim and petite, with
very dark hair.

She was a delightful teacher; she never played favourites, and it was
always obvious that she loved children and wanted us to do well.

Miss Jobb was very fussy about our schoolwork, and we all wanted her to be proud of us. For a Grade One class, there was an awful lot of competition!

One day, Miss Jobb brought five brand-new books to school for her shelves, an embarrassment of riches back then, let me tell you. One of the new books caught my eye right away; it was called *The Little Red Hen*....

During my travels of the past couple of years, I've tried to show people that a well-stocked library is essential to the health of any community. Libraries provide us with knowledge, with inspiration, with entertainment—all the tools we need to grow as human beings.

Libraries are as vital to our civilization as schools, hospitals, police and fire services, the military, the courts—you name it. Our public library system is a focal point of our culture, and I think that to remain truly Canadian, we must remain committed to the principle of equal access.

That principle is nowhere more important than it is when applied to libraries, since so many people, especially those with limited income, depend on them. Perhaps one day libraries will be funded enough so that we can do away with membership fees; that, I think, would be a real step forward.

Public libraries are, I believe, the most important institution in our country, because everything else that's good in our society must flow from knowledge. Few of us can afford to buy all the books we need, and everyone benefits, even the rich, when everyone has full access to libraries. Reading is perhaps the best way to learn about other cultures, new ideas, and different viewpoints.

It opens up our minds to all the diversity and the incredible possibilities that lay before us. The information to build a better world is all there, right on our library shelves; but we all need to read it to make that dream a reality.

I hope that Albertans will support this program with great enthusiasm, not because it bears my name, but because our citizens *need* books. Anyone who's bought even a thin paperback recently knows all too well how expensive books have become, which makes libraries all the more vital to anyone who needs to do research, to study for exams, or simply to read for pleasure and enlightenment.

Any donation is an investment in a brighter, smarter future for the people of this province.

In closing, I must thank the Library Association of Alberta, the Alberta Library Trustees Association, the Alberta Library, and the Alberta Library Conference for making this all possible.

You've really done something wonderful here, and I'm very proud to be associated with such steadfast guardians of the public trust.

Thank you so much.

Lois often told the story of how her father had advised her against becoming a nurse. It was a down-to-earth crowd pleaser. A dinner for the foundation that raised funds for the University of Alberta Hospital also saw her characteristically slip in a suggestion of how more attention to providing books might help build medical research in the province. This speech also saw one of the first references to Martin Luther King, who became a frequently cited figure in speeches in coming years.

University Hospital Foundation
Chairman's Donor Appreciation Dinner
April 27, 2002

GOOD EVENING, EVERYONE, and thank you for asking me to join you tonight. On behalf of all the people who will benefit from your generosity, it's my privilege and pleasure to express our profound gratitude. To begin, I'd like to share a little story about my brush with a career in health care.

My father had always assured me that I could be whatever I wanted to be when I grew up. So one day, after long and careful thought, I told him that I wanted to be a nurse.

"Oh, no," he said, "That's out of the question."

"But you told me I could be anything I wanted to be," I complained.

"Anything except that," he said.

At the time, I didn't understand why my father didn't want me to pursue such an admirable career. As I grew older, I developed two theories.

My first theory was that he didn't want me to see naked men.

My second theory came a little later on; I think my father knew what a difficult life nurses had, and he wanted something less stressful for me.

Dad knew a little bit about the history of nursing, and he was, of course, well acquainted with his sister-in-law, my Auntie Anne, who was a nurse so dedicated to her work that it seemed to consume her entire life; she never married, you see, and I wonder if my father ever subconsciously worried that the same thing would happen to me.

At any rate, obviously I never did become a nurse, and a part of me still regrets that. I have such respect for doctors and nurses and researchers, the people who dedicate their entire lives to helping those in need....

Before I say goodnight, I'd like to offer some thoughts from the renowned civil rights activist, Dr. Martin Luther King.

Doctor King said, "I have the audacity to believe that people everywhere can have three meals a day for their bodies, education and culture for their minds, and dignity, equality and freedom for their spirits. I believe that what self-centred people have torn down, other-centred people can build up."

To me, this is the central truth of philanthropy: that "other-centred" people—donors like you, in other words—will be the ones to ring in the era of true prosperity, of true equality, of true justice....

Thank you all so much for having the compassion and the vision to take that first step towards a healthier future.

A discourse on the importance of immigrants to Canada took on extra meaning with another personal story. Once again, growing up in Buchanan, Saskatchewan, had taught a future lieutenant-governor much about living in the wider world. The list of prominent Polish Canadians included George Radwanski; 13 months later he may have been left off after a scandal about the size of his expense accounts as federal privacy commissioner.

Polish Canadian Women's Federation 45th Anniversary
Edmonton, May 18, 2002

GOOD EVENING, EVERYONE, and thank you so much for asking me to join you tonight.

I grew up in a little town in northern Saskatchewan called Buchanan. In Buchanan, we had a Polish shoemaker, Mr. Hupon. Mr. Hupon could make an old, beaten up pair of shoes look better than a new pair from the store.

In fact, he was so good that when I moved to Edmonton, not even the vast array of shoes at the big department stores really impressed me. The selection was wonderful, of course, but I always doubted that they could match the quality of Mr. Hupon's shoes.

Not only was Mr. Hupon a great shoemaker, he was one of the nicest people I've ever met. I went to school with his daughter Annie, and Mr. Hupon always treated me like a member of the family.

I always wondered, though, if Mr. Hupon was one of the many immigrants to change his name so that English-speaking Canadians would find it easier to pronounce. I don't know, maybe Hupon is a common Polish name, but if he *did* change it, I think it's a shame. After all, Canada's strength comes from its immigrants and our ability to celebrate their cultural diversity.

No one should ever feel the need to smother their original cultural identity. In my mind, we're all better off when immigrants combine the best of their own traditions with the best Canadian traditions. Why not embrace both cultures?

Fortunately, I think that the Poles have done an excellent job of achieving this balance. Certainly there's no question that Canada has been enriched by immigration from Poland. Polish-Canadian scientists, politicians, business people, writers, artists, and actors have all distinguished themselves here.

Just off the top of my head, I can think of Chief Justice Allan Wachowich of the Court of Queen's Bench here in Edmonton, the World War II hero and Victoria Cross recipient Andrew Mynarski, former Deputy Prime Minister Don Mazankowski, one-time Toronto Star editor George Radwanski, and one of my favourite Canadian heroes, CBC broadcaster Peter Gzowski.

Now, I realize that these famous names happen to be male. But perhaps that's because women simply get so focussed on doing the vital work of our day-to-day lives that we're too busy to go out and become famous. That was certainly the case for the vast majority of immigrant women, the Poles chief among them.

And though many of their names may be lost to history, their work in building the solid foundations of this country continues to resonate and strengthen us to this very day.

Even now, Polish-Canadian women band together to better their communities; the charitable work of this very organization has been of immeasurable help to a wide range of Alberta's citizens. I am very proud of your volunteer efforts, and I know that the people you've helped are profoundly grateful for your generosity.

All human beings, regardless of culture or religion, share the same basic goals and dreams. We all want to live in peace, we all want to share in art and music and literature, and we all want enough food for our bellies and shelter over our heads. These are the birthrights of every human being, no matter where you were born. And that's why I believe that immigrants are such a boon to Canada.

They bring all their hopes and dreams, all their talent and passion, to our shores. And, without fail, they make profound contributions to our economic, social, and cultural well-being.

Immigrants made this country great, and they will continue to do so in the 21st century. It's been my privilege to work with and befriend people from many cultures, and I wouldn't give up any of those experiences for anything in the world.

Congratulations on your 45th anniversary. The Polish Canadian Women's Federation has long been a credit to our nation, and I hope you endure for many more years to come. Your presence has helped to make Canada an island of hope in an often troubled world.

Lois took the office of Queen's representative seriously and wanted others to treat it, rather than her personally, with respect. One reason was her tremendous respect for Queen Elizabeth II. This was one of her strongest and most personal statements on the monarchy.

The Monarchist League of Canada
Queen's Jubilee Celebrations

June 1, 2002

GOOD EVENING, and thank you for inviting me to join you in this wonderful celebration. I have to begin with a story.

One of my great honours as Lieutenant Governor of Alberta was the opportunity to enjoy an audience with Her Majesty, Queen Elizabeth the Second. Since the Lieutenant Governor represents the monarchy in our province, it was proper protocol—and I was thrilled to go.

On the plane to London, I was seated beside a nice young fellow from Calgary. We struck up a conversation, and after the usual pleasantries I inquired about his trip. As the conversation progressed, he asked me the question: "Where are you going?"

All I could think of was the children's nursery rhyme:

"Pussycat pussycat, where have you been?"
"I've been to London to visit the Queen."

So I answered, "I'm going to London."
"What are you going to do there?" he responded.
I smiled and said, "I'm going to London to visit the Queen."
He laughed, and then suddenly realized who he was sitting beside. "You're Lois Hole! You're our new lieutenant-governor!" he exclaimed.
I have to confess something else. I took a few of our gardening books along. At the end of my audience with Her Majesty, I asked if she could please give the books to Prince Charles, since he's such an avid gardener. Much to my surprise, the Prince later took time to respond with a handwritten letter. That letter is very special to me, something I will always treasure.[21]

The Queen was, quite frankly, easier to talk to than I expected. But, as befits her station, she also maintained a professional distance; I would never have imagined giving her a hug, for example, though I would have loved to.

Despite that necessary distance, it quickly became apparent that she cares about people from all walks of life; her concern for farmers, for example, came through loud and clear. It was completely genuine. She spoke very lovingly about children and the importance of visiting schools.

She approved of my focus on education, and she told me that talking to children about learning was very important. The Queen is not as cold as some people in the media would have you believe.

During my audience with Her Majesty, I also discovered that this was a woman who was very well informed, very knowledgeable. The amount of information she had to keep track of is phenomenal; her duties demand that she is well prepared to converse on a wide variety of subjects.

It's the only way she can possibly handle the countless functions she attends and the hordes of diplomats and dignitaries she deals with on a daily basis.

Even if I'd never met the Queen, today would still be very special to me. My parents were both strong monarchists, even though my mother was born in Sweden and my father was the son of Russian immigrants. They recognized the truth that there is something of value in the monarchy that transcends nationality, and they passed on that respect of the institution to me.

Never in my wildest dreams did I imagine I would ever meet the Queen, let alone represent her here in Alberta. I am so happy and honoured to help pay tribute to a remarkable woman and a sovereign who has already left an indelible mark on history.

I think we should remember that the Golden Jubilee is a celebration of a bittersweet anniversary.

In 1952, the peoples of the Commonwealth celebrated the ascension to the throne of their new monarch, Her Majesty Queen Elizabeth II, even as they mourned the loss of her father, King George VI.

For fifty years, we have benefited from the presence of a Queen truly regal in stature, manner, and influence.

And during those same fifty years, that same Queen has had to live without a father.

And yet, the tragic nature of succession is part and parcel of the monarchy's strength, for it gives us the most powerful symbol possible of the handing down of values and character from one generation to the next.

Despite this, in recent years it has become fashionable to question the role of the monarchy and to criticize the Royal family. I think it's always wise to question the status quo and to offer constructive criticism when the situation calls for it. But we must remember that the Queen has given up more than any of us can ever know.

From the moment of her birth, she never had a chance at anything resembling a normal life. Her duty, from cradle to grave, has been and will be to serve the interests of the United Kingdom and the many countries of the Commonwealth.

I admire the Queen because she has been constant in her quest to instil the values of acceptance and love in all the peoples of the Commonwealth. Her annual Christmas messages are always eloquent appeals for understanding between peoples of different races, cultures, and religions.

She genuinely believes in the principles of the Commonwealth—that a large group of wildly disparate nations, embracing dozens of different cultures, can work together in pursuit of greater prosperity, greater understanding, greater brotherhood.

From my perspective, this has seemed to be her primary cause, and she's been hammering it home for fifty years, perhaps long enough that people are starting to get the message; certainly we've seen major strides forward on the path to peace in recent years, the current troubles excepted, and I really think the Queen deserves at least some of the credit.

After all, when someone so respected all over the world tells you to get along, at least some people are likely to take that message to heart....

The world has changed a lot in fifty years, but the Queen has always been there, our Rock of Gibraltar, our Northern Star, something fixed and permanent that we can use to orient ourselves. This is the true gift of the monarchy, and we mustn't lose sight of its value. Some people say the Monarchy is anti-democratic; I disagree.

On the contrary, I think the Monarchy provides our democracy with a vital counterweight to short-term thinking. It's an institution that reminds us that the decisions of one generation have huge implications for the next. Elected governments remain in power for five or ten years; human problems span decades, centuries.

The perspective of a Monarch is an incredible resource, one we should take care not to lose. I think it would be a great tragedy if we were to allow this remarkable institution to slip through our fingers due to apathy....

Her Majesty's inspiration is one of the reasons I take my role as Lieutenant Governor very seriously. Having a representative of the monarchy here in Alberta makes the monarchy less distant and more a part of real people's daily lives. When I attend a function, everyone there, I hope, feels like they're a little more involved in our system of government.

And I hope they feel closer to the peoples of all the different nations that make up the Commonwealth. Anything that brings the world a little closer together is all right in my book, and I relish the chance to drum up more support for the institution.

We have been fortunate indeed to live during the era of Queen Elizabeth's reign, a time that has seen great tragedy, to be sure, but also an amazing increase in the world's standard of living, a spreading acceptance of fundamental human rights, and even, we hope, a more peaceful era.

So as we celebrate this Jubilee, let us savour our triumphs, learn from our errors, and find the wisdom to build a brighter future. Queen Elizabeth the Second is a beacon of dignity and poise. She has class and presence, and commands respect.

Her unwavering commitment to the democratic values we hold so dear make me very proud to have her as our Queen, and very proud to be a Canadian and a citizen of a great Commonwealth of nations that recognizes the contributions of the Royal family, Her Majesty the Queen in particular.

She's been our voice of reason, compassion, and tolerance for fifty years. She has served us well. Long may she reign.

By 2002, concern about the environment was hardly new in Alberta. This speech at an awards banquet still contained hints of early awareness. Water started becoming a much more important subject for the provincial government after an unusually hot and dry summer in 2003.

The "vinegar coffee" story was one of her favourites. She and Ted used to go to a local service station to get water for coffee in their early days on the farm because their well water was of marginal quality. The water was carried back in old vinegar bottles. One morning, Lois didn't notice a mix-up and made coffee with vinegar. Ted splurted out the result, gasping, "What are you trying to do, kill me?" They didn't have a good source of drinking water until a city water line was installed in the 1980s. By then, Lois had thoroughly absorbed the respect for water common across much of Prairie farm country, where access to good water was and remains a prime concern. Not wasting water was a big issue at the greenhouse. Lois was known among family and staff for constant reminders about not leaving hoses running or otherwise being prodigal with a resource she knew could not be taken for granted.

Emerald Awards
Alberta Foundation for Environmental Excellence
June 12, 2002

Good afternoon, everyone, and thank you for joining us for the 2002 Emerald Awards.

As a farmer, gardener, and proud patron of this Foundation, I'm very proud of the work you're all doing to encourage and create environmental excellence.

The work you do today is the only thing that can ensure future generations will continue to enjoy the clean air, clean water, and pristine environment that previous generations took for granted.

Cleaning up our environment is a goal with many different avenues of approach, but the one dearest to my heart is probably water.

So tonight I'd like to share a few memories and thoughts on water with you, since this simple, precious fluid is the lifeblood of our natural world.

Just a few days ago, I attended the annual Negev Dinner. In preparation for that event, I learned a lot about the Negev project, in which the

Lois doing what she loved, watering in the greenhouse, spring 2002. [Hole Family Archives]

Israelis are attempting to use tree planting and water conservation to reclaim some of the desert and make it habitable once again for humans and wildlife.

Thinking about what I would say to those people made me remember how stingy my parents were with water, and how they passed that trait down to me and my children.

My parents always made it clear how precious water was; it was a real concern, given how dry our little town in Saskatchewan was. Every drop of moisture was precious.[22]

My parents taught us just how precious water is by how we lived. Spent dishwater had a second purpose: to keep the flower bed moist. And when Saturday night bath time came, we all took turns using the same water. I grew up thinking bathwater should be used more than once.

That conserving attitude toward water continued when Ted and I moved to the farm—and partly out of necessity. We fixed up a little seven hundred square foot bungalow, and for the first few years it had no running water. The telephone was a party line, and the only other amenities we had were electricity and a coal-fired furnace.

On the plus side, our well produced water soft as silk due to high sodium content. It was great for washing clothes—and hair. One drop of shampoo, and you had suds galore. Later on we did get indoor plumbing, but for a long time our water still came from that well. And while it made your hair shiny and soft, it also made the most atrocious coffee.

During the week, I solved the problem by taking empty vinegar bottles down to Roger's Esso and filling the bottles with water from their tap. This was our coffee water—and it was used for nothing but coffee. On the weekends, we often visited friends in the city, and each time we travelled I would take empty vinegar bottles, fill them with water and haul them back home.

Mornings were always a blur at our house, with the hired men coming in for breakfast and everybody rushing every which way. I always liked to make sure a pot of coffee was ready by the time Ted sat down for a quick glance at the newspaper. One morning, while reading his paper, he took a big gulp of coffee and immediately spat it out with a surprised "Lois, what the h... did you do to this coffee?" In the chaos that morning, I'd grabbed a bottle of vinegar that I'd set on the counter while making pickles the previous day.

For many weeks after, as I poured his morning coffee Ted would pause dramatically, carefully lift the cup towards his face and sniff. "Just checking," he'd say with a smile.

Now I think everyone in this audience knows that water is priceless. But the sad truth is, not everyone recognizes this. By and large, we in the Western world still use water like there's no end to the supply. This practice just isn't sustainable, and I'm not the only one saying it.

Professor David Schindler of the University of Alberta, a leading ecological scientist and the winner of the water ecology equivalent of the Nobel Prize, has some pretty dire warnings for us. In an abstract of a recent paper on the effects of human activity on our lakes and rivers, he writes:

At best, we can expect the cost of freshwater to increase by billions of dollars in Canada, with billions more needed for restoration of damaged lakes, rivers and wetlands. At worst, we will lose freshwater sport fishing throughout southern Canada, and Walkerton-like crises will become more common.

I hope people will begin to wake up to the reality that our water supplies are not infinite. What are we going to do in Alberta when water is worth more than oil?

I shudder at the thought, but I believe that day is coming, unless we start cleaning up our act right now.

It makes me sick when I think of all the money being spent world-wide on guns and bombs when we face the gravest crisis the world has ever known: the destruction of our water supply, the very stuff of life for every creature on this planet.

We have to get off our bums and start thinking about water now.

Not tomorrow, not next week, but the next time we flush a toilet or turn on a tap. We're so darn short-sighted about our water use that we're not likely to pay any attention to the problem until we can walk across the ditch where the North Saskatchewan River used to be.

Now, I don't mean to sound too pessimistic; I'm just hoping there's a reporter or two out there who will repeat a few words of warning. The truth is, we do have reason to hope, plenty of reasons: they're all sitting among you in this very room....

A homecoming parade for Edmonton-based soldiers returning from Afghanistan after the first military response to the 9/11 terrorist attacks was among many military events that Lois attended. This one took on added poignancy because of the deaths of four soldiers killed by a bomb dropped by a U.S. fighter pilot who interpreted small-arms gun flashes in a night training exercise as anti-aircraft fire.

Homecoming Parade for Troops Returning from Afghanistan
Edmonton, August 9, 2002

SINCE THE BIRTH OF OUR NATION, Canadians have been called upon time and again to defend the fundamental principles of freedom, democracy, and community. In the defence of those principles, we have lost many fine soldiers, young people in the prime of life, including those who perished in Afghanistan this year: Sgt. Marc D. Leger, Cpl. Ainsworth Dyer, Private Richard Green, and Private Nathan Smith. But those soldiers would be the first to tell you that their sacrifice was not a vain or empty one. They died in the pursuit of a better world, and we owe them our gratitude.

The members of the armed forces have a proud tradition of service to our country. Their contribution to the well-being of Canadians, in times of peace and war alike, cannot be overstated. With dignity, valour, and grace under fire, they have served under the most difficult conditions imaginable, in a hostile and unforgiving environment.

Despite these obstacles, Canadian soldiers have once again proven themselves to be among the world's most elite fighting forces.

Canadian troops are disciplined, dedicated, and ethical, and in a war as complex as the one we face today, the world needs our well-educated, compassionate, professional soldiers.

A Canadian soldier is brave, yet *not* foolhardy; patriotic, yet *not* fanatical; obedient, yet independent; effective, yet compassionate. These moderate qualities make Canadian soldiers much admired throughout the world, and it is these qualities that will carry us through these difficult times.

Like all Canadians, I am very proud of the men and women of our armed forces as they fight to safeguard the lives and freedom of *all* peoples, both here at home and across the oceans.

Now that your tour of duty in Afghanistan is over, I offer my heartfelt thanks for your service and my pride in your dedication to duty and the principles of Canadian democracy. Thank you, and welcome home.

Libraries, literacy, and the arts made up the core of the more than 800 speeches that Lois Hole gave as lieutenant-governor of Alberta. Most of the speeches were relatively brief. Beginning in the summer of 2002, she began making more comprehensive statements of what she believed. She was clearly growing more comfortable with her position and certain about what she wanted to communicate to Albertans.

This address to gardeners in the small central Alberta town of Rumsey consolidated her thinking in these areas. It follows the form of a speech she delivered three weeks earlier at a homecoming in Crowsnest Pass, and was to be followed by many more very much like it. If there are classic Lois Hole speeches, this is one of them.

Red Deer River Garden Club
Alberta Provincial Horticultural Show
Rumsey, August 23, 2002

GOOD AFTERNOON. It's my pleasure to join you tonight, and to welcome everyone participating in this year's Alberta Horticultural Show.

> *One spring morning, years ago, I got a phone call from a friend who taught junior high school in nearby Bon Accord. "Lois," she said, "we're having a career day. Could you come and talk to our Grade Sevens, Eights, and Nines?"*
>
> *"What career are you asking me to talk about, exactly?" I inquired. And she said, "Well, market gardening, of course."*
>
> *"Who else is coming?" I asked, trying to sound casual. She recited the guest list: a doctor, a nurse, a fireman, a police officer, a photographer, a university drama professor—the array of glamorous professions went on and on.*
>
> *"Margaret," I asked, "what teenager in her right mind would want a career in market gardening? With all those wonderful people, the kids will never come to hear me."*
>
> *"Oh yes they will, Lois," she replied. "They have to."*
>
> *Well, before I knew it, there I was walking down the school hallway. I still hadn't the slightest idea what I was going to tell these kids. Just then, two girls passed me, and I overheard one of them*

saying, "If I can just find a way to earn twenty more dollars, I'll finally be able to buy that dress." I snapped my fingers and thought, "Now I know what to say."

As I walked into the room, a very nervous little Grade Seven girl was introducing me. She said, "We're so glad to have Mrs. Holey here today."

I could tell by looking at the kids that they were already thinking ahead to the fireman. So I turned to them and said, "Hey kids, do you want to make some money this summer?" Every kid was suddenly paying close attention.

I told them, "Go home and ask your mother for half of her vegetable garden. In that half garden, you're going to plant peas. And make sure you plant those peas nice and thick! And then you're going to get up in the morning and pick those peas."

You might notice I left a few details out between the planting and picking. But I had their attention and didn't want to lose it.

I said, "You'll pick a great, big bag of peas. Your mother will drive you to the nearest supermarket. When you get there, you'll march up to the first staff person you see and tell them, 'I'd like to see the produce manager, please.' When he comes out, you'll say, 'I have this bag of peas I'd like to sell you.'

"He'll reach over and grab a pod. The peas will be so shiny and squeaky, he'll know you picked them that morning. He'll want them so badly. And when he asks you, 'How much do you want for your bag of peas?,' you will say, 'TWENTY DOLLARS.'"

I thought the little girl was going to fall off her chair.

I told the kids, "You can sell fresh peas anywhere. Put them in big bags, put them in little bags, go to the City Market, go door to door. People will die for fresh peas."

Well, the room absolutely erupted. The kids began talking all at once, excitedly throwing out suggestions. Just then the bell rang and I had to move on to the next class. I thanked the kids for their enthusiasm and began gathering my things.

A little girl in the front row raised her hand. "Mrs. Hole," she begged, "don't tell the other kids about the peas!" [23]

As I was thinking about what to say at this event, it struck me that the only reason Canadians have enough money, leisure time, and knowledge to attend garden shows is because our forefathers and foremothers had the drive and the desire to build a better country.

So tonight, I'd like to talk a little about what I feel we need to do to sustain our prosperous, vibrant culture, to ensure that the work of the pioneers was not in vain and that our children and our children's children will have the opportunity to enjoy the good things in life, whether that means garden shows like this one, the theatre, the symphony, or simply the comfort of a good book by a Canadian author.

Canadians have built a culture to be proud of. And yet, there are signs on the horizon that make me a little nervous, signs that we're becoming a little less compassionate and a little less concerned about the public good, all in the pursuit of nebulous values like "efficiency" and "productivity."

Well, let me tell you. I certainly don't have anything against making money, but it takes more than entrepreneurship to build a culture. To be sure, a vigorous business community is important, even vital, but I believe that Canadian culture rests on three important foundations: public schools, public libraries, and the fine arts.

If you support these fundamentals, everything else becomes much easier to accomplish.

The best place to start building a better Canada, and a better world, is to begin with education and libraries, to improve literacy around the globe.

Why is literacy so important? Well, obviously a literate culture is a richer culture, both in economic and social terms. Literate people require less social assistance, they get better jobs and thus pay higher taxes, and they are more likely to contribute to our cultural and artistic legacy.

In other words, it's in our collective interest to maintain a high rate of literacy. Literacy simply makes good sense; it's practical.

But those are a businessman's reasons to encourage literacy. Literacy is more than a simple economic stimulus. Literacy offers the human race hope.

Hope of escaping our violent past and attaining something better. Ignorance is the great villain of history, and literacy is our best weapon against it.

Once upon a time, reading was a skill reserved only for the upper classes. Allowing the masses to read was dangerous to those who cherished the status quo.

On this very continent, it wasn't so long ago that the law forbade minorities from learning the skill. The ability to read empowers people, and literacy gives us a measure of control over our own lives.

Being literate gives us the capability to form our own opinions and create our own ethical standards.

Reading good books opens our minds to new opportunities, and gives us the ability to ask the right questions. Literacy is a tremendous power, an incredible force for good. It gives each of us the capacity to learn and grow and affect our world.

We know, then, that literacy is more than important; it's vital. Knowing that, we as a society must decide the best means of maintaining and even raising the standard of literacy in our country.

I believe that literacy can only be built upon three important pillars.

One pillar is made up of the various adult and family literacy organizations. Another is public libraries. And the third is public education. These three institutions share two traits: their primary goal is to make people literate, and they are free and open to all citizens.

I cannot stress how important that openness is to the survival of our culture.

The most dangerous problem facing our country, and for that matter, our world, is one hardly anyone recognizes: the division of our population into two classes, the literate and the illiterate.

Now, don't get me wrong; I think we've done a pretty good job of gradually raising our level of literacy since Canada's founding. But if we want to maintain and improve upon that record, we can't take our public institutions for granted. The price of literacy, you might say, is eternal vigilance.

Do you ever wonder why we never hear about it in the media when library budgets get cut? I sure do. And yet, you could argue that library budgets are as important as health care budgets or defence budgets. In fact, library budgets are *more* important, since you can't have professional health care or well-trained soldiers without the resources libraries provide.

Here's why you don't hear about library budget cuts: because too many Canadians have taken literacy for granted. According to statistics, Canada is one of those countries that has a literacy rate of something like 98 per cent. With numbers that high, you tend not to worry too much about library budgets.

But it took generations to create a literate populace, and we all know how much easier it is to destroy than to create, how easy it is to rest on our laurels and let our best institutions slide into disrepair, on both the physical and the metaphorical plane. The three pillars of literacy must never be allowed to crumble, and it is our responsibility to see that they stand.

Those who promote literacy—authors, librarians, teachers, professors—are nothing less than the guardians of democratic civilization and, for that matter, of human existence itself. Why is literacy more important than ever?

Because human beings have gotten so advanced, and our problems so complex and so threatening, that it will take the collective brainpower of millions of people to find solutions. Why are we raising tuition during these times? Do only the rich have brains? No!

We must ensure that every human being has the opportunity to pursue higher learning; we cannot afford to waste their potential for the sake of having a surplus every year.

We can't afford to be illiterate anymore; the world is too complex to leave in the hands of a privileged few.

Being literate means having the ability to exercise political power, to have a voice in how human beings manage our environment and our dealings with each other.

Literacy is the key to not just the economy of our world, but also to developing understanding between the many cultures on our planet.

If we are ever to escape the cycle of violence and ignorance that plagues us, we must all not only learn to read, but to read carefully, and to read as much as we can, by a wide range of different authors.

Literacy isn't just a way to get ahead, and it isn't just about entertainment.

Being literate means being able to really participate in shaping the world, work for peace, and reach understanding with our fellow human beings. Being literate means that you're in control of your own destiny. At the individual level, being literate means you're one very large step closer to realizing your true potential.

At the global level—well, imagine what humanity could accomplish if everyone in the world were literate, if every single living soul could read and write and had free access to libraries and public schools. That's not just a pipe dream, not just a vision of utopia: I'm telling you now, it's an absolute necessity.

There should be fully stocked libraries in every village in the Third World, and I don't think we in the West should hesitate to help pay for them, partly because it's the right thing to do, partly because *it really is necessary for human survival.*

Without literacy, we stumble in the dark, blind to the wonders of the written word, helpless before those who would take advantage of our ignorance, unaware of the wisdom that could save us.

Literacy is our only hope of finding the path to true peace, true justice, and true equality in our troubled world. We must not fail to spread it far and wide.

The great South African human rights activist and leader, Nelson Mandela, once said:

> *Education is the great engine of personal development. It is through education that the daughter of a peasant can become a doctor, that a son of a mineworker can become the head of the mine, that a child of farm workers can become the president of a great nation. It is what we make out of what we have, not what we are given, that separates one person from another.*

And not long ago, thirty CEOs of some of Canada's biggest, most prosperous high-tech firms spoke out to support government funding for a liberal education. Here's part of what they said:

> *A liberal arts and science education nurtures skills and talents increasingly valued by modern corporations. Our companies function in a state of constant flux. To prosper we need creative thinkers at all levels of the enterprise who are comfortable dealing with decisions in the bigger context. They must be able to communicate—to reason,*

create, write and speak—for shared purposes: for hiring, training, managing, marketing, and policy-making. In short, they provide leadership.

For example, many of our technology workers began their higher education in the humanities, and they are clearly the stronger for it. This was time well spent, not squandered. They have increased their value to our companies, our economy, our culture, and themselves, by acquiring the level of cultural and civic literacy that the humanities offer.... It is critical that all universities in Canada receive sufficient funding to ensure a well-educated workforce and a new generation of leadership."

That statement was signed by, among others, the CEOs of Sun Microsystems, Hewlett-Packard, Motorola Canada, Compaq Canada, AT&T Canada, and IBM Canada. Obviously, businesses are beginning to truly understand the value of a well-rounded education.

Sometimes businesses and the government find themselves at odds, but we must realize that in the end, we're all on the same side. We all want to improve our quality of life, and we want to help build our country's economic and cultural strength. Our public schools, from kindergarten to university, are the foundation of our current and future prosperity.

We must help people understand that our future depends on making university more accessible to students. Funding universities, liberal arts programs in particular, is not an expense. It's an investment, one that has proven itself time and again.

Just stop and think for a moment about the enormous contributions to Canada made by liberal arts graduates like W.O. Mitchell, Peter Lougheed, Joe Clark, Margaret Atwood, Pierre Trudeau, Supreme Court Justice Beverley McLachlin, and my personal hero, Tommy Douglas.

Where would Canada be without these remarkable men and women, their attitudes and perceptions shaped by the liberal arts?

We need liberal arts graduates, now more than ever. A complex world demands people who can think on their feet, who have a broad knowledge base, and who understand the values that liberal arts fosters: flexibility, creativity, openness, tolerance, and rigorous critical thought.

The liberal arts offer us a chance to pursue and explore peace, social justice, and the nature of our humanity.

These issues are too important to neglect, and I hope that we can work together to convince the general public and our governments to provide liberal arts programs—which should always include some training in business and economics—with the support they need to meet the demands of the 21st century. It's not just the right thing to do; it's good for business.

Now let's look at the fine arts. Contrary to what some people think, they are not a frill; at their best, they provide us with a means of understanding ourselves and can even help to change our actions and attitudes for the better. Our painters, sculptors, writers, musicians, directors, and other artists all provide essential services.

Their contributions are as vital as those of the entrepreneur, the police officer, the doctor, the custodian, the childcare provider, the construction worker. Our artists should have much more prominence than they currently enjoy; after all, these are often our greatest thinkers and our most passionate idealists.

Imagine how different the world would be if we had more painters, more musicians, more writers, more sculptors serving in our legislatures. Frankly, I think we'd enjoy a saner, more compassionate society.

Every teacher who introduces a child to the world of the arts has performed a great service, not just for the student, but for the world. We *need* more artists, and our teachers are the ones who will help those artists discover themselves.

The fine arts are much more important to the health and security of our nation than many people outside the arts community are willing to admit. Because art is much more than entertainment or a means of bringing aesthetic pleasure.

Certainly art accomplishes these things, but to me, art's most important role is to engage our minds, to encourage us to think in new ways, to use our most precious gift: our imagination. Art gives us an excellent means to examine questions of public policy, philosophy, even the big questions like the meaning of existence itself.

Finally, let's think about libraries for a minute. As you know, I'm a huge fan of libraries, and I believe that the public library is the most important institution devised by human beings.

Libraries make concrete the ideal that all persons have the right to learn all they can about history, politics, art, literature, science, and all the other disciplines and diversions of thousands of years of human civilization.

Libraries are sacred places; they contain both the hard-earned lessons of the past and the seeds for a better future.

Our lives are richer when they are touched by books. I was lucky enough to have parents who always encouraged me to read; from a very early age, I discovered how magical books were, with their power to take you to strange and beautiful places and expose you to new ideas.

My favourite Christmas gifts were books. I'd curl up in the big comfy chair and read all day long.

I was a teenager when I first moved to Edmonton, and I remember well what happened the first time I was exposed to Edmonton's library system. You see, I was in high school at the time, and I had to go downtown to visit the dentist.

Well, I had a little bit of time to kill after the dental appointment, so on the way back to school I stopped in at the public library. I was amazed by the size of it—after using the tiny little library in my hometown in Saskatchewan for years, the rows and rows of books in the downtown Edmonton branch completely overwhelmed me with delight.

I got so excited I spent the rest of the day reading and browsing and exploring, and I missed all of my afternoon classes. But I certainly didn't regret it!

After that, I spent many long afternoons at the Edmonton Public Library, and the books I discovered there brought me so much knowledge and sheer fun that I don't know what I'd be doing today if the library hadn't been there. I certainly doubt I'd have become Lieutenant Governor!

During my travels of the past couple of years, I've tried to show people that a well-stocked library is essential to the health of any community. Libraries provide us with knowledge, with inspiration, with entertainment—all the tools we need to grow as human beings.

Libraries are as vital to our civilization as schools, hospitals, police and fire services, the military, the courts—you name it. Our public library system is a focal point of our culture, and I think that to remain truly Canadian, we must remain committed to the principle of equal access.

That principle is nowhere more important than it is when applied to libraries, since so many people, especially those with limited income, depend on them. Perhaps one day libraries will be funded enough so that we can do away with membership fees; that, I think, would be a real step forward.

Public libraries are, I believe, the most important institution in our country, because everything else that's good in our society must flow from knowledge. Few of us can afford to buy all the books we need, and everyone benefits, even the rich, when everyone has full access to libraries.

Reading is perhaps the best way to learn about other cultures, new ideas, and different viewpoints. It opens up our minds to all the diversity and the incredible possibilities that lay before us. The information to build a better world is all there, right on our library shelves; but we all need to read it to make that dream a reality.

If we hope to sustain a literate, well-educated culture, Canadians must support libraries with great enthusiasm, because our citizens *need* access to a wide variety of books to maintain our cultural edge.

Anyone who's bought even a thin paperback recently knows all too well how expensive books have become, which makes libraries all the more vital to anyone who needs to do research, to study for exams, or simply to read for pleasure and enlightenment.

Any donation to a library, whether it's money or your time as a volunteer, is an investment in a brighter, smarter future for the people of this province.

Libraries, public education, the fine arts; these are the institutions we must support to foster Canada's growth.

Canada has the potential to become one of the world's great civilizations, if we have the vision, the foresight, and the commitment to make it so. We are a young people, but one with great potential, and I think that there are no limits to the good we can do.

The time has long passed when we could rely on other people to secure the future of our country. We must be willing to fight for the institutions we care about, even if it's something as simple as a letter to your MLA or MP or a speech to some friends.

As the British playwright Tom Stoppard has said, "Words are sacred. They deserve respect. If you get the right ones, in the right order, you can nudge the world a little."

Thank you.

A simple appearance at a Grandparents' Day Walk in Edmonton had become
very complicated. An official in the Alberta Council on Aging, which sponsored
the event, had made comments in the summer about opposing government
cuts to seniors programs and using the walk to raise money for the council.
One of Lois's aides told the Edmonton Journal *the lieutenant-governor would*
have to reconsider attending because of the political overtones and the fund-
raising. Well out of public view, Lois's husband Ted entered the palliative ward
at Edmonton General Hospital about this time, suffering from both prostate
cancer and Alzheimer's disease. Any event dealing with seniors would have
taken on new meaning for Lois now, but she kept her husband's condition out
of her speeches.

Alberta Council on Aging
Grandparents' Day Walk
September 8, 2002

GOOD AFTERNOON. I'm very pleased to see you all here today, because
it gives me a chance to discuss an important issue with my peers: the
issue of the role of seniors in our province.

The wisdom of grandparents is a vast resource, one we have yet to
tap to its full potential. The Right Honourable John Diefenbaker once
said something about aging that I really like: "While there's snow on the
roof, it doesn't mean the fire has gone out in the furnace." He was absolutely right.

When seniors can maintain sound minds and bodies, they have as
much to contribute to the world as anyone. As Margaret Laurence said:
"It is my feeling that as we grow older we should become not *less* radical
but *more* so. I do not, of course, mean this in any political party sense,
but in a willingness to struggle for those things in which we passionately
believe."

That's what I'm trying to do during my time as a senior: struggle on
behalf of my passions. I believe that the future of our country depends
upon vigorous support of the arts, of our public schools and universities,
our public libraries, and public health care.

These are the issues that keep me young; as long as I feel that they are
threatened—and believe me, they are—I'll have plenty of fuel for my furnace.

Lois visiting with customers at the greenhouse, late 1990s. [Hole Family Archives]

As I grow older, I've been thinking more and more about what kind of future the next generation can hope to expect.

While human beings have made a lot of progress, especially in the last hundred years, we also have a long way yet to travel, and some of the problems we face—hunger, crime, disease, poverty, racism, war—seem almost insurmountable. It's no wonder that many of our young people have cynical attitudes about their future prospects for employment and a good life.

But we can bury that cynicism if we work together, young and old, to fight poverty, injustice, and racism. And the best way to build a better world for our children is to fight for our public libraries and public schools.

If I could bestow one gift upon young people, it would be a good education, an education rich in literature, science, mathematics, history, crafts, sport, and the fine arts. It would be an education with no shortage of excellent teachers and a full supply of the world's best books.

And part of that ideal education would include teaching youth about community responsibility, public awareness, trustworthiness, respect, and compassion for their fellows.

I believe that grandparents can take a much larger role in this great endeavour....

It also doesn't hurt to have heroes around, everyday people who set an example for youths simply by doing their part to help the community. Every charitable act performed by grandparents doesn't just help the immediate recipients. It does much more than that; it provides young people with some guidance on how to live a truly moral life.

When young people see their grandparents donating to worthy causes or offering their services as volunteers, it plants a seed in their minds: they begin to realize how rewarding helping others can be.

Respect, tolerance, honesty, compassion, trust—these are the values young people need to survive and prosper.

And these are the values, if we have used our years wisely, that seniors are best equipped to impart. These are the values our communities need to hold dearest if we are to successfully face the challenges of the coming decades....

When we use the phrase "Senior Citizen," I think it's important to emphasize the second word: citizen. Whatever our age, I believe we were put on this earth to help each other out. Grandparents are uniquely qualified to do just that, and it's time that we not only made our voices heard, but our actions felt. Getting involved, having a purpose, a reason for being; that's what keeps people alive. It's what makes life worth living, no matter how old you are.

Thank you.

Virginie Durocher again, but from a new perspective. Lois's concern for the
marginalized sprang from life experience rather than from theory.

Alberta Association for Community Living
Community Living Awareness Month Kick-Off
Alberta Legislature, October 3, 2002

GOOD MORNING, AND WELCOME.

I want to tell you a little bit about a friend of mine, a Métis named Virginie Durocher. Mrs. Durocher wasn't developmentally disabled, but she faced many of the same struggles, and my memories of her life continue to inspire me.

Mrs. Durocher had very little formal education. She couldn't read or write, and her spoken English was very poor. She grew up in an era and a community where prejudice was all too common. And yet, despite these obstacles, she was one of the wisest, most ethical, most hard-working women I've ever known.

She knew the secrets of the land and taught me how to be a better gardener, and she also provided life lessons in the power of love. I'll never forget the time she gave birth to a son, a tiny little thing the doctors told her was too frail to live. But she brought that little boy home, made an incubator with blankets and old bottles filled with hot water, and gave that little boy all the love she had.

And the child lived, thanks to Mrs. Durocher's sheer force of will and her boundless love.

A remarkable woman, a remarkable life. But I can't help but wonder what might have been, had she had the chance to pursue an education or simply to enjoy a life without prejudice.

She taught me so much, even without an education; what might she have taught the world had she had the chance? How much better off would her whole family have been, had they been wholeheartedly welcomed as full-fledged members of the community?

We'll never know, and so I can only be thankful for the time I had with her and the teaching she passed on to me. And so I celebrate that, even if I sometimes wonder what might have been.

Working with Mrs. Durocher for so many years helped me to understand that sometimes people react badly to people they find different.

My father always told me never to say something bad about someone just because she had a different religion, or a different skin colour, or because they fell a bit behind in school.

I never completely understood why my father was so adamant until I saw some of the things Mrs. Durocher had to put up with. Many people welcomed her as part of the community, but sadly, most did not.

I've never been quick to judge people on appearances. After all, if people judged me on my appearance most days, I'd be in real trouble! It's impossible to work with plants and soil, or at any physical job, and look as if you walked off the cover of a fashion magazine. I'm a farm woman, after all, and I usually look like one.

This can catch some people off guard. Al White, one of our suppliers, still laughs about the first time he came out to our place. He saw this woman out watering the garden, with a dirt-smudged face and windblown hair, soaked with perspiration and the spray from her water hose. "Boy," he thought, "just wait until the boss gets a load of her! She won't last the week!" Of course, that woman was me.

Too many people rely on first impressions. I remember an incident long ago, when I went hunting for boxes to use for packing our vegetables.

Back in those days, banana boxes were the ultimate prize. We sold a lot of lettuce to wholesalers, and banana boxes were absolutely ideal for that purpose. When we stacked the heads in, a dozen per box, they looked just beautiful. If we had to buy similar boxes new, they would probably have cost us 35 or 40 cents apiece. It was much cheaper and easier to find good-quality used ones. Today, of course, wholesalers are much stricter and would not accept boxes recycled in this way. (And yet, old habits die hard: I still find it hard to throw away a good, sturdy cardboard box. In fact, I often joke that when I'm an old woman, I'll spend my time poking around back alleys looking for boxes!)

One morning, I drove to the city, pulled in behind a large grocery store, and, lo and behold, found a veritable treasure trove of banana boxes. I asked a nearby store employee if I could take them. He said, "Oh sure, we're just throwing them out."

So I started to load the boxes up, stacking them very carefully so they wouldn't blow off the truck. All of a sudden, the manager came out. All he saw was this rather disheveled woman, in jeans and rubber boots, stacking up cardboard boxes.

"What are you doing?" he demanded.

"I'm just taking these banana boxes," I replied.

"You've got no business back here," he snarled. "Clear out!"

I drove home, terribly hurt. It had never before occurred to me that people might look down on me simply because of the way I dressed. That man, I decided, needed a lesson in basic courtesy.

I stormed into the house and marched straight upstairs. I got dressed up nicely, put on my best hat, and drove back to the store. I strode in proudly and asked to see the manager.

"What can I do for you, ma'am?" he asked when he came out. I told him who I was and explained, "I was here earlier this morning getting banana boxes and you were very rude. According to the fellow I asked, those boxes were going to be thrown in the garbage. We live on a farm, and we use those boxes for packing lettuce." He had no answer.

"Next time," I said, "maybe you won't be so quick to judge people." From that day on, he was one of the best suppliers of boxes.

Sometimes my own customers make the same mistake that manager made. Over the years, more than a few have complained to me about the personal appearance of some of our workers.

It started back in the 1960s, shortly after the Beatles became popular. A man came up to me, pointed at one of our best employees, and asked, "Why don't you make that kid get a haircut?" I told him that the young man was hard working, well groomed, smart, and pleasant to the customers. The length of his hair didn't matter to me at all.

It's hard to imagine now, but the length of men's hair was a very hot issue back then. Isn't it funny how things change? In any picture I've ever seen of the classical composers, their hair was long. And I'll bet their hair wasn't as neatly brushed as it is in the pictures, either. Of course, those fellows were radicals in their day, too.

Nowadays, if you walk through our greenhouse, you may spot a tattoo here or there, maybe even a pierced nose. You might also see me in my jeans and rubber boots, looking much as I did gathering banana boxes long ago. [24]

We face the same challenge today with the developmentally disabled, simply because, as my father observed, we tend to fear and shun what we don't understand. So it falls upon us, teachers, parents, community leaders, to help our children learn to accept and understand those who need a little extra help as they make their way through life.

Indeed, we should be working very hard to teach compassion and respect for everyone, from the developmentally disabled, to members of other cultures, to those with different beliefs. We don't have to teach them to meekly agree with every idea that comes along, but we *must* teach them the value of respect and compassion.

Above all, we must teach them that there are no surplus people. Each and every human being has a role to play in building a better world.

And each of those human beings is blessed with but one life; one life to cherish love and friendship, to marvel at nature's wonders, to appreciate the arts, to explore the world; in sum, one life to find happiness and, if we're lucky, to leave the world a better place than it was when we arrived....

Another life lesson, and character study, from Buchanan, Saskatchewan.

St. Josaphat Ukrainian Catholic Church
100th Anniversary
November 10, 2002

GOOD EVENING, and thank you so much for asking me to join you tonight. I really couldn't turn this opportunity down, because I've grown up with a profound respect for Ukrainian culture and its effect on Canada.

When I think about the tremendous contributions that Canadians of Ukrainian heritage have made to our country, I'm always drawn back in time to my own experiences with the Ukrainians in my old home town of Buchanan, up in northern Saskatchewan. When I was seven or eight years old, you see, the town was getting ready for a municipal election.

One of the fellows running for mayor was a very humble, hard-working man named Alex Yunick. Now, Mr. Yunick wasn't the kind of person who usually runs for mayor. He was a very humble person, and he was happy serving as the town's de facto official handyman. Mr. Yunick was the person to call whenever there was an odd job to be done.

He picked up the mail shipment from the train and took it to the post office, and then carried the outgoing mail from the post office to the train. He helped install the town's sewer and water facilities, house by house, as the homeowners decided to modernize. He even brought in wood from the forest and chopped it into kindling for the town's widows.

Mr. Yunick couldn't read or write very well, but there was no disputing that he was the hardest-working man in town.

One of Mr. Yunick's two daughters was a very close friend of mine; her name was Albina. Albina told me that her father really didn't want to run for mayor, but that several of his friends convinced him that he'd be the best man for the job.

And when the votes were tallied up on election night...well, wouldn't you know it, he'd won. I was very glad, and very proud of Mr. Yunick; he was Albina's father, after all, so I knew that he was a kind and generous man.

Now, Mr. Yunick had a unique governing style. Whenever someone phoned up the mayor's office with a complaint, Mr. Yunick didn't pass the buck—he just went out and fixed the problem himself. If there were potholes to be filled or sidewalks to be repaired, there was the mayor, out there with his tools, doing his civic duty.

His staff often had to tell him, "You know, Mr. Mayor, we have people who can do that for you…"

But Mr. Yunick was happier getting his hands dirty. He was an excellent mayor, and I think it's fair to say that the townspeople loved him.

Ukrainians like Mr. Yunick taught me a lot—about the value of working hard, yes, but also about pride and simple human dignity. Alex Yunick was never too proud to let his status as mayor interfere with the work that needed to be done to build a stronger, safer, more generous town.

As life went on, I found myself grateful time and again for the presence of Ukrainian Canadians. When Ted and I started our farm, we didn't know anything about agriculture but what Ted had learned at university. Neither of us had any practical experience on a farm.

But we were lucky.

Our neighbours were Ukrainian, and they were more than generous with their help, their advice, and their friendship. I don't know what we would have done without their help.

> One year, early in April, Ted and I were out in the field. We'd had a very warm spring, and it looked as if we would be able to begin planting soon.
>
> Along the riverbank where we live, the land is divided into long, narrow strips, so our neighbours are actually quite close. I noticed Mrs. Sernowski out in her field. I could clearly see what she was doing, although I couldn't quite believe my eyes.
>
> "Ted," I said, "Mrs. Sernowski is over there planting potatoes."
>
> "She's making a big mistake," he replied. "It's way too early. They'll freeze for sure."
>
> "Ted, she's been in the business for 25 years. Maybe she knows something we don't know."
>
> "Nope," said Ted, "they're going to freeze. Mark my words."

I wasn't about to give up. "But Ted," I pointed out, "she's planting three acres!"

"Well," he persisted, "she's going to be sorry."

Mrs. Sernowski didn't strike me as the sort of person who would take a foolish risk. Born in Ukraine, she had farmed all her life. She was a short, stocky woman, just over five feet tall, and a hard worker. She always had a friendly smile or a word or two of gardening advice. She also had a natural way with kids. My son Jim would often wander over to her house for a visit, and to this day Bill can ask for a cup of coffee in Ukrainian.

Above all, Mrs. Sernowski was down to earth—literally! She never wore shoes, except on special occasions, and the kids often marvelled at the thick, tough soles of her feet. A woman who had such close, constant contact with the soil would know more about gardening than most people.

Ted and I kept a close eye on Mrs. Sernowski's potato field that spring. The fine weather continued, and within a few weeks, the potato plants were a foot high. Sure enough, just as Ted predicted, we did get a frost. Down went the potatoes, as black as can be. Although he hated to see something like that happen to a neighbour, Ted couldn't help being the tiniest bit smug.

Well, Mrs. Sernowski was no April fool. The next day it rained. Later in the week it got warm—and up came the potatoes once again. She was selling them at the City Market before the end of June.

I'm never too proud to ask advice, and Mrs. Sernowski was more than willing to share her secrets. In addition to planting early, she said to choose an early variety of potato. She told me to leave them whole, so they wouldn't rot in the cool soil.

She also paid me one of my most cherished compliments. One summer, she brought visitors over to my yard. "I just had to show them your beautiful garden," she explained.

When I give talks each spring, I always tell my audiences to get those potatoes in early. And every year in June, as I enjoy that glorious first meal of new garden potatoes, I always think of Mrs. Sernowski. [25]

So tonight, I think that in addition to celebrating the centennial of this wonderful church, we should also be very grateful for the entire history of Ukrainian Canadians. Without the Ukrainians, Canada, particularly the Canadian West, would be a very different place. And I don't think it would have turned out nearly as well as it has.

Thank you so much again, and congratulations on the church's centennial.

The history of the Canadian Prairies is partly the history of Chinese Canadians. A standard speech on multiculturalism in November 2002 began with specific recognition of their contribution to the country.

Chinese Garden Society
November 16, 2002

GOOD EVENING, welcome, and thank you so much for asking me to join you tonight.

For a long time, I've been very conscious of the vital contributions the Chinese Canadian community has made to our country. Back when I was in the market garden business, I often had wonderful conversations with the Chinese vendors at the market, and let me tell you, I quickly found out that no one knows more about vegetables than those Chinese gardeners. I learned a lot from them, and they really helped make our business a success.

In fact, when you think about it, the Chinese helped make Canada itself a success. We need only look back to the construction of the railroads, and the sacrifices the Chinese immigrants made to link East to West. I think it's fair to say that without the Chinese, Canada as we know it today would never have come into being.

Now of course, you know better than I the terrible price many of those immigrants paid. The treatment of the Chinese during those days will always be a stain on our history, but thanks to our efforts to remember that history, it's a mistake we need never make again.

That's why I'm so glad that the story of the early Chinese immigrants continues to be told in our public schools. Our children need to know the full details of our history, the bad right along with the good, if we hope to build a stronger, fairer, more peaceful nation....

Lois Hole's audience with Queen Elizabeth II, November 8, 2000. [Hole Family Archives]

2003

The year 2003 marked the 50th anniversary of the coronation of Queen Elizabeth II. Presentation of Queen's Jubilee medals began to take up more and more time; there were several more such events in January alone. For Lois, each such event offered another opportunity to ask people to contribute to their community.

Queen's Jubilee Medal Presentation
Edmonton, January 11, 2003

GOOD AFTERNOON.

Today I am very pleased to present some of Canada's greatest citizens either the Queen's Golden Jubilee medal or the Governor General's Caring Canadian Award. I consider it a true privilege to share a room with people who have played such a tremendous role in building a stronger country.

This Jubilee medal is granted to Canadians whose contributions have shaped the Canada we enjoy today, while the Caring Canadian Award recognizes Canadians who have made voluntary, extraordinary contributions to their community for many years.

These dedicated people have shown us what it really means to be Canadian: to work for the common good, to alleviate suffering, to push the boundaries of what can be accomplished in community service and building a better nation.

Today's medal recipients have been of immense service to Canada. Their talents, their creativity, and their commitment to their fellow citizens have been and will be tremendous assets to our nation.

They haven't just excelled in their respective fields; they've served as excellent role models for other Canadians, role models who show us how to effectively work for positive change in our country. There is no greater accomplishment.

As I look upon the thirteen recipients gathered here today, it strikes me that they are Canada in the microcosm, a small sampling of a large country. And it also strikes me that many of their accomplishments would have been impossible without our strong historical commitment to public education and public libraries.

Public education serves two very important purposes. The first, the one that the general public already knows, is that public education gives students a huge storehouse of useful information as well as the fundamental ability to learn. Public education provides the basics; reading, writing, arithmetic, history, the fine arts, science, and all the rest.

But public schools have a second, perhaps even more important, function. Public schools welcome people of all cultures, all economic backgrounds, of any religion or no religion at all. And by providing an environment where people of very different natures can mix and become friends, public schools provide a great service to this country.

It's very hard, for example, for a Muslim to hate an atheist if he makes friends with an atheist study partner in science class—and for her part, the atheist learns something about the Muslim faith. Similarly, when you put blacks and Chinese on the same basketball team, an important bond is formed. Cultural walls are slowly taken down, and the basis of a pluralist society is strengthened.

But public schools are under increasing attack these days, and so today I'm going to take a few moments to ask all of you to think about the role of public education in our society. Personally, I believe that the destruction of the public school system would be a catastrophe beyond anything this country has ever experienced.

And just imagine a country without public libraries and school libraries. Students, no matter what their age, must have free access to books, and the public library is the only source of that access.

If we are to maintain a high rate of literacy, if we are to continue to expand the depth and breadth of our cultural knowledge, we must ensure that libraries are given at least as much funding, care, and attention as our sports stadiums. I *dream* of a day when teachers and librarians are valued as much as hockey players, pop musicians, or movie stars.

Don't get me wrong; I enjoy popular culture and sports as much as anyone. But wouldn't it be a saner country if we gave teachers and librarians half the attention and support we give celebrities?

I have to mention one more thing, another facet of our country's educational future: I would love it if we could strengthen this country's bilingualism. Let me tell you, since I've taken up this role, I've met ambassadors and consuls from all over the world, and every one of them speaks at least two languages; a few speak up to five. And *all* of them knew French.

Frankly, it's a little embarrassing that I can't speak French myself, and I would love it if we could revamp our school systems so that every young person in this country grew up fluent in both English and French. What a huge economic and cultural advantage that would be for the next generation of Canadians!

As recipients of the Golden Jubilee Medal or the Caring Canadian Award, the men and women we honour today have a lot of moral clout. So I would ask you, if you can, to speak out for public schools, public libraries, and bilingual education....

If a runner-up to hockey were ever selected as Canada's national game, the choice might well be curling. A native of rural Saskatchewan who moved to another curling hotbed in Alberta naturally knew the game well and was happy to help celebrate the 100th anniversary of Edmonton's Thistle Curling Club. She didn't mention it, but the first Alberta legislature, elected after the province's founding in 1905, met in the original Thistle Club in what is now downtown Edmonton.

Strathcona Cup Competition—100th Anniversary Thistle Curling Club
Edmonton, January 20, 2003

GOOD EVENING, everyone, and welcome to the 100th Strathcona Cup, truly a milestone in the history of one of the greatest sports ever invented. For a century, curlers from Alberta have met their Scottish counterparts in the spirit of friendship and good-natured competition.

And no matter who prevailed on the ice, all the participants shared in the kind of victory that only comes when people of goodwill come together to share in a mutual passion: in this case, the love of a great game.

You know, this event has a very special meaning for me, because there's a long history of curling in my family.

My mother was on a team that took the Edmonton city champion-ship, my dad won a provincial championship in Saskatchewan, and my brother took home a regional championship here in Alberta. My husband Ted even curled with Hector Gervais, a terrific curler who actually went to Scotland to play in the world championships.

Actually, I have a quick little story about Hector. When he arrived in Scotland, you see, he discovered that the teams there liked to leave the rocks in the house, which was the exact opposite of the way they played in Canada back then, taking rocks out willy-nilly. Well, Hector did what I like to call the Canadian thing and played the game their way. When in Scotland…leave the rocks in the house.

As for me, I started curling when I was a little girl. You see, during the winter in small-town Saskatchewan, there weren't many options when it came to recreation. But everyone had a homemade rink, and we filled up jam cans with water, let the water freeze, and those were our rocks. And brooms?

Well, it was never hard to find one in the closet, even if they weren't exactly regulation curling brooms. We always had a wonderful time, and when I was old enough to play on a real rink with real rocks, well, I'll tell you, that was the biggest thrill of my life.

Now, I never won any bonspiels, but I wasn't a *bad* curler either.

And win or lose, I loved every moment on the ice. I imagine a lot of amateur curlers feel the same way; it's a game that rewards participation, no matter what your skill level. So when I see all you people gathered here tonight, it brings back a *lot* of happy memories.

Curling requires skill, strategy, and most importantly of all, good sportsmanship. Tonight we're going to see all three in abundance, and I know everyone is going to have a wonderful time. Thank you all so much for coming, and for inviting me to share in this event.

Lois's husband Ted had been in hospital for half a year with Alzheimer's disease when she made this speech, which she reprised the next day in Edmonton. She almost never talked about his illness in public. She did when the occasion made her personal experience relevant.

Alzheimer Society of Calgary
Calgary, January 30, 2003

GOOD AFTERNOON, welcome, and thank you for coming. This gathering is an expression of the hopes and dreams of many thousands of Canadians, fine people who come together with hope and compassion, daring to dream that one day a cure for Alzheimer's will be found. That makes me very proud to be here, despite the pain and sadness that currently afflict my own family.

> *My husband Ted is a terrific sport and always laughs along whenever I haul out one of my old anecdotes. Good thing, too, because he's a central figure in so many of my funny stories.*
>
> *But Ted has always been a man of great vision, with an inventive and innovative mind. I saw that the very first day we came out to the farm. There we stood, side by side, two kids from the city, while he told me how we were going to make a wonderful life on this little patch of land, with its aging barn and tiny house. He painted the picture so clearly that I could see it myself.*
>
> *Of course, once we got down to the actual business of farming, that picture was clouded by dozens of day-to-day details. People who grow up on farms absorb so much knowledge that it becomes second nature. Ted and I, on the other hand, had to learn as we went along.*
>
> *In the long run, Ted turned his lack of experience into his greatest advantage. Farmers are creatures of habit: if they grow up doing things a certain way, it can be next to impossible to convince them to change. Ted, on the other hand, had absolutely no preconceived notions. He constantly questioned our methods and looked for ways to improve them.*
>
> *When we started market gardening, the industry was in its infancy in central Alberta. Very few people here farmed vegetables, and those*

Ted and Lois Hole during the bedding plant industry conference, fall 1986. [Hole Family Archives]

who did weren't operating on the scale Ted envisioned. As a result, we had a terrible time finding appropriate equipment. As far as the manufacturers and suppliers were concerned, we might as well have been growing vegetables at the North Pole.

Ted subscribed to dozens of magazines and catalogues from the United States, where the industry was much better established. He'd go through them page by page, looking for new ideas, methods, and tools. After days of research, he chose a John Deere 1020 because, with its adjustable wheel spacing, it was the most suitable for row-crop work. And if he couldn't find the things he needed, he'd adapt the things he had on hand.

Ted relied a lot on our neighbour Len Adams, a talented welder. He would wander down the road to tell Len his latest idea and Len, always the pessimist, would mutter, "Nope, can't be done. It's not gonna work." Ted would ask, "Well, can you at least give it a try?" He'd go back an hour later, and the tool would be built.

After a few years of digging carrots by hand, which is a terrible job, Ted invented a carrot lifter. He had Len weld two grader blades onto a cross-brace, and hitched it to the 1020. As he drove the tractor along a row, the blades loosened the soil on either side. The carrots just popped right out of the ground, ready to gather.

Ted also loved to experiment with new seed varieties. When we first started market gardening, our neighbours told us not to bother trying to grow corn. Ted shopped for the latest hybrids and kept trying different varieties very year. After several years of experimenting, we grew crop after crop of beautiful corn.

Ted also developed a close relationship with the horticulturists at the Brooks Research Centre, at a time when most farmers were skeptical of scientific approaches to farming. From those gentlemen, we learned to try new technologies, many of which we were able to employ successfully.

Of course, not everything Ted tried worked. But when it did, the rewards could be enormous. For instance, if you could find ways to grow an especially early crop, your profits multiplied. Dill cucumbers, which might fetch fifty cents a pound in August, were worth two or three dollars a pound in July. Ted invested a lot of time and effort in his ideas, and it usually paid off for us.

If people poked fun at his unorthodox thinking, Ted never let it bother him. In the later 1960s, I was on the board of the Rural Safety Council. At the time, we were fighting to have roll-bars installed on tractors and to make their use mandatory. Ted saw it as an issue of simple common sense: by spending a couple of hundred dollars, he might save his life or that of one of his kids. When the neighbours got a look at Ted's tractor, all fitted out with a roll-bar, canopy, and radio, they were beside themselves. One of them even climbed right up and danced on the canopy. Ted just stood there and watched, not saying a word.

Of course, his foresight has since been proven right, as roll-over protection systems (ROPS) are now legally required on all new tractors. Ted was also an early advocate of hearing protection, another *development that has substantially reduced injury on farms in the last few decades. (In fact, Ted swears he lost much of his hearing operating our first potato harvester—hearing protection came a little too late for him.)*

But not all of our neighbours made fun of Ted. Other families in the market gardening business began to keep a close eye on him and often followed his example. For years we had people stopping by our house to check out our crops or borrow equipment.

Ted still helps shape our business and his bold spirit continues to be reflected. Customers often tell me how much they look forward to the new plant varieties we offer each year, and our garden centre is always well stocked with ingenious gardening tools.

So when you read one of my anecdotes about Ted, don't forget that behind the laughter stands a most remarkable man.[26]

Now, I know that many of you have similar stories, and that many of those stories are far worse than mine. To tell the truth, on some days, I feel very fortunate that Ted has as many good moments as he does.

And I have to tell you, I know that a cure probably won't come in time to help Ted. It's hard—very hard—to admit that, but that doesn't mean that I've given up. Not on Ted, and not on the thousands of others who are fighting Alzheimer's. As citizens, I believe we each have a duty to keep fighting, not only for our own loved ones, but for future generations.

The simple truth is, the longer it takes to find a cure for Alzheimer's, the more people will suffer.

We need a cure as quickly as science and politics will allow, and by coming out today to show your support, you've helped not only yourselves and your families, but countless potential Alzheimer's patients, people who, thanks to your generosity and hard work, may never have to deal with the pain you've suffered.

I know dealing with Alzheimer's isn't easy. In fact, I wish I didn't know. But at least we can share the pain and find some comfort in knowing that brilliant, compassionate people are working so hard to find a cure. We owe these men and women so much, even if a cure doesn't arrive in time to help our own loved ones.

We owe them for the effort, for giving us hope, for building a future in which no other children and grandchildren, husbands and wives, will have to endure what we have endured.

I think the Alzheimer's Society is a priceless organization, one that provides not only support for the families of Alzheimer's patients, but the information and influence that are so vital to finding a cure. That cure will come, and when it does, the thanks will be to you.

Thank you so much, and I wish you and your families the very best. Your strength and compassion is an inspiration.

Music was never far away. An appearance at the annual Johann Strauss Ball in Edmonton became another place to support music and the arts generally. Lois emphasized that she had found practical benefits in studying music. The quotation from Byron showed up in many of her talks that featured music.

Johann Strauss Foundation
28th Annual Johann Strauss Ball
Edmonton, February 8, 2003

GOOD EVENING. As an enthusiastic lover of all things musical, I am immensely thrilled to be here tonight, especially because this gathering is such an important stepping stone for talented young musicians to hone their skills and move towards professional status.

As an amateur musician myself, I have direct experience with the liberating power of music. I took music lessons for years, first in my hometown of Buchanan, Saskatchewan; I was fortunate enough to have a mother who encouraged me to play. In a sense, I was a little spoiled; given the choice between having me practise piano or do chores, Mom always urged me to practise.

Later on, I continued my studies at Alberta College in Edmonton, and eventually I earned a degree in music from the Royal Conservatory. That's always been one of my proudest achievements. Just don't ask me to sing!

I'm so very grateful I had the opportunity to learn an instrument; it's something I feel every Canadian should have the chance to try. The skills I picked up during those times did more than develop my piano and organ playing abilities—they sharpened my wits, too.

Learning music theory and practising for hour upon hour helped me learn how to focus my attention and to see patterns in things beyond the music. It was an immense help in my education, my career as a businesswoman, and my current role as Lieutenant Governor. I firmly believe that without my education in music, I wouldn't be standing here before you today.

Unfortunately, certain people—some of them very influential— believe that the fine arts are an extra, a pleasant but nonessential component of life and education. These people seem to think that

Lois Hole and University of Alberta Youth Orchestra in the greenhouse, 1986. [Hole Family Archives]

funding should be diverted from fine arts programs to other, more "practical" faculties. Nothing could be further from the truth.

Fine arts teach us how to think critically, with a keen eye for both the smallest details and the big picture. The arts enrich us all; they are not a frill, they are an absolute necessity. Music education should be available to everyone, regardless of age or wealth. Indeed, if we are to continue as a nation proud of its culture, that education *must* be made available.

It is an absolutely vital investment in our future. I realize that I'm preaching to the converted here, but as we enjoy the ball tonight, I think we should commit ourselves to doing even more to spread the word about the richness that the Fine Arts add to our lives.

Whenever I can, I like to tell people that the world would be a much better place if we had more artists in our legislatures; more musicians, more painters, more dancers—I can't help but believe that if we had just a few more artists in government that we'd have a much more balanced approach to governance, and perhaps a world just a little bit saner and more compassionate would arise.

As a gardener, I appreciate very much what Lord Byron wrote in
Don Juan:

> *There's music in the sighing of a reed;*
> *There's music in the gushing of a rill;*
> *There's music in all things, if men had ears;*
> *Their earth is but an echo of the spheres.*

And while Byron was right—there is indeed music in nature,
surrounding us every day—I must admit that I prefer the music created
by humans.

So to the musicians, who fill our lives with the glorious gift of music:
thank you. Thank you so much for stirring our souls with your magnificent performances. Your music reaches out to touch the threads that
connect every human being, and gives those threads a subtle vibration
that brings us all a little closer together.

To music teachers everywhere: thank you for keeping the song alive
in your hearts, for passing your love of music and your skills and passion
on to the next generation, so that these precious art forms are not lost to
our culture....

This speech to a Lutheran church group included a rare statement of purpose. In addition to talking about what was important to her, Lois cited some personal heroes and told the group what she hoped to achieve during her time as lieutenant-governor. She had accepted the post knowing that she would use it to try to make a difference. Within weeks of this speech, she entered hospital to begin treatment for peritoneal cancer. After the reminder of her mortality, she pursued her goals with new commitment and vigour.

R.A.R.E. (Retired and Retired Early) of Ascension Lutheran Church
Edmonton, February 13, 2003

GOOD AFTERNOON, and thank you for asking me to join you this afternoon. I hope you're all enjoying a healthy, comfortable, but still challenging retirement.

You know, I suppose you could consider me retired in one sense: although I'm still working as Lieutenant Governor, I have retired from the greenhouse business. And now that my professional involvement with the farm, the greenhouse, and the world of plants is pretty much over, I have a chance to reflect on the things that made our business successful. Beyond a doubt, the number one contributor to our success was education.

You see, back when we started out on the farm, neither Ted nor I had any experience farming. All we knew was what Ted learned in university, and his textbooks became our gospels. I remember so well how we'd be out in the field, sowing or harvesting or what have you, following the measurements and guidelines in those books.

In fact, in the beginning we used to carry those books along with us. This, of course, led to some jokes from our neighbours, who liked to point at Ted and say, "There's an expert in his field."

Now, they did tease us a little, but they also gave us a lot of help, and in those early years, I can tell you that we needed it.

Without the advice and experience of our neighbours, we would never have made it....

Many of the folks who helped us out are retired now, but that doesn't mean I've stopped looking to them for advice. The wisdom and experience of the retired is a vast resource, and we have yet to tap that resource to its full potential. The Right Honourable John Diefenbaker once said something about aging that I really like:

"While there's snow on the roof, it doesn't mean the fire has gone out in the furnace." He was absolutely right.

When retired folks can maintain sound minds and bodies, they have as much to contribute to the world as anyone.

Look at people like Harriet Winspear; she's 98 years old, but she still goes out to read to children, and she's incredibly active as a philanthropist. Or consider Dr. Stuart Davis, for that matter, the man who donated that magnificent pipe organ to the Winspear Centre. The artistic and cultural scene in Edmonton would be much diminished without their activism.

Naturally, those two had an advantage over many of us; they had a bit of extra money to spread around. But remember Tommy Douglas, who fought for the good of this country right to the end; though not poor, he certainly wasn't rich, and his contributions weren't monetary, anyway.

Their examples bring to mind something Margaret Laurence said: "It is my feeling that as we grow older we should become not *less* radical but *more* so. I do not, of course, mean this in any political party sense, but in a willingness to struggle for those things in which we passionately believe."

That's what I'm trying to do during my time as Lieutenant Governor: struggle on behalf of my passions. I believe that the future of our country depends upon vigorous support of the arts, of our public schools and universities, our public libraries, and public health care.

These are the issues that keep me young; as long as I feel that they are threatened—and believe me, they are—I'll have plenty of fuel for my furnace....

We need to show our young people that there's more to life than the temporary satisfactions of popular entertainment. Life isn't a video game or a rock concert—not that these things aren't fine in moderation. Life needs to be engaged. Life is about helping people, enriching your mind and your spirit by learning, reading, and doing good works.

It also doesn't hurt to have heroes around, everyday people who set an example for youths simply by doing their part to help the community. Every charitable act performed by seniors doesn't just help the immediate recipients. It does much more than that; it provides young people with some guidance on how to live a truly moral life.

When young people see retired people donating to worthy causes or offering their services as volunteers, it plants a seed in their minds: they begin to realize how rewarding helping others can be.

Only by remaining active in our communities can seniors drive home a very important message: we need each other....

Lois soon hit the speaking trail again. She took an optimistic view of her health and rarely talked about it. However, Norman Cousins now appeared on the short list of famous persons she enjoyed quoting. He was a noted U.S. writer and editor and the words she borrowed from him centred on books. But he had famously recovered from an obscure and usually fatal form of arthritis after having a movie projector installed in his hospital room and watching old comedies by the Marx Brothers, Charlie Chaplin, and others. He found that laughter let him have two hours of uninterrupted sleep, and for the rest of his life he wrote about and investigated the power of emotions to help heal ill bodies.

Strathcona County Library
Grand Reopening & Kickoff for the Lois Hole Library Legacy
March 17, 2003

GOOD MORNING. I am absolutely delighted to be here today, to congratulate the Strathcona County Library on both the wonderful new renovations and 25 years of outstanding service. I think the people of Sherwood Park deserve a lot of credit for helping this library become a focal point in the development of the community.

And now these renovations will help the library play an even larger role in Sherwood Park's economic and cultural growth.

And that's just as it should be, because the library isn't merely a quiet repository for books and magazines.

No, libraries play a much more important role in our lives, a role I think we should be far more outspoken in defending.

Norman Cousins, the famous author, editor, and spokesman for peace and literacy once said:

The library is not a shrine for the worship of books. It is not a temple where literary incense must be burned or where one's devotion to the bound book is expressed in ritual. A library, to modify the famous metaphor of Socrates, should be the delivery room for the birth of ideas—a place where history comes to life.

In other words, the library must be a gathering place for everyone, a free and open public square where men, women, and children from every economic and cultural background can share equally in the collective wisdom and imagination of humanity. In the library, it's not just history that comes to life: it is science, art, music, politics, philosophy, the wonders of fiction, and so much more.

A library is a place where we can uncover the deepest truths, where we can examine the thoughts and actions of others and in so doing find better ways of conducting ourselves. It is a place where we can find escape or confront our most difficult social problems. Libraries are as crucial to our survival as schools, hospitals, farms, or any other institution you can name....

Today, of course, we're also kicking off the Lois Hole Library Legacy Program in Strathcona County. And while I feel more than a little strange in speaking out for a program that was named for me, I do hope that you will encourage your friends and neighbours to support the initiative.

Above all else, a library's book collection must have both depth and breadth; it needs to address a wide range of subjects, and it needs a sufficient number of books to give those subjects the coverage they deserve.

Books are the lifeblood of the library, and when you donate to the program, you're contributing to the legacy of literacy that took Canadians many, many decades to build.

I truly believe that every Canadian has a duty to support our libraries. We owe it to ourselves, to our descendants, and to every librarian, schoolteacher, parent, and mentor who ever took it upon themselves to introduce another human being to the liberating world of literature. As Cousins said, the library is not a shrine.

It is a living, breathing institution that requires all the love and care we can give it. Libraries don't just preserve the wisdom of the past; they contain the seeds of a better future.

Thank you so much for coming out today, and enjoy your newly renovated library.

A speech to the Canadian Cancer Society two months after she was diagnosed marked the first time that she spoke publicly on her illness. It sparked a return to her familiar theme of the importance of education.

Canadian Cancer Society
Annual Fundraiser
April 26, 2003

HELLO, EVERYONE, AND WELCOME.

A few months ago, I spoke to volunteers at the Cross Cancer Institute. One of the things I said to them was that one way or another, every Canadian is touched by cancer. Even if we ourselves are never afflicted, odds are a family member, friend, or mentor will fall victim to this disease.

Everyone here knows that, and everyone here knows what a terrible scourge cancer is; the betrayal of our own cells, the corruption of our own bodies.

Well, like many of you, I now have personal experience with cancer; I lost my husband to it, and I'm fighting it myself. In fact, if I seem a little tired today, it's because I just had a chemo treatment a couple of days ago.

The strange thing is, it hasn't been all bad. The love and support I've received from the doctors, nurses, friends, family, and well-wishers from all over Alberta has given my spirits a huge lift. I don't know what I'd do if I weren't surrounded by so many wonderful people. I think the only thing I miss is giving out hugs, because the chemo treatments are tough on my immune system.

But let's be realistic—I'm in a pretty privileged position. A lot of people know who I am, so naturally I have lots of support. But we mustn't forget that there are thousands of Canadians who aren't so lucky, and who need just as much (*or more!*) support and compassion as I've enjoyed.

That's why it's so important that we continue to fight for a strong, innovative, and technologically advanced public health care system. It's also why we must support the restoration and modernization of our public schools and libraries.

Cancer is very much a disease of the industrialized world, and to successfully combat this disease, we're going to need every ounce of creativity and innovation our wealthy society can muster. We need the young people of today to pursue careers in science, medicine, public service, and the arts, and we need to give them the tools to successfully pursue such careers.

Perhaps you read a story in the paper a few days ago, a story that extolled the virtues of an increasingly prosperous Alberta, particularly the Edmonton-Calgary corridor, an area with one of the highest living standards in the entire world. Now, there's no question that our prosperity is good news. But there was a very disturbing downside to that story, one that really bothers me.

According to the report, there has been a significant decrease in the number of students pursuing higher education in Alberta, thanks in great part to the skyrocketing cost of tuition.

We may be doing well today, but let me tell you, if we decide that university education is only for the rich, in five or ten or twenty years we're going to find ourselves with a shortage of doctors, nurses, writers, musicians, engineers, and all the other people who make our society work. You want to know why the Edmonton-Calgary region is doing so well?

Obviously, oil plays a large role. But we mustn't forget that Edmonton and Calgary both have a very strong university presence, and both play host to wonderful fine arts communities. We mustn't neglect the role that public education and the arts play in our prosperity. But what, you may ask, does this have to do with cancer?

Well, fighting cancer isn't just about donating to a specific cause; it requires a systematic analysis of where our country is going on a number of fronts. Without a strong public education system, without affordable university degrees, how can we discover the fundamental causes of cancer? We need environmental experts to examine the role industrial toxins play in cancer.

We need artists to communicate the issues surrounding cancer patients, as well as giving those patients much-needed comfort. (Let me tell you, I wouldn't be doing nearly as well as I am if it weren't for the Edmonton Opera, the symphony, the theatre, the CBC, good books, and all the other works of art that have given me comfort over the past few weeks.)

We need researchers to probe the mysteries of the human body. And above all, we need the wealth generated by our universities and our artistic communities, wealth that increases our standard of living and therefore gives us the means we need to battle cancer.

None of these things are possible without our unwavering support for a robust system of public schools, universities, hospitals, and libraries. So even as I thank you all for coming out tonight to support cancer research and victims of cancer, I would ask you to go one step further and push your MLAS and MPS to strengthen the societal foundations that make a cure possible....

One of her frequent addresses at a military event produced a fusion of ideas that reads almost like a spontaneous joining of thoughts. She never felt bound to restrict her subject matter to fit the presumed nature of the group she was talking to. She was more interested in stretching boundaries.

Exercise Mercury Trek 2003
Communications & Electronics Branch, Canadian Forces
Northwest Territories & Yukon Radio Systems Memorial
Edmonton, April 29, 2003

GOOD MORNING.

I am very proud to welcome the participants of Exercise Mercury Trek to Edmonton.

The principal aim of this noble trek is to raise money for the Military Communications and Electronics Museum in Kingston, Ontario.

I fully endorse this endeavour; to preserve our history and keep it alive for young people is one of the most important roles of any Canadian citizen. Museums form a vital part of our public education system; each one is a rare treasure that should be nurtured and maintained for the benefit of all Canadians.

So I must thank the individual and corporate sponsors who have contributed to the cause thus far, and I hope that the Mercury Trek team enjoys more and more support as it continues its journey across this great country.

The other goal of this exercise is to encourage Canadians to explore their own history, a history too often neglected. This year we celebrate 100 years of service from the Military Communications and Electronics Branch of the Canadian Forces.

During those years, we have lived through a genuine revolution in communications. If one were to trace the history of this science, some of the highlights would include runners, carrier pigeons, horsemen, motorcycle couriers, the telegraph, the telephone, radio, and in today's information-saturated world, e-mail, the Internet, and cellular phones.

I guess it won't be too long now before we're all wearing one of those two-way TV video watches like Dick Tracy used to have.

No one can deny that communications technology has shaped the history of our nation and our world, and the armed forces have always been at the forefront in exploring and exploiting new ways of delivering and receiving messages.

So in the spirit of the dedicated Canadians who have spent time in the Communications and Electronics Branch over the past hundred years, I would like to deliver a message of my own.

Usually, communications sent through military channels are routine; but in times of crisis, as everyone here knows far better than me, those messages can mean the difference between victory and defeat.

Today, I would argue that we live in times of profound crisis, as the peoples of the world struggle to come to terms with the problems of the 21st century. More and more often, the battles we face today involve not hostile armies, but instead the forces of fear, poverty, ignorance, and prejudice. The noted scientist and author Stephen Jay Gould once said, "I am somehow less interested in the weight and convolutions of Einstein's brain than in the near certainty that people of equal talent have lived and died in cotton fields and sweatshops."

The crisis we face is one of lost potential.

Today uncountable millions toil in conditions we in the Western world cannot imagine, and yet we find ourselves distracted by far less important messages—which Hollywood star is pregnant by which politician, and other such trivia.

Civilian communications channels are full to the brim with meaningless fluff, and unless we can find some signal in all that noise, we risk being drowned in useless data. Communications are meaningless unless we think about the messages we're sending.

And yet, I remain an optimist. I believe that the Canadian military and the Canadian people are in an excellent position to win the battles of the new millennium. We have the wealth, we have the expertise, and I believe we have the ability to find the will and the generosity necessary to bring freedom and social justice to the peoples of the world.

The compassion and professionalism of Canadian soldiers is world-renowned, and I wish more Canadians would look to the men and women of our armed forces as the sterling role models they are.

The members of the armed forces have a proud tradition of service to our country.

Their contributions to the well-being of Canadians, in times of peace and war alike, cannot be overstated. With dignity, valour, and grace under fire, they have served under the most difficult conditions imaginable, in the most hostile and unforgiving environments.

Canadian troops are disciplined, dedicated, and ethical. A Canadian soldier is brave, yet *not* foolhardy; patriotic, yet *not* fanatical; obedient, yet independent; effective, yet compassionate. And, as this event proves, our soldiers understand the importance of history and of reaching out to their fellow human beings, searching for better understanding.

As the participants of Exercise Mercury Trek continue their journey across Canada, I hope that all Canadians will learn something about the important role our soldiers have played in advancing not only communications technology, but also in spreading Canadian values of peace, tolerance, and understanding all over the world. Thank you so much, and best of luck on the rest of your trip.

Lois was no fan of U.S. President George W. Bush. She still came up with a
warm welcome to Alberta for his mother, the wife of the first President Bush.
Not only that, she managed to invoke the presence of Mrs. Bush to support her
advocacy of libraries and public schools.

An Evening with Barbara Bush
Hyatt Regency, Calgary
May 8, 2003

IT'S CERTAINLY A PLEASURE to welcome Barbara Bush to Alberta. Her work on behalf of education has been exemplary, and her passion for the subject clearly matches my own. As a former school trustee, I'm always thrilled whenever someone speaks out on behalf of public education, the indispensable foundation of all we hope to achieve in the future.

Public education serves two very important purposes. The first, the one that the general public already knows, is that public education gives students a huge storehouse of useful information, as well as the ability to learn. Public education provides the basics; reading, writing, arithmetic, history, the fine arts, science, and all the rest.

And I believe that public education does this job better than any private institution. To be sure, there are many fine private schools, full of excellent, dedicated teachers. And these schools are wonderful for addressing certain special needs. But the public schools will always be my first choice for any young Canadian....

We must all remember that the future is in our hands; we are the masters of our own destiny.

If we can only find the will to make the right decisions, if we can only find it within ourselves to support the causes we know are just, then we will build a better world for our children.

Thank you.

Appreciation for multiculturalism extended to Alberta's Buddhist community.

The International Buddhist Friends Association
Rinchen Khando Choegyal Visit—Fundraising Dinner
Edmonton, May 10, 2003

GOOD EVENING, and thank you so much for inviting me to this once-in-a-lifetime event. I've long been an admirer of Buddhist culture, with its emphasis on peace and harmony with the natural world and our fellow human beings.

I've also admired the example of His Holiness the Dalai Lama, who has led a nonviolent struggle for a free Tibet with wisdom and patience that all world leaders should aspire to.

It's certainly a great pleasure to have Mrs. Rinchen Khando Choegyal and Dr. Elizabeth Napper visiting our city; I hope that their presence will give many Albertans a chance to learn about and appreciate the contributions and the very important values of Tibetan and Buddhist culture.

Exposure to different peoples is so very important; in fact, that's why I'm so glad organizations like this one exist....

Canada's strength is built upon our willingness to embrace the best aspects of all the world's cultures. In doing so, we are building a society unique to this planet, a true multicultural state.

Canadians have much to be thankful for. We have been blessed with abundant natural resources and incredible natural beauty.

But we should be even more grateful for the depth and breadth of our cultural strength. We have a rich, dynamic culture, thanks to our founding nations, Great Britain, France, and the First Nations peoples, as well as immigrants from all over Europe, Africa, the Middle East, South Asia, the Far East, Latin America—well, from all over the world, including, of course Tibet.

We have friendly neighbours and an excellent international reputation. We have one of the strongest economies in the world, and a legacy of technological and artistic innovation that has had and will continue to have a lasting positive impact on the history of human civilization.

But most importantly, I think we have managed to strike a unique balance between the importance of individual rights and the needs of the community. We respect individual expression of artistic and political views, while pulling together to create a better life for everyone.

Despite our success in building a generally prosperous, open, and free multicultural society, we must not become complacent. Each year, we should move a few steps closer to our goal of building a society free of poverty, free of greed, free of hate, and full of harmony.

And we should also look beyond the borders of this nation and understand that if we are truly dedicated to building a better country, then we must also commit to building a better *world*. I've had too many conversations with friends and colleagues in which someone says, "We have to take care of our own, first."

Well, the trouble is, these people don't realize that "our own" extends to every person on this earth. We owe it to our children and to ourselves to put an end to needless suffering wherever it exists, from the streets of Edmonton to the mountains of Tibet.

Don't let the selfish and the ignorant silence the voice of justice, a voice that tells us what we already know deep in our hearts: there can be no prosperity until there is global prosperity. There can be no justice until there is global justice. There can be no peace until there is global peace.

Human civilization has a long way to go, and we will never be *truly* civilized until every single man, woman, and child on this planet has access to a solid education, clean water, clean air, healthy food, good books, great art, and freedom from the spectre of war and tyranny.

Those are the days worth fighting for, ladies and gentlemen, and the struggle will never be easy. But we owe it to ourselves and to the generations to come to rally to the cause, as you have tonight by participating in this fundraising dinner....

Thank you, and may you all be blessed with peace, harmony, and good health.

This excerpt is the first part of what by now had become a standard speech on education and the arts. The language was strong but no longer unusual for Lois. She had been saying off and on for months that losing the public education system would be a "catastrophe." This time, however, she was speaking at a high-profile event at the Winspear Centre, the most prominent arts venue in Edmonton. A reporter followed up on her "catastrophe" remark. If members of government were upset they didn't show it. A spokesman for Learning Minister Lyle Oberg said, "We agree 100 per cent with the lieutenant-governor on the importance of public education." By June 2003, Lois had become too popular to attack. She had even become an asset to the government. And policy had changed from the mid-1990s, allowing for constant increases in the education budget, despite the government's sometimes rocky relationship with the Alberta Teachers' Association. The controversy faded after a few days.

Crown Imperial Concert
The Edmonton Symphony Orchestra Tribute to the Golden Jubilee of Her Majesty, Queen Elizabeth II
Winspear Centre, June 6, 2003

GOOD EVENING.

Today I am very pleased to present fifty-six members of the Edmonton Symphony Orchestra with pins commemorating the Queen's Golden Jubilee.

I consider it a true privilege to present these pins to the members of our orchestra, who have played such a tremendous role in transforming Edmonton into one of Canada's most dynamic cultural centres, and who will make tonight's concert one of the very best tributes of the entire Jubilee.

This Crown Imperial Concert is just another example of world-class music being performed by world-class musicians in a world-class facility. I think Edmontonians, and indeed all Canadians, should be very proud of the accomplishments of the ESO. I know I certainly am.

These fifty-six talented artists have shown us what it really means to be Canadian: to work for the common good, to serve the community, to explore the musical heritage of Canada and the world, and to explore new artistic frontiers. I know that if Her Majesty were here tonight, she would be very pleased that Edmonton has shown so much artistic maturity and innovation.

As I look upon the members of the Edmonton Symphony Orchestra, it strikes me that they are Canada in the microcosm, a group of diverse men and women with different cultural backgrounds, different ideologies, and different personal histories.

Nonetheless, they share two important goals: to produce beautiful music, and to enrich the lives of all Canadians.

I believe most people would like to participate in that last goal, to play their own role in enriching our nation.

I think it's possible for everyone to do so, if we remember that the success of the Edmonton Symphony, and indeed nearly all Canada's progress, would have been impossible without our strong historical commitment to public education, public libraries, and the fine arts.

Public education serves two very important purposes. The first is that public education gives students a huge storehouse of useful information as well as the fundamental ability to learn. Public education provides the fundamentals; reading, writing, arithmetic, history, the fine arts, science, and all the rest.

But public schools have a second, equally important, function.

Public schools welcome people of all cultures, all economic backgrounds, of any religion or no religion at all. And by providing an environment where people of very different natures can mix and become friends, public schools provide a great service to this country.... But public schools are under increasing attack these days, and so today I'm going to take a few moments to ask all of you to think about the role of public education in our society. Personally, I believe that the destruction of the public school system would be a catastrophe beyond anything this country has ever experienced.

For years music and drama programs have been suffering, because people think that the fine arts are some kind of frill. Well, you and I know how wrong they are, and it's up to us to show people how vital fine arts education is to the nation and the world.

In a time when the shifting politics and evolving cultures of our world seem to be dividing us, we need the arts, our great unifying common interest, more than ever.

Archeological discoveries have shown that human beings embraced art long, long ago, and that art took root and flourished all across our world, each culture expressing universal questions in superficially similar and yet astonishingly unique ways.

When answers seemed impossible to find, when the terrors of the night seemed omnipresent and the challenges of the day insurmountable, people turned to art to fortify their courage, to explain the world around them, and to ask the great questions of existence.

Though our art forms have grown ever more sophisticated with time, the basic purposes of art remain the same.

First and foremost, the arts invite us to reach within ourselves and explore our motivations, our prejudices, our very reasons for being.

And secondly, when the artists are men and women of character and conscience, the arts are a powerful tool for promoting the values that will enable our species to survive and prosper.

Those values include curiosity, tolerance, compassion, honesty, and most importantly, love for our fellows.

In a world where votes cast on one side of the planet can result in vast suffering or renewed prosperity on the other, we depend on the arts to ask the questions that will help us make those decisions correctly.

Great art gives us the chance to explore all the possibilities of life, philosophy, relationships, and what it means to be a human being. By asking important *questions*, theatre forces us to think about the *answers*, and sometimes it even forces us to *do* something to change our world for the better....

The world needs artists more than ever these days, and even more importantly, it needs people who are willing to commit to helping their fellow human beings. Thank you.

The arts and horticulture mixed easily in Lois Hole's world. There she shared common ground with Prince Charles. A handwritten letter from him held a place of honour in her suite in the Legislature Building.

Edmonton Horticultural Society
Third Annual Garden Gala
July 7, 2003

GOOD EVENING, everyone. It's wonderful to join you again. These days, it's not often that I get the chance to speak to an audience of gardeners.

You know, I must begin by congratulating your Society for your remarkable work.

You've done such an amazing job of encouraging young people to garden, helping novices, organizing useful garden workshops and tours, and of course holding events like this one. Everything you do really helps gardeners enjoy their hobby and find a deeper appreciation for the wonders of nature and science.

And I speak from experience when I say that you've been of immense help to Alberta's economy; certainly anyone who operates a garden centre, greenhouse, or show garden should be immensely thankful for your support.

Now, I know you wanted me to talk a little about Prince Charles's gardens, but the truth is I haven't visited them yet. I do have an invitation to go, but I probably won't have a chance until this fall at the earliest. I can tell you that he sent me a beautiful book on Highgrove, and if the gardens look even half as good as the photographs, then it's going to be simply astounding.

Prince Charles is a man deeply concerned with social issues, so while I may not have the experience yet to speak about his garden, I can address some of the issues that are close to his heart—and indeed, to mine. So tonight I'd like to talk a little bit about what I think it takes to keep the pursuit of gardening healthy and growing in the future.

As gardeners, each and every one of us knows how important it is to plant healthy seeds.

Lois Hole giving a talk at the Edmonton Home and Garden Show, 1995. [Hole Family Archives]

And as a gardener, I believe that the future of gardening depends on planting a seed in the mind of every Albertan, a seed that says, "Get out there and support your public schools, public libraries, and the fine arts."

The reason I emphasize the arts, libraries, and schools so often in my talks is because all too often I see them being taken for granted by both citizens and public officials. Libraries are often even more neglected than schools; some people think of libraries as an extra, or even a frill.

Well, I'm here to tell you that maintaining well-stocked libraries is as important to the future of Alberta, and to our beloved gardens, as maintaining our roads and sewers and clean supplies of fresh water.

Of all the things that humans build, libraries are among the most noble, the most precious....

What would an Alberta summer be without a rodeo? What other lieutenant-governor would have a speech for the opening ceremony of a major rodeo filed in her Arts and Culture folder?

Medicine Hat Exhibition & Stampede Opening Ceremony
July 24, 2003

GOOD AFTERNOON, AND WELCOME.

Since the days of the earliest settlers, it has been a Western tradition to celebrate our good fortune with an exhibition of athletic and artistic talent, by the cowboys and cowgirls on the rodeo ground and by artists of all persuasions in the streets, arenas, and meeting halls.

In these modern times, we enjoy a level of prosperity unimagined by our forebears, and so too do we enjoy a much wider range of artistic expression than our Prairie ancestors. Our celebrations have become much more organized, formal, and complex, but the need to let loose and have a good time remains the same.

And as we gather together to enjoy ourselves this week, we must always remember that our diverse and prosperous society, the one that makes summer festivals possible, is a result of both very good luck and very hard work.

Our public schools and libraries, our public health workers and artists, dedicated volunteers, philanthropic entrepreneurs, and committed public servants all worked together for many decades to build the culture we enjoy today.

This exhibition and others like it, all across Canada, are possible only because ordinary people gave of themselves so that others could have a better life.

And you know, I don't think we've forgotten that lesson, because this very Stampede was organized by volunteers and public servants who also gave of themselves so that all of us could enjoy a terrific summer festival. They remember the gifts of the pioneers and of all the public-minded citizens who followed in their footsteps.

It is therefore a great pleasure to thank everyone who worked on this project and to declare the Medicine Hat Exhibition, Stampede, and Rodeo officially open. Have a wonderful time, everyone.

Lois appeared at a little known event and delivered this capsule summary of her beliefs. It was not reported in the media, but it clearly states the foundations of her thinking.

Alberta Society of Youth for Democratic Values International Convention
August 19, 2003

GOOD EVENING. It is a pleasure and a privilege for me to welcome young delegates from here at home and all over the world to Edmonton. I hope all of you make new friends, learn about each other's cultures, and strengthen your commitment to democratic values.

But what are "democratic values," exactly? The phrase means different things to different people, so in the hopes of giving you some food for thought for this convention, I'd like to offer what I feel are the most important democratic values.

First, there is literacy. Only a society of well-read individuals with keen critical thinking skills can maintain democracy. Citizens of a democracy should read voraciously. They should use and support their public libraries and public schools. They should question authority, and they should, in turn, question those who question authority. And they must always be willing to think, and to think hard.

Then, there is empathy. A democracy cannot function unless its people are concerned with the welfare of their fellow citizens. Charity is not enough; we must work towards addressing the systemic inequalities in our society, towards bridging the gap between rich and poor. There's a saying I quite like: "When we all do better, we *all* do better." In other words, the more help we give the less fortunate, the more we resolve issues of pay equity and discrimination, the better off everyone, the rich, the middle class, and the poor alike, will be.

Thirdly, there is creativity—both using it and appreciating it, particularly when it comes to the arts.

Good books, plays, movies, operas, photographs, paintings, and all the other forms of artistic expression provide valuable commentaries on contemporary culture, commentaries citizens can use to examine the most important issues of the day. Democratic citizens, therefore, have a vested interest in supporting the fine arts.

Those are some of the democratic values that I cherish, and as you convene, I encourage you to discuss and explore the other values that are essential to a fair, prosperous, and free society.

We in Canada are fortunate indeed to have the opportunity to host this important convention. Our democracy, like all the world's democracies, thrives only because individual men and women are willing to expend the time and effort it takes to be responsible, informed, compassionate citizens.

I salute you all for attending this convention; it proves that you are all dedicated to strengthening democracy, and to extending democratic values around the world. Thank you for your commitment to building a more democratic, a more just, tolerant, literate, and compassionate world.

Not every speech to high school students followed the same course. This one saw Lois emphasizing the importance of having fun, along with the importance of what students had been accomplishing. The mention of listening to the CBC reflected a passion. She kept about six radios in different rooms of her house tuned to the national network.

F.G. Miller Junior/Senior High School Graduation Ceremonies
August 29, 2003

GOOD EVENING, EVERYONE, and thank you so much for inviting me to be a part of this milestone in your lives.

To begin, I must offer my most sincere congratulations to tonight's graduates. You have taken the first step towards a brighter future. The question for many of you now becomes, what's next?

Venturing into the unknown always involves a little uncertainty. Many of you will be heading to university or college; others will head straight into the workforce. I suspect that some of you may even have avoided thinking too much about what happens after tonight—but that's all right. Don't be afraid to take a little time to consider your future.

Whatever your eventual choices in life, it's important to remember that your success is based on two things: your willingness to keep learning, and your belief in yourself....

My sons Bill and Jim run our business today, and even when they were your age, they did a lot of work on the farm.

They took fresh vegetables to market and sold them, they worked in the fields planting and harvesting, and they worked hard at school and later at university to prepare themselves to handle the business.

But, as the old saying goes, all work and no play makes Jack a dull boy, or Jill a dull girl.

I always made sure that Bill and Jim were allowed to pursue other interests. As it turned out, both boys developed a love of football, and they also had some fun by participating in opera. Mind you, they accidentally set the stage on fire one time and put a hole in it with an anvil, but never mind that. At least they had fun.

Ted, Jim, Lois, Michael, Valerie and Bill Hole around the lunch table, 1986. [Hole Family Archives]

And as for me—I like to find balance in my life by taking some time off to relax at the symphony, to enjoy a play, to listen to CBC radio, or to find a nice comfy chair and get lost in a good book.

So that's how my family finds balance; we juggle work and play, education and experience. Your lives might be similar, and they might be very different.

My only advice to you is this: do what you love. Pursue it with all the passion and energy you can muster, whether it's sports or creative writing or music or gardening or drama or whatever excites you most. But take some time to explore the other things in life, too; if you're nuts about hockey, try a game of chess, or spend some time browsing at the library.

If you love science fiction novels, go see a football game. If you need to take a break from astronomy, take a dance class or join the drama club. There's a whole world out there to explore, and none of us can ever experience all it has to offer. But we can have a lot of fun trying. And in the attempt, we can bring balance to our lives....

You have no idea how proud I am of each and every one of you, and I salute you for overcoming the struggles you faced in achieving your diplomas. Congratulations, one and all, and best of luck.

Chester Cunningham was one of Alberta's most prominent Métis citizens because of his work with Native Counselling Services. This address honoured his contributions. Lois also cited him at the end of November when she spoke at a social justice award dinner organized by the Institute for the Advancement of Aboriginal Women, founded by another prominent Alberta Métis, Muriel Stanley-Venne.

Native Counselling Services of Alberta
Official Opening of Cunningham Place
Edmonton, September 9, 2003

HELLO, EVERYONE, AND WELCOME. First, I must say that it is a tremendous honour and a personal thrill for me to be invited to participate in this event. One of the greatest influences in my life was a Métis woman by the name of Virginie Durocher, a woman who taught me about gardening, humility, perseverance, compassion, and the enduring power of love.

I'll always be grateful for the presence of Mrs. Durocher and her children in my life; I think it's fair to say that my life would have been much the poorer without them.

So as someone who grew up on a farm and enjoyed the wisdom and assistance of many Native Canadians, I feel very privileged to be here today to help celebrate the existence and the potential of Native Counselling Services of Alberta. The work you have done here is vitally important, and it's crucial that more Albertans start to recognize that fact.

I believe that Canada is a wonderful country, and that we have the potential to be world leaders in ethics, culture, and prosperity. But that potential cannot and will not be realized until the peoples of Canada's First Nations have achieved a cultural, social, and economic standing equal in full measure to the other peoples of this country.

We cannot move forward as a united people until all of us have the security that others take for granted.

So I congratulate everyone who has participated in the creation of this new facility. You are all men and women of vision, who have taken it upon yourselves to help us move forward, towards better days.

One day, we will all be one people: First Nations, whites, blacks, Asians, Catholics, Protestants, Muslims, wiccans, pagans and atheists. But it's going to take a lot of work to reach that day, and I'm so very proud of anyone who works towards that future.

Today we are here not only to open a building, but to recognize the outstanding contributions of a man who has changed countless people's lives for the better, a man who has dedicated his life to the service of others.

It is with great pleasure that the people of Alberta dedicate this new facility to Dr. Chester Cunningham, a man who has done so much to ensure that our Native peoples will one day enjoy all the status, prosperity, and happiness that is their birthright as Canada's first stewards of the land.

Dr. Cunningham, thank you for making a difference in the lives of not only Alberta's Natives, but to all her citizens.

Those who come to Cunningham Place will find all the tools and support they need to fulfil their vast potential.

The completion of this project and the goodwill of the men and women who will work here represents an important step on the road towards true equality in this country, and we should welcome it with open arms.

Thank you, and may this building be the birthplace of not only dreams of hope, but of the knowledge and wisdom we all need to build a better future.

Lois had spoken many times now on education. She still occasionally added new thoughts. This speech to a university women's group also produced an example of her increasingly emphatic tone, using phrases such as "absolutely depends" to ensure the audience understood how serious she was. This speech was delivered two days after the death of her mother, Elsa Veregin, at age 97 after three years in a nursing home. Lois did not refer to the loss in her speeches.

Canadian Federation of University Women (CFUW) Red Deer & District Fundraiser Luncheon
September 18, 2003

GOOD MORNING EVERYONE, and thank you for asking me to join you today. I really couldn't say no, once I learned about all the good work you do: the literacy projects for elementary schools, the Red Deer college endowment fund, the awards for high school students. So I must begin by offering you some well-deserved congratulations. Since I accepted the role of Lieutenant Governor, I've been telling people that they need to do more to support our public education system, and here in Red Deer you're doing exactly that. I want you to know that your efforts are a source of great joy to me; you give me hope that people really do care enough to build a better world, and that's why I consider it such a great honour to be made a lifelong member of the CFUW.

Learning, as your organization understands so well, is a lifelong process, and to me, lifelong learning is not so much about taking extension courses and the like; it's about being involved in your community, about being an activist. You can learn so much simply by participating in the life of your province, the day-to-day struggles of the sick, the poor, and of our young people.

Margaret Laurence said:

It is my feeling that as we grow older we should become not less radical but more so. I do not, of course, mean this in any political party sense, but in a willingness to struggle for those things in which we passionately believe.

That's what I'm trying to do during my time as Lieutenant Governor: struggle on behalf of my passions. As I've said before, the future of our country *absolutely depends* upon vigorous support of the arts, of our public schools and universities, our public libraries, and public health care.

As I grow older, I've been thinking more and more about what kind of future the next generation can hope to expect.

While human beings have made a lot of progress, especially in the last hundred years, we also have a long way yet to travel, and some of the problems we face—hunger, crime, disease, poverty, racism, war— seem almost insurmountable. It's no wonder that many of our young people have cynical attitudes about their future prospects for employment and a good life.

But we can bury that cynicism if we work together, young and old, to fight poverty, injustice, and racism. And the best way to build a better world for our children is to fight for our public libraries and public schools.

If I could bestow one gift upon young people, it would be a good education, an education rich in literature, science, mathematics, history, crafts, sport, and the fine arts. It would be an education with no shortage of excellent teachers and a full supply of the world's best books.

And part of that ideal education would include teaching youth about community responsibility, public awareness, trustworthiness, respect, and compassion for their fellows.

Education doesn't just provide the next generation with the knowledge and skills they need to prosper; it also gives them the tools they need to make ethical choices....

Her own arts award dinner provided a larger than usual platform to reiterate her belief in the importance of the arts. Once again, she lightened the serious message with personal stories. Usually she described her son Bill's adventures in opera in brief form. On this occasion, she recounted the story in full detail. The more closely she described the episode, the funnier it became.

Lieutenant Governor of Alberta Arts Awards Program Fundraising Dinner
Edmonton, October 14, 2003

WHILE MY SON BILL WAS ATTENDING UNIVERSITY in the mid-seventies, he and three of his football teammates had been asked to be supers in the EOA production of *Il Trovatore*. The evening of one of the rehearsals, Bill took the anvil from his father's workshop and loaded it into the back of his truck. The anvil belonged to Grandpa Hole, and it was over 75 years old. Naturally, I was curious.

"I thought you were going to an opera rehearsal," I said.

"I am," Bill said.

"Why are you loading up the anvil, then?"

"Mom," Bill explained, "Lorne, Dave, Leo, and I are playing anvils in the Anvil Chorus."

Well, I was thrilled. I'd tried and tried to teach Bill to play the piano, with no success, and here at last I was vindicated: Bill was learning an instrument.

[Pause for (hopefully) laughter]

When Bill came home that evening, I asked him how the rehearsal went. He explained that they worked with the conductor, which I thought was a good sign; normally, supers only work with stage managers. He told me how the conductor worked with them extensively on timing, rhythm, and tone. Well, you can imagine how thrilled I was. Perhaps Bill had some promise as a musician after all! And not only that, it was *Il Trovatore*, a wonderful opera that I've loved for years. I couldn't wait to see Bill perform. "Just imagine," I thought, "My son, playing tenor anvil at the Jubilee Auditorium!"

At last, the evening of the performance came, and I was there, excited beyond words. The anvil chorus occurs about midway through the opera, and at the appointed moment, there were Bill and his friends, all dressed up in period blacksmith clothing, hammering away on those anvils with all the strength in their arms. It was really quite something to see these huge, mean-looking, sweaty football players, all coated in grimy makeup, banging out the chorus. It was deafening, but to me it sounded absolutely wonderful. I really was incredibly pleased and proud.

When Bill came home after the performance, I asked him how *he* felt about the evening.

"How did it go?" I asked.

To my surprise, Bill's response was less than enthusiastic.

"Not so well," he replied.

"Why?" I asked.

Bill explained that the heavy anvils had to be moved offstage rather quickly once the anvil chorus was complete. Normally the set workers moved the props around between scenes, but the anvils were so heavy that it took several workers to move each one, and there just wasn't enough time between scenes to complete the job. So the set workers, seeing that my son and his friends were all huge football linemen, asked them to help out. It was relatively easy for the boys to lift up their own anvils and carry them away.

Bill and his anvil were located high up at the left side of the stage, so he had to carry the anvil down several levels and all the way across the stage. The last level was a platform about two feet above the stage. Now, each of these platforms were supposed to be securely fastened down, but wouldn't you know it, this one was not. When Bill stepped onto the platform, the plank when flying straight up and Bill began to fall. He was headed straight for the floor, and that anvil was going to come down right on top of him. So, to prevent a potentially serious injury, Bill threw the anvil away from his body as he started to fall. The anvil flew out of his hands and came down point-first, KABOOM, making a huge hole right through that beautiful, three-inch hardwood floor.

You know, thinking back, I thought I'd heard a crashing sound on the stage....

Anyway, I told Bill not to worry about it—it wasn't really his fault, no one got hurt, and besides, the anvil chorus really sounded great. As far as I was concerned, that was a happy ending, and not many operas have those.

Bill and his younger brother Jim participated in a few more operas over the years, and I've always been so glad they had those experiences. There's no question in my mind that their flirtation with performance enabled them to think outside the boundaries of their agriculture degrees. The fine arts are not something "outside" the real world, as many believe; they are, in fact, an integral part of how we live and work.

My son Jim once had a chance to talk to Mike Wilson, who used to play as an offensive lineman for the Edmonton Eskimos. To Jim's surprise, Wilson told him that the key to being a great lineman was to first become a great dancer. Wilson took dancing very seriously, and if you ever watched him play, you couldn't fail to notice that he was indeed very light on his feet. Interestingly, Charlie Turner, another Eskimo, went on to illustrate children's books. I can't help but think that his creativity on the field was directly linked to his creativity as an artist.

Perhaps the greatest scientist of the 20th century, Albert Einstein, was also a devoted amateur violinist. His groundbreaking work is proof that the arts teach you to think unconventionally, that practical problems can often be solved by creative thinking. Einstein himself is famous for saying, "Imagination is more important than knowledge."...

An address to a United Church women's conference in October 2003 reiterated familiar themes but introduced some new features. Quotations from famous persons were beginning to show up more frequently. Martin Luther King had appeared in her speeches before. Now, World Bank president James Wolfensohn and legendary U.S. oilman Clint Murchison showed up, as did Nelson Mandela, Charlie Chaplin, and, rather more unexpectedly, Jimi Hendrix. All became fixtures in Lois's speeches over the coming year. The relative avalanche of quotations may have detracted from her usual speaking style; the words of others began to replace the stories she would tell from her life in Saskatchewan and on the farm at St. Albert. Nevertheless, her address to the United Church women set out a model she would follow for the rest of her time in public life. Chaplin's movie script was quoted at length and has been shortened here.

United Church of Canada Women's Conference

Camrose, October 19, 2003

Good morning, and welcome.

All my life, I've had the good fortune to be inspired by remarkable women—by Mrs. Durocher, the Métis woman who taught me so much about courtesy, compassion, and humility; by my mother, who instilled in me the importance of public education and the fine arts; by people like Mary Robinson, once the United Nations Commissioner for Human Rights, or Nellie McClung, Margaret Atwood, and all the remarkable women I've been privileged to meet and work with as a farm woman, mother, wife, school trustee, business owner, chancellor of the University of Alberta, and Lieutenant Governor.

I would never have been able to perform in any of those roles were it not for the guidance and inspiration of those women.

And in fact, it seems like every day I meet another remarkable woman who's building shelters for the homeless, or working with abused children, preparing aid packages for victims of famine, performing a beautiful piece of music at a charity event, or simply providing her students with a world-class education.

All of these women have one thing in common: they were never afraid to use their gifts and talents in the service of humanity. They recognized that one of the sacred duties of being human is to use whatever gifts we've been blessed with to not only pursue our own dreams, but to pursue the larger dream of building a safer, more peaceful, more plentiful, more equitable world.

Of course, I've also been inspired by men; men who also recognized their gifts, and who, like the women I so admire, used those gifts to preach the power of love, some with religious messages, some with secular.

In fact, just a couple of weeks ago, another man spoke out for a fairer world. World Bank President James Wolfensohn told World Bank delegates, "Our planet is not balanced. Too few control too much, and too many have too little to hope for."

Putting it a bit less tactfully, as well as many years earlier, the famous entrepreneur Clint W. Murchison said, "Money is like manure. If you spread it around, it does a lot of good; but if you pile it up in one place, it stinks like hell."

[Short pause for (hopefully) laughter]

Economic disparity must surely be the chief sickness that afflicts our world, the prime obstacle to a lasting, loving peace. As it stands, a privileged few enjoy wealth undreamed of in history, while billions must suffer under the soul-crushing weight of terrible poverty. This is not a status quo conducive to peace and brotherhood.

And even worse, it is a *criminal* squandering of potential. The world's poor, whether they live in the struggling developing nations or forgotten on the streets of the Western world's richest cities, have the potential to not only lift themselves out of terrible poverty, but to lead the rest of the world into a new age of peace, enlightenment, and brotherhood.

We're talking about billions of human beings, an incredibly broad and deep pool of talent. Just imagine what an engine of economic, social, and cultural progress a rich, well-educated Third World could be. Just imagine how much the homeless people of Toronto, New York, London, or Edmonton could do for their neighbours if they only had the means.

I cannot help but mourn all the progress the human race has lost to poverty. How many brilliant young minds are withering this very moment because of malnutrition or lack of access to education? How many great composers, painters, scientists, and peacemakers will never see their tenth birthday, their gifts lost to the world forever?

The truth is, the poor people of this earth need our help. And since it is our children who have the potential to build a better tomorrow, part of our help must come in the form of investment in education. As one of my personal heroes, Nelson Mandela, once said,

> *Education is the great engine of personal development. It is through education that the daughter of a peasant can become a doctor, that a son of a mineworker can become the head of the mine, that a child of farm workers can become the president of a great nation. It is what we make out of what we have, not what we are given, that separates one person from another.*

This quote is a great inspiration for me, and reinforces my determination to support public education and public libraries here in Canada and in all the corners of the globe.

It is only through education and art—through music, through books, through theatre—that we will find the wisdom to trade hate for compassion, to trade competition for co-operation. Education and the fine arts engage the human mind, forcing us to think in new ways, forcing us to use our most powerful tool for progress: our imagination.

Albert Einstein himself once said that imagination is more important than knowledge, and history, I believe, vindicates his statement.

Dr. Martin Luther King, for example, had a pretty good imagination. In his famous "I Have a Dream" speech, he imagined a world where his children would be judged "not by the colour of their skin, but the content of their character." And when he accepted his Nobel Peace Prize, he went on to say,

> *I refuse to accept the view that mankind is so tragically bound to the starless midnight of racism and war that the bright daybreak of peace and brotherhood can never become a reality. I believe that unarmed truth and unconditional love will have the final word.*

Or consider the imagination of the famous explorer of the seas, Jacques Cousteau, who said,

If we were logical, the future would be bleak indeed. But we are more than logical. We are human beings, and we have faith and we have hope, and we can work.

And Charlie Chaplin had a great imagination, too. In the late 1930s, he wrote and directed *The Great Dictator*, a thinly veiled attack on Adolf Hitler.

It was released in 1940, before most North Americans realized the full extent of Hitler's evil. In the film, Chaplin's character, a Jewish barber in the mythical European country of Tomania, is mistaken for Adenoid Hynkel, Tomania's ruthless dictator, and so the Jewish barber rules in the dictator's place.

He has a series of misadventures, and at the film's end, with the people of Tomania still believing that he is the dictator, he gives an impassioned speech that astonishes the gathered masses. Here, in part, is what he says:

...To those who can hear me, I say "Do not despair." The misery that has come upon us is but the passing of greed, the bitterness of men who fear the way of human progress.... Let us fight for a new world, a decent world that will give men a chance to work, that will give youth a future and old age a security. By the promise of these things, brutes have risen to power. But they lie! They do not fulfil that promise. They never will!

...Wherever you are, look up! The clouds are lifting! The sun is breaking through! We are coming out of the darkness into the light! We are coming into a new world; a kindlier world, where men will rise above their greed, their hate and their brutality. Look up! The soul of man has been given wings and at last he is beginning to fly. He is flying into the rainbow! Into the light of hope! Look up! Look up!

What a beautiful vision, what an impassioned call for love and brotherhood.

I love that speech, and I wish more politicians would echo those sentiments, for to embrace the grim alternative, hate, is to foolishly cast our destiny into the unforgiving sands of an brutal emotional desert.

Love and acceptance, on the other hand, are like a garden, green and growing, lush and vibrant, sustaining our bodies and our souls. We, all six billion human beings, have a choice to make; will we live in the garden, or die in the desert?

Is it too much to ask for a desert turned green, or a lasting and heartfelt peace between all the peoples of the world?

Is it too grand a thing to strive for a world without hunger, without injustice, without hate? I don't think so. I think we can build an Eden right here on Earth, if we can only drum up the will to do it.

I believe if we keep on planting seeds of hope and trust every year, the generations to come will sit under trees of peace and prosperity, sheltered from hate, from ignorance, from fear. Perhaps one day the Negev, the Sahara, the Gobi will be rich not only in vegetation and animal life, but in spirit.

Perhaps our deserts will become gathering places, living memorials to the triumph of love over despair.

Growing a new Eden here on earth means that we must first plant the seeds of compassion in our hearts. We must learn to accept the suffering and hardship of others as our own suffering and hardship.

We must feel the loss of an anonymous Bangladeshi child as keenly as a famous and beloved leader.

Only then—only when we finally realize that the death or suffering or lost potential of any human being diminishes us all—only then will we have the capacity to put hatred to rest and give birth, at long last, to peace, after a millennia-long labour. Only then will the soul of humanity be given wings.

The famous American guitarist and songwriter Jimi Hendrix once said, "When the power of love overcomes the love of power, the world will know peace." Untold thousands of men and women, through their work, their sacrifices, their wisdom, and their compassion, have shown us the power of love.

Very few of these people gained fame; most toiled in obscurity for little earthly reward. But if enough people follow in their footsteps, then, as Hendrix predicted, the world will indeed know peace.

So where does all this leave you and I, and all the other women who decide to put their potential to use?

The important thing, in my view, is not to try to solve all the world's problems, or to become some kind of superwoman.

The important thing is to do what you can, a little every day, to do your part to make the world a better place. If all you have time for is to volunteer an hour a week to read to children, that's fine.

If all you can afford is a twenty-five dollar donation to your favourite charity, that's fine.

Be proud of anything you can do for your fellow human beings, because no matter how small it seems, you're making a difference. And let me tell you: someone's going to see it, and they're going to follow your example.

And when enough people start doing some little thing, it suddenly becomes something really big.

That's how the world changes: bit by bit, because someone took a little bit of time and decided that they would pitch in, that they would lend a hand, that they would make a difference.

Never, ever forget that your contributions matter, and that your role in building a better society is absolutely essential. The first duty of every woman, and of every man, is to our fellows. If we can remember that, then we have a pretty good chance of making some progress here on our troubled, but promising, world.

Again, thank you all so much for inviting me to join you this morning, and enjoy the rest of the conference.

Book clubs had become very popular by 2003. It was likely only the small size of most that had kept Lois from talking to one before. She evangelized for libraries and retold the story of Miss Jobb, but carefully recast her usual remarks to include the club.

Riverside Book Club 75th Anniversary
Medicine Hat, October 20, 2003

GOOD EVENING, and thank you so much for asking me to participate in tonight's celebration. 75 years is a long time to keep a club going, and I think you all deserve a huge amount of credit for maintaining such a worthwhile organization for so long.

So tonight, I'd like to share a couple of stories with you about my experiences with reading, and how they led me to appreciate libraries....

Book clubs such as yours also act as a kind of library, a closely-knit group of people with a common purpose: to share the richness of the books they enjoy, to discuss the ideas and style within these books, and to propose new authors and subjects to explore.

I think book clubs are a wonderful way to tie the people of the community together, and I wish that more people would start them up and participate. In fact, your book club is the longest-lived and most successful one I know of.

In fact, I hope that you use some of the knowledge and influence you've accumulated to introduce as many people as possible to the world of books. Perhaps you have nephews or nieces, children or grand-children, who can be convinced to get a little volunteer experience at the library. Or perhaps you have some well-to-do relatives who are looking for a worthwhile charity to bequeath some of their accumulated wealth to.

Well, I can't think of a better way to promote the values of a book club than to donate some time or funding to literacy organizations or libraries. And please, let's remember to look beyond our own borders; there are so many libraries and educational institutions across the world that could benefit from our help.

Just imagine what a difference it would make if all the children of Africa and Asia had access to well-written, up-to-date textbooks; they'd lead longer, healthier, richer lives, and by doing so, they'll contribute not only to the prosperity of their own countries, but the benefits will eventually come right back to Canadian shores.

If literature teaches us anything, it is that the human race is one large, inexorably connected family, and that the suffering of one member of the human family affects us all. Knowledge hoarded is knowledge wasted, while wisdom shared may lift us all from the abyss.

All that being said, I must say once again how pleased and proud I am by your club's mission and its longevity. You really are an inspiration to anyone who loves to read.

So congratulations once again, and here's to 75 more years of new books, new discoveries, fascinating discussions, and the next generation of readers.

Dealing with Alzheimer's in a small town, and revealing a little more of how tough her husband's illness had been to bear.

Myrnam Alzheimer Home Development Association
Myrnam, October 22, 2003

PROVIDING CONSTANT CARE for those suffering from a terminal illness isn't a task to be taken lightly, and before I say anything else today, I must salute you for taking on the responsibility. Those who suffer from Alzheimer's are among our society's most vulnerable members, and caring for them presents special challenges.

It's hard not to take the pain and confusion of an Alzheimer's patient into yourself, to share in their suffering, and if you're not careful, it's all too easy to fall into hopelessness and depression. That's why caregivers like yourselves need all the support we can offer....

It takes a very special kind of dedication and empathy to be a caregiver.

For instance, your commitment to provide the highest standards of care to the seniors of Myrnam is truly inspirational.

Your compassion epitomizes what being Canadian is all about—making sure that our neighbours have the dignity of proper, civilized care.

Martin Luther King said, "I have the audacity to believe that people everywhere can have three meals a day for their bodies, education and culture for their minds, and dignity, equality and freedom for their spirits. I believe that what self-centred people have torn down, other-centred people can build up."

To me, this is the central truth of volunteerism: that "other-centred" people—volunteers, in other words—will be the ones to ring in the era of true prosperity, of true equality, of true justice. For volunteers act not out of self-interest, but altruism; the hope that all people can enjoy a standard of living and of health commensurate with dignity and self-respect.

This is especially true when it comes to fighting Alzheimer's. My husband Ted had it in the long months before he passed away this spring, and as you can imagine, it was one of the most difficult times in my life.

Ted was a terrific sport and always laughed along whenever I haul out one of my old anecdotes. Good thing, too, because he's a central figure in so many of my funny stories.

But Ted was always been a man of great vision, with an inventive and innovative mind. I saw that the very first day we came out to the farm. There we stood, side by side, two kids from the city, while he told me how we were going to make a wonderful life on this little patch of land, with its aging barn and tiny house. He painted the picture so clearly that I could see it myself.'

Of course, once we got down to the actual business of farming, that picture was clouded by dozens of day-to-day details. People who grow up on farms absorb so much knowledge that it becomes second nature. Ted and I, on the other hand, had to learn as we went along.

In the long run, Ted turned his lack of experience into his greatest advantage. Farmers are creatures of habit: if they grow up doing things a certain way, it can be next to impossible to convince them to change. Ted, on the other hand, had absolutely no preconceived notions. He constantly questioned our methods and looked for ways to improve them.

When we started market gardening, the industry was in its infancy in central Alberta. Very few people here farmed vegetables, and those who did weren't operating on the scale Ted envisioned. As a result, we had a terrible time finding appropriate equipment. As far as the manufactures and suppliers were concerned, we might as well have been growing vegetables at the North Pole.

Ted subscribed to dozens of magazines and catalogues from the United States, where the industry was much better established. He'd go through them page by page, looking for new ideas, methods, and tools. After days of research, he chose a John Deere 1020 because, with its adjustable wheel spacing, it was the most suitable for row-crop work. And if he couldn't find the things he needed, he'd adapt the things he had on hand.

Ted relied a lot on our neighbour Len Adams, a talented welder. He would wander down the road to tell Len his latest idea and Len, always the pessimist, would mutter, "Nope, can't be done. It's not gonna work." Ted would ask, "Well, can you at least give it a try?" He'd go back an hour later, and the tool would be built.

After a few years of digging carrots by hand, which is a terrible job, Ted invented a carrot lifter. He had Len weld two grader blades onto a cross-brace, and hitched it to the 1020. As he drove the tractor along a row, the blades loosened the soil on either side. The carrots just popped right out of the ground, read to gather.

Ted also loved to experiment with new seed varieties. When we first started market gardening, our neighbours told us not to bother trying to grow corn. Ted shopped for the latest hybrids and kept trying different varieties very year. After several years of experimenting, we grew crop after crop of beautiful corn.

Ted also developed a close relationship with the horticulturists at the Brooks Research Centre, at a time when most farmers were skeptical of scientific approaches to farming. From those gentlemen, we learned to try new technologies, many of which we were able to employ successfully.

Of course, not everything Ted tried worked. But when it did, the rewards could be enormous. For instance, if you could find ways to grow an especially early crop, your profits multiplied. Dill cucumbers, which might fetch fifty cents a pound in August, were worth two or three dollars a pound in July. Ted invested a lot of time and effort in his ideas, and it usually paid off for us.

If people poked fun at his unorthodox thinking, Ted never let it bother him. In the later 1960s, I was on the board of the Rural Safety Council. At the time, we were fighting to have roll-bars installed on tractors and to make their use mandatory. Ted saw it as an issue of simple common sense: by spending a couple of hundred dollars, he might save his life or that of one of his kids. When the neighbours got a look at Ted's tractor, all fitted out with a roll-bar, canopy, and radio, they were beside themselves. One of them even climbed right up and danced on the canopy. Ted just stood there and watched, not saying a word.

Of course, his foresight has since been proven right, as roll-over protection systems (ROPS) are now legally required on all new tractors. Ted was also an early advocate of hearing protection, another development that has substantially reduced injury on farms in the last few decades. (In fact, Ted swore he lost much of his hearing operating our first potato harvester—hearing protection came a little too late for him.)

But not all of our neighbours made fun of Ted. Other families in the market gardening business began to keep a close eye on him and often followed his example. For years we had people stopping by our house to check out our crops or borrow equipment.

Ted still helps shape our business and his bold spirit continues to be reflected. Customers often tell me how much they look forward to the new plant varieties we offer each year, and our garden centre is always well stocked with ingenious gardening tools.

So when you read one of my anecdotes about Ted, don't forget that behind the laughter stands a most remarkable man.[27]

Ted was a vital, funny, inventive, hard-working, compassionate man, and it was so hard to lose him like that. Now, I know that many of you have similar stories, and that many of those stories are far worse than mine. To tell the truth, on some days, I felt very fortunate that Ted had as many good moments as he did.

The only thing that made it bearable was the incredibly professional and compassionate treatment he received from his caregivers—people like you.

Ted lost his fight with Alzheimer's, but there are thousands of Canadians that can still be helped.

As citizens, I believe we each have a duty to keep fighting, not only for our own loved ones, but for future generations....

Your example shows people that Alzheimer's patients still deserve our respect, our love, and our health care dollars. Because *you* have not forgotten them, you've shown us that *we* cannot forget them, either.

I know dealing with Alzheimer's isn't easy. In fact, I wish I didn't know. But at least we can share the pain and find some comfort in knowing that brilliant, compassionate people are working incredibly hard to find a cure, and that volunteer caregivers are devoting so much love and attention to Alzheimer's patients.

We owe you men and women so much, even if a cure doesn't arrive in time to help our own loved ones.

We owe you for the effort, for giving us hope, and for doing your part in building a future in which no other children and grandchildren, husbands and wives, will have to endure what we have endured.

I think the Myrnam Alzheimer Home Development Association is a priceless organization, one that provides not only support for Alzheimer's patients, but the inspiration and influence that are so vital to finding a cure. That cure will come, and when it does, the people of Canada—indeed, the world—will owe you a great debt of gratitude....

At first glance, citing the words of former U.S. President (and Second World War commander of Allied Forces in Europe) Dwight Eisenhower may seem a surprise. However, both Eisenhower and Lois were independent thinkers raised in small prairie communities and in families that nurtured both an appreciation for education and a confident pragmatism.

Remembrance Day Ceremonies
University of Alberta Butterdome
November 11, 2003

LADIES AND GENTLEMEN—

I'll begin today by thanking the Canadian Fallen Heroes Foundation for a new initiative that will help all Canadians remember those who gave their lives for freedom. The Foundation is creating remarkable posters that pay visual tribute to our soldiers, posters that will remind us of their sacrifice.

It is a tremendously important project, because, after all, the lessons of history are lost if we allow our memories to die, even if those memories cause terrible grief. So to founder Mark Norman and everyone else who made the project a reality, I offer gratitude and congratulations. You've done history a great service.

Art alone, of course, cannot keep the past alive; we need to keep the memory of the fallen in our hearts, and we need to pass that respect down to each generation. That is why, every year, we continue to recognize those who came to Canada's defence in the hours of her greatest need.

The 20th century was wracked by terrible wars time and again, but each time, without fail, Canada's sons and daughters heard the call and restored peace and order to our world. And as the 21st century dawns, these brave and loyal soldiers continue to give up their lives as they try to bring peace, freedom, and stability to the world's poorest, most desperate people.

We can never truly repay our veterans for their heroism, but we can, and must, remember it. Not just for the sake of honouring the fallen, but for the sake of the millions of people on our planet—the current generation of Canadians among them—who have never had to endure the horrors of war, thanks to their sacrifices.

November 11 is the most significant national event of the year, for without Remembrance Day—or rather without the soldiers who gave us cause to *create* Remembrance Day—we might not be celebrating the other national holidays we enjoy. We might not have reason to celebrate anything at all.

Remembrance Day is one of our country's most important and solemn rituals, an event that pays tribute to those who died in defence of our freedoms, and the surviving veterans who continue to be haunted by the memories of war. It is the duty of every Canadian to respect and honour the contributions of our soldiers.

But at the same time, we have a still greater duty, an obligation to ensure that the efforts of our veterans were not in vain. For if we remember what our soldiers endured, perhaps we will someday find the wisdom to put war behind us.

The great American general and later President Dwight Eisenhower, certainly no pacifist, nonetheless recognized the tremendous waste and loss of human potential inherent in war. At a speech in 1953, he said:

> *Every gun that is made, every warship launched, every rocket fired signifies in the final sense, a theft from those who hunger and are not fed, those who are cold and are not clothed. This world in arms is not spending money alone. It is spending the sweat of its laborers, the genius of its scientists, the hopes of its children. This is not a way of life at all in any true sense. Under the clouds of war, it is humanity hanging on a cross of iron.*

Eisenhower was right. Each war must be seen as a great failure of human imagination: a failure to identify the root causes of war, a failure to accommodate the genuine needs and grievances of our neighbours, a failure to address the conditions that give rise of dictatorships, a failure to repudiate violence as a means of effecting change.

Our soldiers pay the price for our lack of imagination, and if we ever hope to close that bloody account, then we must find a way to bring lasting prosperity and freedom to all the peoples of the world.

Peace will never come until all human beings enjoy good food, clean water, strong shelter, excellent schools, modern hospitals, fully stocked libraries, and the fundamental freedoms that we in the Western world take for granted.

Therefore, the best way to remember the sacrifices of Canadian soldiers is to keep working towards the day when all human beings will at last put aside their petty differences and live as we were meant to: in peace. To do that, we must fight and win one last war: the war on poverty and ignorance.

And given their dedication, bravery, and compassion, I have no doubt that Canadian soldiers will be leading the way, as they always have.

So this Remembrance Day, I believe all of us should do two things: we should pay our respects to the thousands of Canadian soldiers who gave their lives for freedom, and then we should look for ways to ensure that one day, we can enjoy peace and prosperity without those sacrifices. It is the only meaningful way to pay the debt we owe our veterans.

Lois kept her days full—sometimes more than full, somewhat to the conster-
nation of her staff. October and November were particularly busy times of the
year. The following speech is only a sample of what she was doing in the fall of
2003 and illustrates the range of events she attended. The comment at the
end about Edmonton "revitalizing itself" refers to the end of about a decade of
slow growth that saw the city worry about both its economic prospects and its
future directions. Lois's strong relationship with the city and the surrounding
region tended to serve as a counter-balance at a time when the city was trying
to recover its confidence. McDougall United Church, in the heart of downtown
Edmonton, is one of the city's finest early buildings and most important
historic sites. In the late 1900s it began to see frequent use as the site of small
concerts and of Kiwanis Music Festival performances.

McDougall United Church
130th Anniversary
Edmonton, November 23, 2003

IT'S A GREAT PLEASURE to offer a few words of gratitude and congratulations to the congregations, both past and present, of McDougall
United Church, an institution that has served the people of Alberta for
over a century. McDougall has endured because people like you have
taken the time and effort to participate in church life, and by doing so,
you have made irreplaceable contributions to this city.

Inner-city churches like this one have played a vital role in the growth
of many cities, chiefly on three fronts: they have provided spiritual
shelter, live-saving aid to the less fortunate, and a means of developing
Edmonton's musical scene.

McDougall has provided all of these, particularly to those who needed
it most, and especially during the years when the downtown core started
to decline in importance. Not everyone can afford to move to the
suburbs, and thank goodness there were stalwart parishioners who
stuck by the church and the people who depended upon its mercy.

McDougall's musical heritage shares an equally important place in
my heart. Long before we had the Jubilee or the Winspear,
Edmontonians gathered here to share good company and good music,

and that is among the most precious gifts we has human beings have the pleasure to enjoy.

Ted and I took in many great performances here, and I'll always remember how the music resonated so beautifully within these walls. Without your patronage and generosity, Edmonton's cultural landscape would have been far bleaker.

Now that downtown Edmonton is slowly revitalizing itself, I hope that the people of this community will recognize the historic, cultural, and spiritual value of this church, and that they will offer support accordingly. The church offered help to the helpless for decades; now, it's time for Edmonton to help the church.

So to the thousands of men and women who have kept McDougall Church thriving, despite these obstacles, I offer my thanks and admiration. Your stewardship—both of this church and the larger community it serves—is truly inspiring. Congratulations again on 130 years of charity and fellowship.

Athabasca University was an experiment in distance learning that quickly developed into a success. Lois had served on its board. She looked back here at the controversial decision to locate the university in a town at the edge of the boreal forest. Her support for the move showed that her interest in the arts did not efface her ability to make tough-minded business decisions. She also revealed more of her mother's influence and once again stepped close to the boundaries of politics. Abrioux was the university's president.

Athabasca University
Reception for Dominique Abrioux
November 24, 2003

GOOD EVENING.

British author H.G. Wells once wrote, "Human history becomes more and more a race between education and catastrophe." It's clear that the race begun so long ago continues to this day.

All of the people here tonight are like members of a relay team, passing the baton from runner to runner as we strive towards the goal of creating a populace that has the tools to prevent catastrophe and bring about a smart, healthy, compassionate society.

My mother carried the baton for many years. Like many others, she taught under less than ideal conditions, conducting classes for children in Grades 1–9 within the confines of a tiny one-room schoolhouse about 17 miles away from the nearest community, my hometown of Buchanan, Saskatchewan.

The schoolhouse was generously equipped with chalk, a chalkboard, and a fireplace that never seemed quite adequate to heat the place in the winter. It had a well-stocked library of seven books—all of which, if I remember correctly, were supplied by Mother.

And, naturally, there wasn't enough money to pay her, so the school board gave her an old piano in lieu of money.

My mother wasn't the only member of the family to be involved in education. I've had cousins, a brother-in-law, and a sister-in-law that have all taught.

And my husband's parents made darn sure that every one of their children got a university degree. But it was really mother who showed me how important education is to our well-being. It's because of her that I decided back in the '60s to get involved in public education.

I served as a school trustee for many years, of course, and I'm proud of the work I did for Sturgeon County schools. But working on the board of Athabasca University was equally important to me; that's why I kept at it for over ten years.

Like many of you, I was there when the controversial decision was made to move the University from Edmonton to Athabasca, and I remember all the fights and the pain and the worry that the move caused. Sure, there was upheaval, and I don't intend to diminish the sacrifices many professors, students, and families had to make to accommodate the move. But I don't think there's any doubt that we made the right decision.

After all, Athabasca University was founded in a period of concern about access to post-secondary education, a concern that remains all too real to this day.

Athabasca University was given a mandate to be experimental and innovative, and moving the university was one way to meet our access goals. Moving towards credit co-ordination was another part of the process, as well as recognizing the importance of workplace learning and lifelong learning.

Athabasca University was asked to focus on distance education, not just to give better access to those traditionally denied such access, but also to ensure that the new students would successfully achieve their degrees. And with pass rates in excess of 65 per cent, I think it's clear that we've achieved those goals....

It's a pleasure to see it not just surviving, but thriving as a centre of excellence and a beacon of innovation for Alberta.

And that leads nicely into an important point I'd like to make tonight. In this province there's an awful lot of talk about the Alberta Advantage.

Let me tell you what I think the real Alberta Advantage is: a well-educated population. We have that advantage today because years ago there was an understanding that investment in education had positive long-term effects on the country.

We must not let that advantage slip away, because public education benefits everyone: you, me, our children, our seniors—it even benefits the banks, large corporations, and politicians. I can't think of a single reason why everyone in this province shouldn't be solidly supporting our public schools.

They're the cornerstone of a strong democracy, one overflowing with citizens who know how to think critically and vote according to rational choices. Public schools, simply put, are the source of our future prosperity. They're what holds back catastrophe and encourages invention, thought, debate, creativity, and wisdom.

I think one of the things we need to do is be more assertive about the importance of public schools. We need to be better at promoting ourselves, of telling people about what we get out of public education.

So let your MLA and the minister of education know how you feel about public schools. Let them know that you support a system that provides every child with a quality education, regardless of ethnicity, religion, income, or ability. Let them know you support a system that has accountable, elected representatives. Write a letter to the paper.

Ask a reporter to cover a special event or a typical day at your school. Just letting people know you care about the system can make a difference....

Christmas was not necessarily a season for respite from politics. If anything, the meaning of Christmas was likely to push Lois more toward trying to influence political decisions. She delivered much the same speech two days later to the Edmonton Realtors' Charitable Foundation.

Christmas Bureau Breakfast

Edmonton, December 17, 2003

GOOD MORNING.

It has become an unfortunate cliché, but it is nonetheless the truth: while Christmas is a time of great joy for millions of people around the world, so too is it a time of sadness and desperation for millions more, including thousands right here in our own city.

For the less fortunate, Christmas is a time of painfully raised expectations, expectations that are, all too often, out of reach.

But thanks to the Christmas Bureau and your own individual and corporate generosity, these families will have at least one reason to celebrate: their own festive meal.

For a few hours, thousands of Edmontonians will have the opportunity to put aside their worries and simply enjoy good food. This is a remarkable gift, one not only of material sustenance, but spiritual renewal. I'm very proud to share a room with such giving people.

That being said, however, I think we should consider what else we can do to improve the situation of the poor on a more permanent basis. We need clean and comfortable low-income housing, fair wages, and more resources for mental health care, just for starters. And we need to tell our MLAS and MPs that we support our public institutions: our libraries, our schools, our hospitals.

Our primary goal as citizens should be to build a truly just and prosperous society, where everyone has a chance to enjoy a fair share of our collective wealth, and to do that, we need to keep those public institutions accessible, modern, and fully equipped with excellent staff and equipment.

Just *imagine* what we could accomplish as a nation if every one of us was well fed, well educated, and at the peak of health. *Those are days worth fighting for*, and we should not rest until those days arrive.

For now, though, we can be happy to enjoy a significant victory over despair. Your contributions have brought a little light into the hearts of thousands of people, and I know that they are extremely grateful. Thank you so much for your selflessness and for embracing the true spirit of the season. I hope you and yours enjoy a happy holiday season.

Christmas was not the only end-of-year religious holiday that Lois enjoyed. Her comments at a Jewish ceremony in Edmonton indicated that this event meant far more to her than just a dutiful nod to another community.

Chabad Lubavitch of Edmonton
12th Annual Candle Lighting Ceremony
Edmonton, December 21, 2003

As much as I love Christmas, I must admit that I feel equal affection for Hanukkah, the beautiful Festival of Lights. Hanukkah brings so much joy, to millions of people all over the world, and not just to members of the Jewish faith.

There's no question in my mind that Hanukkah, along with countless other cultural, scientific, and social advances, has contributed immensely to our world's slow but steady progress towards enlightenment.

Our country—indeed, many countries—wouldn't have achieved nearly the measure of cultural and economic success they have without the active and willing contributions of the Jewish community. In fact, Jews have been instrumental in building modern Canada, a nation that is in many ways the envy of the world.

And yet, we must not become complacent. As we celebrate this season of renewal, as we commemorate the triumph of light over darkness, we must remember that there are still greater battles against injustice to come.

Each year, we should move a few steps closer to our goal of building a nation where no one goes hungry, no one lives on the street, and where everyone can reap the benefits of a world-class public school system.

And we should also look beyond the borders of this nation and understand that if we are truly dedicated to building a better country, then we must also commit to building a better *world*. I've had too many conversations with friends and colleagues in which someone says, "We have to take care of our own, first."

Well, the trouble is, these people don't realize that "our own" extends to every person on this earth. We owe it to our children and to ourselves to put an end to needless suffering wherever it exists, from the streets of Edmonton to those of Tel Aviv.

We already know deep in our hearts that there can be no prosperity until there is global prosperity. There can be no justice until there is global justice. There can be no peace until there is global peace. I think that Jews know this better than anyone, and I think that Canadian Jews in particular have a very important role to play in forging a more peaceful world.

Human civilization has a long way to go, and we will never be *truly* civilized until every single man, woman, and child on this planet has access to a solid education, clean water, clean air, healthy food, good books, great art, and freedom from the spectre of war and tyranny.

Those are the days worth fighting for, ladies and gentlemen, and the struggle will never be easy. But we owe it to ourselves and to the generations to come to rally to the cause.

If we hope to set an example as a multicultural state, it's people like you who will lead the way, by showing your neighbours, families, friends and co-workers that Edmonton is a place where character matters more than ethnicity, and where compassion prevents conflict and brings peace to troubled hearts.

Thank you for being such an indispensable thread in the fabric of our culture. I hope you and yours enjoy a happy Hanukkah and a wonderful new year.

Lois Hole and Harriet Winspear celebrating Mrs. Winspear's 95th birthday, 1999. [Hole Family Archives]

2004

Early in the last year of her life, Lois delivered a brief address on the theme of hope. This was not a perfunctory choice. Through the next few months she spoke with heightened certainty, and with her strongest language, about the importance of education, the arts, and humanity working together for the common good. Everything she said rested on the belief that people's lives could and would get better. Hope dominated her thinking and became the theme of her last public speech as well as of this one.

Hope Foundation of Alberta
Reading of Proclamation for Hope Week
City Hall, Edmonton, January 26, 2004

BECAUSE IT IS AN ABSTRACT CONCEPT, hope can be difficult to grasp; it is all too often ephemeral, fleeting, especially when the times we live in seem so unjust, so unfair to the majority of people who struggle to eke out an existence on our world.

Fortunately, hope is often personified by very special individuals, those men and women we're lucky enough to meet or simply be inspired by.

So whenever I'm saddened by the evils human beings visit upon each other, I think about those special people who give me reason to hope:

Tommy Douglas, perhaps the greatest of all Canadians, father of public health care, champion of the working class.

Mary Robinson of Ireland, champion of human rights, a woman of peace whose example has shown us that a better world is possible, if we're willing to work hard enough for it.

Mahatma Gandhi, who showed that violence is not the answer to the world's problems.

Nelson Mandela, who led the fight against apartheid and now fights for the rights of Africa's children.

And perhaps most importantly, the men, women, and children of Alberta, the countless volunteers who have given their time, money, and souls to organizations and charities supporting the fine arts, our public schools and libraries, the homeless, the illiterate, the abused, the lost, the disabled, the critically ill, the elderly, and to anyone who needs a helping hand.

Simply serving as Lieutenant Governor gives me hope, because I can see hope in the eyes of our citizens—and not only hope, but the fierce glow that you see when someone is determined to change things for the better.

Hope is not an illusion, and it is not invisible. We can see it every day, in the selfless actions of our friends and neighbours, in the outstretched hands of compassionate strangers.

As we celebrate Hope Week, let us not only seek out hope; let us give it, through kind words, kind deeds, and kind hearts.

Thank you.

Hope and literacy always came together in Lois's view. Here she participated
in the launch of a program that promised to deliver both. Justice Minister
David Hancock, who became minister of advanced education after the election
of November 2004, made a good partner for her at the launch. He was an
Edmonton member of the legislature whose own views on education came
closer to Lois's than some other members of the government. Part of this
speech will be familiar from earlier speeches. She delivered the same message
on scores of other occasions.

Centre for Family Literacy
Prairie COW Bus Launch with Hon. Dave Hancock
Government House, Edmonton, January 26, 2004

GOOD MORNING, and welcome. As Honorary Patron of the Centre for
Family Literacy, I am thrilled to participate in today's launch of the
Prairie COW Bus, a Classroom on Wheels that will bring the gift of
reading to hundreds of Alberta families.

The COW Bus will perform a mission that's absolutely critical to
Alberta's continued prosperity: maintaining and improving the literacy
of our people. So before I read to the children today, I'd like to say a few
words about the importance of a literate community.

Learning to read is the first duty of every citizen; teaching another to
do so is the second; using that ability to maintain your education and the
education of others is the third. As Gandhi once said, "The best way to
find yourself is to lose yourself in the service of others."

With those words in mind, I think we owe it to ourselves and to
future generations to serve others by keeping learning and literacy alive.
One day, hopefully not so very far in the future, everyone on this Earth
will enjoy the gift of literacy, and when that day arrives, we'll be one
giant leap closer to building a more just, more peaceful, more prosperous world.

The future of our country *absolutely depends* upon a literate population, and attaining that goal involves not only vigorous support of our
public schools, universities, and public libraries, but also public health
care and the fine arts.

Lois Hole, Dave Hancock and Joyce Fairbairn at the launch of C.O.W., 2004. [Hole Family Archives]

All of these institutions, when taken together, form the foundation of a prosperous, literate culture, and we must not neglect any one of these institutions for the sake of another.

As I grow older, I've been thinking more and more about what kind of future the next generation can hope to expect.

While human beings have made a lot of progress, especially in the last hundred years, we also have a long way yet to travel. Some of the problems we face—hunger, crime, disease, poverty, racism, war—seem almost insurmountable.

It's no wonder that many of our young people have cynical attitudes about their future prospects for employment and a good life.

But we can bury that cynicism if we work together, young and old, to fight poverty, injustice, and racism.

And the best way to build a better world for our children is to fight for our public libraries and public schools and to reach out to Alberta families with wonderful programs like the Classroom on Wheels....

The Italian author Luciano De Crescenzo wrote, "We are each of us angels with only one wing. We can only fly when we embrace each other."

He was right. Adults can't change the world without the support of the young, and the young can't perform to their full potential without the wisdom and the experience of adults.

Building a better world won't be possible until we establish permanent bonds of respect, acceptance, and trust between generations.

As long as we retain our mental and physical health, as long as we still have something to give, we have a responsibility to remain active in our democracy and to keep learning.

Whenever I wonder why we've been put on this Earth, the example of the men and women I've known gives me my answer: we're here to help and to make the world a better place. Any chance we have to make a positive difference, as you have by supporting the Classroom on Wheels, should be taken: it's a blessing.

And now, let's have a story for the children.

By early 2004, Lois had delivered addresses hundreds of times on her favourite topics. Increasingly through this year, she combined those ideas into one lengthy speech, a grand tour of all the most important messages she wished to impart. This address to a rural women's conference was a typical early example. It was repeated with minor variations throughout the rest of the year.

Rural Women's Conference

Edmonton, February 11, 2004

GOOD MORNING, and welcome. Today I'll be sharing some of my experiences as a farm wife, but mainly I'll be focussing on how those experiences have shaped my perceptions of the world around us.

What I've learned is this: prosperity and fulfilment on the farm, and across the country at large, depends upon healthy public institutions, most especially libraries and schools, and a vibrant arts scene.

In the beginning, I would never have guessed that I would become a rural woman. When I was a teenager, I told my mother, very firmly: "I'll never marry a farmer."

I loved towns and cities, you see, and all the attractions they held. When I thought of farms, all I could think of was loneliness.

Fortunately, my mother gave me two very special gifts, gifts that would be absolutely vital to enjoying the life that was to come. First, she taught me to enjoy gardening.

And secondly, even more importantly, she taught me to love the arts, particularly music and literature.

While my mother would often ask me to help with the gardening, she made sure that it never became a chore by allowing me to take frequent breaks. Much of the time, I used those breaks to practise on the piano or to read a good book.

I got pretty good at the piano as I grew older, and eventually I took up the organ, too, playing in church. And there was always plenty of opportunity for me to read. The public library became one of my favourite places.

So by the time I met Ted, the man I'd eventually marry, I had plenty of interests to keep me entertained.

And thank goodness, because Ted's heart belonged to the soil, and if I were going to marry him, I'd be marrying the farm, too. I said yes, and I've never looked back. It was the best decision I ever made....

For new farmers like us, our experiences in the public school system were invaluable.

My years on the farm, at the public library, and in the public school system showed me how important public education and libraries were to all the prosperity I enjoyed.

It was thanks to my wonderful teachers and the city's libraries that I developed a love of reading and learning, and it was during those years that I really began to appreciate how much the fine arts enriched my life and the lives of everyone around me.

I grew up with a profound appreciation and respect for public education, libraries, and the fine arts, and that respect has influenced my business, my public service, and my activism.

So today, I think we should dedicate ourselves to ensuring that the next generation of students, whether they decide to stay on the farm or pursue other careers, has all the advantages we did, and more.

As lucky as we have been in Canada, we need to understand that our quality of life is built upon a foundation of public institutions that must be continually reinforced if we hope to perpetuate our status as a nation both prosperous and free.

Our success as individuals and the beautiful, rich, tolerant, and peaceful country we live in exists today thanks to hard work, abundant natural resources, a lot of luck, and our commitment to public schools, public libraries, and the fine arts.

These institutions are the bedrock that supports our current good fortune, and if you're looking for a worthwhile way to spend your free time, if you're looking for a cause to support, I ask you today to focus your efforts on keeping our public institutions and the fine arts alive and well.

The most important institution that needs our help, without question, is our system of public schools. While it's true that our public schools were recently found to be among the world's very best, this is one area where we can never afford to be complacent, for public education serves two very important purposes.

The first is that it gives students a huge storehouse of useful information, as well as the ability to learn. Public education provides the fundamentals; reading, writing, arithmetic, history, the fine arts, science, and all the rest. And you could argue that private schools provide these, as well.

But public schools have a second, equally important, function, one that I feel private schools have a lot of difficulty matching: public schools build tolerance. They welcome people of all cultures, all economic backgrounds, of any religion or no religion at all.

And by providing an environment where people of very different natures can mix and become friends, public schools provide a great service to this country.

It's very hard, for example, for a Muslim to hate an atheist, if he makes friends with an atheist study partner in science class—and for her part, the atheist learns something about the Muslim faith. Similarly, when you put Canadians of, say, Jamaican and Chinese descent on the same basketball team, an important bond is formed. Cultural walls are slowly taken down, and the basis of a pluralist society is strengthened.

But despite decades of proven success, both academically and socially, public schools are under increasing attack these days. So today I'm going to take a few moments to ask all of you to think about the role of public education in our society. Personally, I believe that the death of the public school system would be a catastrophe beyond anything this country has ever experienced.

As citizens, we are all on the front lines of the fight to keep our public schools viable. We are the ones who have to speak out for funding for teacher-librarians, music programs, physical education facilities, updated textbooks, and all the other essentials.

In a society as rich as ours, it is unconscionable that parents must resort to bake sales and working casinos to make up for funding shortfalls. We have a responsibility to stand up and examine this country's priorities, because as citizens, we are the guardians of a sacred public trust. *We* hold the keys to a better future.

Our governments know very well that the only way Canada can compete with other nations is to maintain a public education system that's the best in the world. Well, that takes money, and if it means that our taxes need to be a little higher, then so be it.

Public education isn't some kind of luxury item, teacher-librarians aren't a frill, music education isn't just for the rich. These are *crucial*. They are as vital to the economic and cultural future of this country as our oil and gas reserves, as our freshwater supply, as our international trading partners.

We simply cannot compete without a robust public school system. And if we don't invest in public education now, we'll all be paying a terrible price just a few years down the road.

Public education is nothing less than the cornerstone of culture, peace, and prosperity.

Henry Adams said, "A teacher affects eternity; he can never tell where his influence stops." That's the absolute truth.

Let me give you an example. People like to look at big companies and gauge their success by saying, "Wow, look at how much money they made this year."

But where would those companies be without their employees, from their CEO right down to the people in the mailroom, the vast majority of whom were educated by the public school system?

We all know exactly where they'd be, and it wouldn't be on the Fortune 500 list.

The truth is, much of what we accomplished in the last century can be attributed to our public education system and government-funded research and cultural support. And I'm not just talking about our great advancements in science, medicine, engineering, and so on.

I'm talking about the vast wealth of great new literature and film, art and dance, music and sculpture and photography and all the rest of it. I firmly believe that the historians of the future will look back and consider the concept of public education the most important instrument of social progress the human race has yet produced.

Well, there's *one* other institution that rivals public education in importance: our libraries.

The library isn't merely a quiet repository for books and magazines. No, libraries play a much more important role in our lives, a role I think we should be far more outspoken in defending.

Norman Cousins, the famous author, editor, and spokesman for peace and literacy once said:

The library is not a shrine for the worship of books. It is not a temple
where literary incense must be burned or where one's devotion to the
bound book is expressed in ritual. A library, to modify the famous
metaphor of Socrates, should be the delivery room for the birth of
ideas—a place where history comes to life.

In other words, the library must be a gathering place for everyone, a
free and open public square where men, women, and children from
every economic and cultural background can share equally in the collective wisdom and imagination of humanity. In the library, it's not just
history that comes to life: it is science, art, music, politics, philosophy,
the wonders of fiction, and so much more.

A library is a place where we can uncover the deepest truths, where
we can examine the thoughts and actions of others and in so doing find
better ways of conducting ourselves. It is a place where we can find
escape or confront our most difficult social problems. Libraries are as
crucial to our survival as schools, hospitals, farms, or any other institution you can name.

In his famous bestseller *Cosmos*, the American scientist Carl Sagan
wrote:

The library connects us with the insight and knowledge, painfully
extracted from Nature, of the greatest minds that ever were, with the
best teachers, drawn from the entire planet and from all our history,
to instruct us without tiring, and to inspire us to make our own
contribution to the collective knowledge of the human species. I think
the health of our civilization, the depth of our awareness about the
underpinnings of our culture and our concern for the future can all be
tested by how well we support our libraries.

Compared to many countries, it must be said that Canada does a fair
job of supporting its libraries. But we can do better, and I think that
sometimes, because Canada enjoys such a high rate of literacy, we take
libraries for granted. Well, we can't afford to do that anymore.

In an age where giant media conglomerates try to shape our opinions
with sound bites, we need books more than ever before. Good documen-
taries and news programs have their place, but when you really need to
understand an issue in depth, you've got to turn to books.

And because books are so expensive these days, libraries have become even more important, to ensure that reading doesn't become a hobby for the rich.

Without true literacy, democracy becomes impossible; the real battle of the 21st century, I believe, will be between those who would use ignorance to serve their own greed and those who selflessly open the doors of knowledge to anyone who cares to listen. By building a culture that venerates the principles of literacy, we may yet save ourselves from a grim future of literacy haves and have-nots.

Libraries are the cornerstone of civil society, of the liberal democracy that we've come to depend upon. We must not allow them to crumble into disuse.

I truly believe that every Canadian has a duty to support our libraries. We owe it to ourselves, to our descendants, and to every librarian, schoolteacher, parent, and mentor who ever took it upon themselves to introduce another human being to the liberating world of literature. As Cousins said, the library is not a shrine.

It is a living, breathing institution that requires all the love and care we can give it. Libraries don't just preserve the wisdom of the past; they contain the seeds of a better future.

If we are to maintain a high rate of literacy, if we are to continue to expand the depth and breadth of our cultural knowledge, we must ensure that libraries are given at least as much funding, care, and attention as our sports stadiums. Frankly, I dream of a day when teachers and librarians are paid as much as hockey players.

Not so much because I want teachers and librarians to be rich (though that might be nice!), but because it would signal that our society finally has its priorities in order.

Alternatively, and I believe this *must* happen, I'd love to see more teachers and librarians—as well as more painters, poets, filmmakers, playwrights, and musicians—serving in our legislatures. Can you imagine how different our country would be if we had more teachers and artists in government?

Perhaps then we'd see public education and public libraries being given the respect and, incidentally, the funding, that they need.

Nor should we ignore the role of the fine arts in our quality of life. For years music and drama programs have been suffering, because people think that the fine arts are some kind of extra.

Well, you and I know how wrong they are, and it's up to us to show people how vital fine arts education is to the nation and the world.

In a time when the shifting politics and evolving cultures of our world seem to be dividing us, we need the arts, our great unifying common interest, more than ever.

Archeological discoveries have shown that human beings embraced art long, long ago, and that art took root and flourished all across our world, each culture expressing universal questions in superficially similar and yet astonishingly unique ways.

When answers seemed impossible to find, when the terrors of the night seemed omnipresent and the challenges of the day insurmountable, people turned to art to fortify their courage, to explain the world around them, and to ask the great questions of existence.

Though our art forms have grown ever more sophisticated with time, the basic purposes of art remain the same.

First and foremost, the arts invite us to reach within ourselves and explore our motivations, our prejudices, our very reasons for being.

And secondly, when the artists are men and women of character and conscience, the arts are a powerful tool for promoting the values that will enable our species to survive and prosper.

Those values include curiosity, tolerance, compassion, honesty, and, most importantly, love for our fellows.

In a world where votes cast on one side of the planet can result in vast suffering or renewed prosperity on the other, we depend on the arts to ask the questions that will help us make those decisions correctly.

Great art gives us the chance to explore all the possibilities of life, philosophy, relationships, and what it means to be a human being. By asking important *questions*, theatre forces us to think about the *answers*, and sometimes it even forces us to *do* something to change our world for the better.

For that reason, artists are as important to the welfare of the nation as policemen, doctors, businessmen, lawyers, any vital profession you can name.

What the peoples of this planet need right now are *visionaries*, men and women who have the imagination to develop and implement the solutions to our most pressing problems.

I think that artists have this kind of vision, this kind of imagination.

We need their wisdom, their passion, and their creativity, and, in turn, they need our support.

I have to mention one more thing, another facet of our country's educational future: I would love it if we could strengthen this country's bilingualism.

Let me tell you, since I've taken up this role, I've met ambassadors and consuls from all over the world, and every one of them speaks at least two languages; a few speak up to five. And *all* of them knew French.

Frankly, it's a little embarrassing that I can't speak French myself, and I would love it if we could revamp our school systems so that every young person in this country grew up fluent in both English and French. What a huge economic and cultural advantage that would be for the next generation of Canadians!

Public schools, public libraries, the fine arts—these are the most important causes, but there are many more that deserve our attention. Public health care. The proliferation of arms. The ever-growing gulf between rich and poor. Widespread economic exploitation. The environment. Homelessness.

And the ongoing struggle to keep family farms alive.

Frankly, it's a little overwhelming, and it's no wonder that so many of us retreat into our comfortable homes and hope that it will all turn out for the best.

[Dramatic pause]

Well, it won't turn out for the best, not unless we take an active role in our world, by reading, by listening, and by taking positive action.

It can be as simple as writing a letter to your MP, volunteering at the library, donating to your local theatre group, or as profound as joining a mission and working for change in the world's poorest nations. If we could only convince each of our friends and neighbours to do a little, the long-term effects could be astonishingly profound.

We need only find the will to make the difference.

Now, all that being said, I must acknowledge that many of you have already done remarkable work to benefit your communities. For that, you deserve our thanks and congratulations, and I hope your example inspires many Canadians to follow in your footsteps.

More than ever, the world needs people who are willing to commit to helping their fellow human beings. And we rural women, who have enjoyed the benefits of robust public schools, public health care, public libraries, and a healthy arts community, should do all we can to give something back to those institutions.

If we hope to live up to the expectations of our children, then we must realize that hard work and sacrifices are necessary. We have a duty to build a better tomorrow for them, and indeed for all the children of this beautiful but troubled world. As Canadians, we have been blessed with peace and prosperity; now, it's our turn to see that someone else enjoys the same advantages we had.

I believe it's time for rural women to make their voices heard, to take a more active role in the issues that shape our common destiny. Rural women have to be mothers, scientists, engineers, businesswomen, artists, and so much more, just to keep the farm running smoothly. Just think of the good we could do if we transformed some of that experience into positive action.

There's no force more potent than a farm woman with a cause, if she's willing to stand up and fight for it. Let's all renew our commitment to rural values: compassion, curiosity, protecting our environment, and building a better future for our children.

Thank you so much, and please enjoy the conference.

Not only could business and the arts mix; in Lois's view they had to mix. An address to a college student business conference gave her a chance to deliver her message to future leaders. It previewed the "butterfly effect" observations that made their way into many of her speeches over the coming months. And it offered the audience a glimpse of a little-known piece of local history—awkward in some respects but inspiring in others.

Grant MacEwan College—School of Business Student Business Conference

Edmonton, March 2, 2004

GOOD MORNING, and welcome to the Grant MacEwan College Student Business Conference.

I trust you will use this conference as a means to not only further your own interests as future business leaders, but to grow as individuals, to discover joy in your chosen career, and most importantly, to find new ways to contribute to Canadian society and the world at large.

For every entrepreneur has two responsibilities: to run an honest, successful business, and to play an active role in improving the quality of life of the surrounding community.

While profits are important, the greater good must be foremost in our minds.

To be truly successful, a businessperson must do *more* than make money. A good business not only provides goods and services at a fair price, it contributes to the quality of life of the community, through volunteerism, donations of money or goods to worthwhile causes, and simple neighbourliness.

Take, for example, one of Edmonton's most famous and respected businessmen, Henry Singer. Back in the 1940s, some of the black players for the Eskimos football club were refused admission to Edmonton hotels.

Well, when Henry Singer heard about that, he used his influence to make sure that those hotel owners did the right thing and gave the players rooms.

When that principled businessman stood up for the rights of those football players, he was making a powerful statement about human dignity, one that, thanks to his esteemed position in the city, no one could ignore.

He proved that business leaders have power, and that such power must be used not for selfish ends, but to right wrongs, to uphold truth and justice, to lift up human beings instead of crushing them underfoot. As an influential businessman, Henry Singer enjoyed great power, power that he never abused, but instead used to *improve* the human condition.

This kind of perspective—one that values people over profits—is especially important in the 21st century, when the forces of hate, hunger, and fear threaten to tear us apart, right at the very moment we need to be working together.

No legitimate business can prosper unless its host nation is peaceful, its government stable and democratic, and its people well-fed, well-educated, and given ample opportunities for entertainment and personal development. Certainly my own business would have been impossible had not these elements all existed in Canada....

And learning what's going on beyond the borders of our own province, our own country, is more vital to our future than ever.

Scientists speculate that something as seemingly insignificant as the fluttering of a butterfly's wings in China can, by setting in motion a long string of equally minor atmospheric events, build up to a hurricane in Florida.

This phenomenon is called the Butterfly Effect, and it's taken seriously by a number of leading scientists.

Now I'm no physicist, but that speculation rings true to me, because it highlights a very important truth: simply put, no man or woman is an island.

The suffering of a starving child in Zimbabwe, the policies of a former Soviet republic, the publishing industry in the United Kingdom; all this and more has an effect on our daily lives, and on our businesses.

And the reverse is also true; the decisions we make every day, as individuals, as consumers, as entrepreneurs, have a profound impact on our brothers and sisters across the globe. To make those decisions wise and just, we depend upon information.

And the lifelong learning we need to collect that information is impossible without the solid foundation that our public schools, universities, colleges, and libraries provide....

The business leaders of tomorrow must have access to excellent public schools and libraries to learn and research the fundamentals entrepreneurs so desperately need: not just math, science, and English, but also strong knowledge of history, music, and the arts.

In other words, a solid liberal education is vital for businesspeople, and without our public schools and libraries, that education will gradually become impossible.

So my message to you is this: don't be the last generation of Canadian entrepreneurs. Build successful businesses, and by all means earn all the money and prestige that you can. But at the same time, don't neglect your duty to uphold the institutions that helped you achieve success.

The greatest entrepreneurs aren't the ones that turn the largest profits. They're the ones that build stronger communities, the ones that help shape a more peaceful, more prosperous, more sensible world. No man or woman ever achieved greatness by serving themselves; we can only do so by serving others.

Thank you, enjoy the conference, and please accept my hopes for a bright and bountiful future.

The host at this prayer breakfast was Leduc Mayor George Rogers. He was elected to the legislature eight months later. Lois delivered one of her "grand tour" speeches that collected several of her favourite themes into one big package. This, considerably shortened here because many of the passages duplicate themes developed elsewhere in this book, was one of her longest. But she inserted some new comments into the opening and closing portions. One of the new ideas was the Earth Charter. It made its way into several other addresses through the rest of the year.

City of Leduc/Leduc Ministerial Association Mayor's Prayer Breakfast
Leduc, March 20, 2004

GOOD MORNING, and thank you for inviting me to join you today.

Recently I was introduced to the Earth Charter, a very important new document that outlines a set of guidelines humanity must follow if we truly want to move forward as a united people. As the Charter's Preamble states:

> *To move forward, we must recognize that in the midst of a magnificent diversity of cultures and life forms we are one human family and one Earth community with a common destiny—it is imperative that we, the peoples of Earth, declare our responsibility to one another, to the greater community of life, and to future generations.*

I believe that the Earth Charter clearly states principles that we must embrace if we hope to build a global society, one based on mutual trust, respect, and compassion.

Indeed, when I think about the privileged life we enjoy here in Canada and the incredible challenges that face the peoples of the developing world every day, I can't help but feel a little ashamed of our disproportionate wealth and the excesses of our culture.

That's not to say that we shouldn't enjoy our prosperity, but I believe that we could temper our desires for material wealth and perhaps divert some of our good fortune to those who simply weren't lucky enough to be born in Japan, western Europe, or North America.

Surely if our citizens and corporations can spend billions of dollars on countless trivialities, there's got to be some wealth left over for more useful purposes.

And I can't think of a better cause than investing in the future of humanity by giving a helping hand to the world's less fortunate, both at home and abroad, and to building systems that will distribute the world's limited resources more fairly.

As human beings, we have a moral obligation to offer our help to those who need it. Failure to do so is a failure to follow the dictates of our own conscience, and every time we commit that failure, we lose a little piece of our soul. *We must speak for those who cannot or will not speak for themselves....*

*Another "grand tour" speech followed within days of the Leduc prayer break-
fast. This excerpt from the middle of it illustrates Lois's ability to weave a new
passage or new way of putting things into a settled general structure as the
occasion suggested or as new ideas cropped up.*

The University of Alberta Sorority Annual Awards Night
University of Alberta, March 23, 2004

...THE STRENGTH OF A CIVILIZATION is built upon the depth and
breadth of her educational and literary institutions. For those institutions, if they are healthy, teach us first how to learn and also how to
think critically.

Education's primary purpose is to nurture our natural curiosity, to
encourage us to ask new questions and seek out truth: *historical* truth,
scientific truth, *moral* truth, *artistic* truth. Good teachers introduce
students to the discoveries and wisdom of the past, while at the same
time showing them how to build upon those discoveries.

It's elementary; the human species moves forward because we take
the time to pass knowledge from generation to generation. It seems to
me self-evident that education should be the *number one priority* for any
civilization.

And yet, in the 21st century, we seem to be losing our judgement,
turning education into nothing more than a factory for producing cheap
labour and eager consumers.

Many members of the business and political elite would like nothing
better than to have our schools churn out hordes of conformists who
can't be motivated to improve the system or even their own lives. And
why should these elites want quality education? It's against their interests.

Educate the masses, and they might decide that smoking is bad for
you. Or fast food. Or reality shows!

Of course, many (I would hope most!) businesspeople and politicians
realize that in the long run, an educated populace is vital to security and
prosperity.

And I hope they also realize that public education is especially important in a multicultural country like ours, for it brings people of many
different races, religions, and economic and social backgrounds under
one roof and treats them all with equal dignity and respect....

A speech about education could easily be redrafted to emphasize the role of teachers. On one level this was both inspiring and innocuous. On another, it had political implications. Relations between the Alberta government and teachers had been chronically strained for years. The teachers' strikes of 2002 saw relations reach a low point. A subsequent arbitrator's award that gave teachers a 14 per cent salary increase did not endear the profession to Progressive Conservative members of the legislature. They did not attack teachers. They sometimes expressed support for the profession—but never with as much warmth as Lois.

Literacy & Learning Day
Parent Conference
Edmonton, April 17, 2004

GOOD AFTERNOON, EVERYONE. I'm very glad to join you today, because it's such a pleasure to talk with parents who are obviously so dedicated to education.

To wrap up this parent conference, I want to share just a few thoughts on what we need to do to ensure that not just our children, but our children's children and the children of all our countrymen enjoy the educational opportunities that so many of us take for granted. In a sense, parents must become more fully rounded teachers.

You already teach your children values and ethics, but to be truly effective, I believe that you must also teach your neighbours and your fellow citizens to appreciate and support our public institutions.

What qualities does a person need if he or she chooses to take up the role of teacher? I think they must have some very special qualities, including, of course, intelligence, but also curiosity, perceptiveness, a desire to share knowledge, the ability to communicate effectively, a sense of humour, a finely honed capacity for critical thought, and, most important of all, a passion for seeking truth.

Josef Albers, the German artist who was also a teacher, summed up that search for truth in one sentence: "Good teaching is more a giving of right questions than a giving of right answers." Thinking along similar lines, the author Joseph Campbell wrote, "The job of an educator is to teach students to see the vitality in themselves."

And Galileo said, "You cannot teach a man anything; you can only help him find it within himself."

By asking the right questions, our best teachers help students along in their journey towards truth: scientific truth, artistic truth, spiritual truth, ethical truth.

And while few of us ever find an ultimate truth, the search itself often gives our life here on Earth some kind of meaning. That's an amazing gift, and I don't think teachers, whether professional or amateur, are recognized often enough for giving it.

It bothers me when I hear stories about "self-made men," those people who achieved wonders in life without the benefit of a good education. It's not that I don't admire these people; I really do. What I dislike is the unspoken commentary, that because a few special people changed the world without a degree, well, obviously we don't need public education at all.

Well, let's face it: if we counted on those very few self-made geniuses, we wouldn't be enjoying our very high standard of living, one of the best in the world. The fact is, if we hope to maintain a decent standard of living, if we hope to lead the world in arts, in science, in medicine, in philosophy, then we must continue to support our teachers, our public schools, and our public libraries....

Without good schools and libraries, many of these countries will have a tremendously difficult time building a more prosperous society. (In fact, I believe the western world should be doing much more to help the poorer countries develop good school and library systems, but that's another story altogether.)

Education is a "can't lose" investment because knowledge and wisdom never lose value. In fact, knowledge and wisdom become more valuable as time passes, especially these days, when critical thinking is so impaired by a media so focussed on rabid consumerism and cheap entertainment.

Every child deserves to be taught the ability to discern fact from fiction, to look deeper than the surface of the world, to search for hidden truths. If we surrender to the forces that are trying to turn education into just another commodity, we risk losing all the progress we've made over the last century. Our children deserve better than that.

Education has been my number one cause during my adult life, and that's never going to change, because it's just too important to the future of the human race.

Each human being is blessed with but one life—one life to cherish love and friendship, to marvel at nature's wonders, to appreciate the arts, to explore the world—in sum, one life to find happiness and, if we're lucky, to leave the world a better place than it was when we arrived....

Each time we allow public education and public libraries to stagnate and degrade, we take one step closer to the final erosion of our critical faculties, and that can only lead to disaster.

Therefore, learning to read is the first duty of every citizen; reading widely and critically is the second; and using that ability to improve the lives of others, the third. If we neglect our own education and that of our children, *then we are also neglecting our responsibility as citizens.*

Much of my success—and, I believe, much of the success enjoyed by any living Canadian—has its roots in our public education system and our public libraries, particularly the teachers and librarians who serve as the custodians of knowledge.

I always felt very fortunate to have the teachers I did, men and women who taught me so much more than music or mathematics. Their influence taught me how to be a better human being, to give back to the community, to search for better answers.

It was *teachers* who got me here today, it was *teachers* who made Canada's entrepreneurs rich, and it was *teachers* who got every prime minister we've ever had into office. Teachers are humanity's engines of progress, the mentors of our children, the custodians of our most cherished values.

Albert Einstein once said that setting an example is not the main means of influencing another, it is the only means. Needless to say, I feel incredibly grateful to all the teachers who have touched my life and the lives of countless other Canadians.

Your influence, your wisdom, and your example have given us the means and the desire to seek out truth, to respect others, and to pursue the dream of a better future....

I want to leave you with one more quote, this time from the great ancient historian Plutarch: "The mind is not a vessel to be filled, but a fire to be ignited." And I want to thank all of you, parents and teachers alike, for being so very good at lighting fires. Thank you.

A return visit with the Hope Foundation ended with a passage that demonstrated the way Lois had begun trying to impress her audiences with the urgency of what she was saying. Her views were not official boilerplate. She wanted her listeners to act.

Hope Foundation of Alberta Gala
Edmonton, April 30, 2004

...PUBLIC EDUCATION is nothing less than the cornerstone of culture, peace, and prosperity. So much of what we accomplished in the last century can be attributed to our public education system. And I'm not just talking about our great advancements in science, medicine, engineering, and so on.

I'm talking about the vast wealth of great new literature and film, art and dance, music and sculpture and photography and all the rest of it. I firmly believe that the historians of the future will look back and consider the concept of public education the most important instrument of social progress the human race has yet produced.

That is, *if* we make sure that concept remains true to its roots. Public education has a bit of an image problem these days, and it's up to us to make sure that our fellow citizens realize how important public education is to our continued peace and prosperity.

So please, take every opportunity you can to show business and political leaders that where public education is properly supported, crime rates go down and more income tax flows into government coffers. Get the message out in any way you possibly can, because we're talking about nothing less than the future of our country. It's *that* important.

If you want to foster hope, you can do nothing better than to support public education.

And so we return to hope, which keeps the dream of a better tomorrow alive. By contributing to the Hope Foundation, you have become architects of that future world, a world more just, more compassionate, more caring than the one we inhabit today.

Thanks to all of you for giving Albertans the hope they need to overcome tremendous obstacles and find joy once again. Never doubt that your generosity has made a difference in someone's life, because it most certainly has.

Now have a wonderful evening, and thank you again for asking me to join you.

I consider it a privilege to visit with such kind-hearted people, people who understand not only the *power* of hope, but that we can all do our part to *fulfil* those hopes. Simply put, the hope you provide keeps the dream of a better tomorrow alive.

Thank you, and goodnight.

Calgary Construction Association
Calgary Exhibition & Stampede Round-Up Centre
May 12, 2004

GOOD EVENING, AND WELCOME. It's a great pleasure to be here tonight, both to congratulate the Calgary Construction Association for its 60th anniversary and to encourage young women to consider a career in an industry that is not only personally rewarding, but also provides great benefits to society.

Tonight, I hope to offer you some thoughts that should give you the means to not only further your own interests as future professionals, but to grow as individuals, to discover joy in your chosen career, and most importantly, to find new ways to contribute to Canadian society and the world at large.

No matter what career she pursues, every woman has two lifelong responsibilities: to enjoy a rewarding, fulfilling job, and to play an active role in improving the quality of life of the surrounding community.

While profits and personal satisfaction are important, the greater good must be foremost in our minds.

To be truly successful, a professional or businesswoman must do *more* than make money. A good business not only provides goods and services at a fair price, it contributes to the quality of life of the community, through volunteerism, donations of money or goods to worthwhile causes, and simple neighbourliness.

Professionals and business leaders have power, and that power must be used not for selfish ends, but to right wrongs, to uphold truth and justice, to lift up human beings instead of crushing them underfoot. Every successful businesswoman enjoys great power, power that must never be abused, but instead used to *improve* the human condition.

This kind of perspective—one that values people over profits—is especially important in the 21st century, when the forces of hate, hunger, and fear threaten to tear us apart, right at the very moment we need to be working together....

If we hope to move forward as a civilization, then we must reach out: to the disabled, to the disadvantaged, to minorities, and most of all, to all the forgotten peoples of the third world. It's good for them, it's good for us, it's good for business, and *it's the right thing to do!*

I'd love it if Canadian construction companies suddenly had the opportunity, thanks to more generous foreign aid budgets, to start building libraries and schools all over the world. Just imagine how much good we could do, and how much we could learn.

It's not an investment that would pay off immediately, but in the long run, I think the returns would be handsome indeed, not just for the construction companies involved, but for the entire world.

Entrepreneurs, scholars, artists, construction workers—citizens of all occupations, in fact—can accomplish great things, if we only agree to work together for the common good.

There are more important things in this world than amassing huge profits or owning a mansion, and I think building a better quality of life for Canadians and for our brothers and sisters in other nations is one of those things. In fact, perhaps that's the *most* important thing.

So as you pursue your studies and decide upon a career, whether it happens to be in construction or not, I encourage you to live your life with passion, and to pursue your dreams with all the vigour and gusto you can muster. But I also urge you to use your considerable talents and intelligence to build a better world.

A truly principled and savvy professional understands that there is a balance between building healthy profits and building healthy societies. A great entrepreneur knows how to motivate his or her colleagues, to make decisions, to create sound business strategies, and how to help everyone perform to the best of their abilities.

In short, great entrepreneurs are also *leaders*, leaders who know that building a truly worthwhile business means more than making a lot of money. (Though that never hurts.)

Leaders know that they exist within a larger society, and they know that supporting that society, especially through public education and public libraries, is the best way to ensure the long-term health of their business.

After all, without top-notch public schools and well-stocked modern libraries, there will be a greatly reduced pool of young talent for the business community to draw upon in the years to come.

So I would encourage all business leaders and professionals to let the government know that the taxes you pay should be used to properly fund our schools and libraries....

What looked like a routine and simple acknowledgement sometimes had a subtext. Eric Newell was one of the most important business executives in the province. He had been chief executive at the Syncrude oilsands operation. But Newell had also long been interested in education, especially at the university level. In the mid-1990s, at the height of provincial budget cuts and of a moderate wave of anti-intellectualism, he spoke at a provincial Progressive Conservative convention. He told delegates that post-secondary education brought great benefits and it might be time to consider investing more in it. The reception was less than enthusiastic. He was much closer to Lois in outlook and willingness to take risks than many Albertans might have imagined.

Installation Dinner for Chancellor Eric Newell
University of Alberta
Edmonton, June 11, 2004

TONIGHT IT IS MY VERY GREAT PLEASURE to join you in welcoming Eric Newell to the University of Alberta Senate. I'm sure it's no secret that I've been a great admirer of Eric's for many years, and I'm absolutely thrilled that he's been chosen as our new chancellor.

Eric Newell has never been afraid to speak his mind. He's called people and institutions to account when they've failed their constituents, and he's spoken eloquently and forcefully on behalf of the poor, the fine arts, minorities, and of course education.

He's probably this province's strongest voice for social justice, and that makes him a powerful ally not just of students and professors, but of anyone who cares about a stronger, smarter, more compassionate Canada.

I think the reason I admire Eric most is that he truly understands how vital public education is to our country's future. Canada's prosperity, its cultural heritage and potential, and its health as a society all depend absolutely upon our willingness to maintain and improve our public institutions, most especially our schools and universities.

And I can't think of anyone who will fight harder for this cause than our own Eric Newell.

Congratulations, Eric. I know that this university and its students will benefit tremendously from your guidance.

The second half of this speech reprised the capsule version of Lois's frequently delivered message on education. The first half took her and her audience on a detour through her thoughts on gardening. Most of her speeches were straightforward; this one had moments approaching lyricism.

Claresholm Care Centre
Horticulture Therapy Program
Claresholm, June 14, 2004

GOOD MORNING, everyone, and thank you so much for inviting me to join you today.

First of all, you should know that I'm no expert when it comes to horticulture therapy.

All I can do is speak from my personal experience as a gardener and share with you how gardening has helped me and some people I've known.

Five or six years ago, a business associate of mine retired. He left behind a high-stakes, high-stress job with a major corporation, and on the day he retired, he looked drawn-out, exhausted, and worn down by years of constant pressure. Even so, he was worried about retirement. What would he do all day?

Naturally, I suggested that he get outside and give gardening a try. And he took my advice, building an arbour to grow some hops on and filling up his yard with plants of all kinds. And you know, today that man looks about ten years younger, and he's full of energy. He's smiling every time I see him.

I see this kind of thing all the time. In my experience, gardeners tend to be more robust and relaxed than most people are.

But don't take my word for it. During a recent study in Japan, ten students were placed in rooms and surrounded with different combinations of decorative plants.

Their brainwaves were measured, and the researchers discovered evidence of mental satisfaction among all of the students. Even a few plants placed on a windowsill had a beneficial effect.

Gardening also keeps you fit—as an exercise, it's roughly equivalent to volleyball, basketball, or brisk walking.

And gardening provides a common ground for people of different attitudes, philosophies, and cultures. Over the years, I've spoken to thousands of people, many from different ethnic groups, some of whom had reason to distrust each other.

But all that negative emotion seems to fade into the background when they start talking about gardening. At worst, there have been a few good-natured disagreements over which plant has the most spectacular blooms, or the best way to grow a tomato.

Of course, gardening isn't all a bed of roses, so to speak. An unseasonable frost or insect invasion that wipes out your entire garden can create loads of stress. And you should have seen my reaction when my husband Ted ploughed under an entire row of perfectly good beets!

But then, sometimes a good release of rage can be therapeutic, too.

Despite the occasional frustrating moment, gardening remains one of the best therapies I know. It's the perfect escape from a world that is becoming increasingly stressful. It soothes the mind, hones the body, and eases the heart.

Let me amend that: gardening isn't an escape, but a refuge, a temporary sanctuary from which you emerge revitalized and ready to face the world again. The energy I get from a couple of hours in the garden is more than enough to prepare me for whatever challenges lay ahead.

The scent of a lilac, the whisper of the wind through the trees, the feel of dirt on my hands, the brilliant colours of all those beautiful blooms, the deep and meditative solitude—this is why I love to garden. It's the ultimate therapy.

Of course, it's not the *only* therapy I rely upon. From the time I was a girl, I've always associated gardening with the fine arts. As a girl, much of my leisure time was spent helping my mother in the garden, practising the piano, or reading a good book. As I grew older, my love of the fine arts matured right along with my knowledge of gardening.

Ted and I used to make regular trips from our farm into Edmonton to see the symphony, to catch a movie, to attend a play, a musical, or an opera. Now that Ted's gone, this kind of therapy has become even more important; I still go to as many live performances as I can.

Gardening and the fine arts are my top two means of therapy, and I know that millions of people find renewal and inspiration from these same sources. So before I leave you today, I ask you to think about what we must do as citizens to make sure that gardening and the arts flourish in the future.

Personally, I think what we have to do is pretty easy to define: we have to support our public schools and public libraries, for it is these institutions that keep gardening and the arts, as well as every other human endeavour, alive and growing....

Wildwood was a community of about 350, located a little over an hour's drive west of Edmonton. Like many other small Alberta communities, it attracted Lois because of its support for the local library.

Wildwood Public Library 50th Anniversary
Wildwood, June 18, 2004

GOOD AFTERNOON.

It's a real pleasure to join you today, to celebrate the 50th anniversary of Wildwood's public library. To all those who helped build this library, who stocked it with books of all kinds, and who have helped introduce countless Albertans to the joy of reading over the course of a half-century, we owe our thanks.

We owe our thanks because librarians, and the people who support libraries—the men and women who sit on library boards, community officials, those who volunteer at libraries, and the patrons who make use of the library's wonders—are, to my mind, the unsung heroes of civilization.

These people, in their quiet way, have maintained one of civilization's great traditions: the gathering and dissemination of hard-won human wisdom. In this way, libraries have been and shall always be the engines of civilization's progress.

In fact, without libraries, such progress would be impossible, especially in the modern era. These days, we all depend upon libraries, whether we know it or not.

Because in the library, those with sufficient drive and curiosity can uncover the deepest truths, using books to explore the thoughts and actions of others and to inform their own creativity.

Books are the gateway to a better tomorrow, for books challenge us to use our minds, to find better ways of conducting ourselves and managing the great problems of human existence.

In the library, we can find the resources to examine and confront our most difficult social problems.

Or we can find solace there in times of stress, indulging in the great works of literature, or even the not-so-great—whatever suits your particular taste.

Libraries are as crucial to our survival as schools, hospitals, farms, or any other institution you can name, because they ensure that we need not learn the same lessons over and over again, from scratch. Unlike our stone-age ancestors, we can learn from the experience of those who came before.

And that gives us a remarkable power to change and grow and do things better....

Homelessness was becoming increasingly obvious in Alberta's richest city when Lois made this speech to the Calgary Homeless Foundation. She also made one of her first public references to the province's 2005 centennial, which she looked forward to helping celebrate. When she died, staff already had about 100 appearances booked and had thought she might be attending as many as 700 events through 2005. Note the mention of Donne. An earlier speech had attributed the same thoughts to Ernest Hemingway, who had in turn borrowed them from Donne.

Calgary Homeless Foundation
"Hope for Humanity" Rose Campaign
2004 Garden Party
June 22, 2004

GOOD AFTERNOON, AND WELCOME.

Though we've worked hard in Canada to build a network of social programs that protect our citizens from economic hardship, we cannot deny that the system is far from perfect and that every year, despite our best efforts, people fall through the cracks.

But thanks to you, we can compensate for some of the shortfall, providing aid to those who need it most.

As Canadians and as human beings, one of our most sacred duties is to protect our neighbours, to care for them when they lack the means to care for themselves. Today, you are doing just that.

You're making a huge difference in the lives of real people, people who, thanks to you, may get the chance to realize their full potential.

Without proper shelter, not to mention the other basic necessities, the poor have no chance to further their education, to get better jobs, to develop their own best qualities.

And that doesn't just deprive *them*; it deprives us all. To paraphrase John Donne, the suffering of one person is my *own* suffering; their pain diminishes us all, because we are *all* involved in humanity.

There's one other thing we can all do to help our neighbours escape the cycle of poverty: we must support our public schools and libraries. With the world becoming more and more competitive, the less fortunate desperately need the educational resources our public schools and libraries provide.

So don't be shy about asking your MPS and MLAS what they're doing to improve these crucial institutions. If we hope to enjoy continued peace and prosperity, we must ensure that our schools and libraries have the tools they need to meet the tremendous challenges of the coming years.

I hope you'll all return—and that you'll bring a few friends—to next year's event at Heritage Park, where the Hope for Humanity Rose Garden will be unveiled, just in time for Alberta's Centennial.

As Alberta heads into its second century, that rose garden will stand as a testament of our determination to find homes for the homeless, help for the helpless, and hope for the hopeless. We have the power to transform our nation and our world into a better place; we only need find the will to do so.

Thank you for finding that will today, and for your generosity. By supporting the Hope for Humanity Rose Campaign, you've given *me* hope for humanity.

A chance to combine support for international aid with a salute to one of her personal heroes.

Canadian Friends of the Nelson Mandela Children's Fund Reception

July 22, 2004

GOOD EVENING, AND WELCOME.

Despite our best intentions, Africa remains the world's most troubled continent. With each passing day, the news worsens, and sometimes it seems that there is no end in sight, that there is no hope for the people of Africa.

Yes, the news is disheartening. But we *cannot* and *will* not allow that to become an excuse for inaction.

No one can deny that there is great suffering in Africa. But the situation is far from hopeless. The people of Africa are brilliant, industrious, and passionate; I have no doubt that their day is coming, and that day will be a great one not just for Africans, but for the world.

But for now, the people of Africa, and especially the children of Africa, need our help: to defeat HIV and AIDS, to provide nutrition, health care, and education, and to bring the most important gift of all—hope. I'm so thankful that you have heard the call of the children of Africa, and that you have stepped forward to answer that call with action.

I am never prouder to be Canadian than when citizens of goodwill donate their time and their passion to provide help for those who need it.

I'm *very* proud tonight, because you're bringing the children of Africa one step closer to their birthright: a full and happy life.

Nelson Mandela once said, "There can be no keener revelation of a society's soul than the way in which it treats its children." By supporting the Nelson Mandela Children's Fund, you have revealed a little of *our* society's soul.

You have shown that our hearts are in the right place and that we are willing to build a world where children can realize their full potential.

And that world could be an amazing one, if we make a serious, dedicated investment in children, not only in Africa, but in all corners of the world, including right here at home.

Thank you so much for coming forward tonight to make a difference. One day, all children of Earth will enjoy a world far more fair, far more just, far happier than the one we inhabit, and when that day arrives, our descendants will be in your debt.

One of Lois's last big speeches took place at a conference of international students. It was a variation of the "grand tour" speech that had appeared earlier in the year. She spoke at length again on few occasions and delivered the "grand tour" for a last time at an economic development conference in the northern town of High Level on September 30. August 6 was also the anniversary date of the first wartime use of the atomic bomb, at Hiroshima, Japan, in 1945.

2nd International Student Representative Conference
Harry Ainlay High School
Edmonton, August 6, 2004

GOOD MORNING, and thank you so much for inviting me to participate in the Second International Student Representative Conference. I'm very pleased to be here today, because it gives me a chance to share my thoughts with the young men and women who, I hope, will be leading humanity's efforts to build better communities, and in turn, a better global society.

I'd like to begin my thoughts by pointing out that we should be very proud of what we've accomplished in this country thus far.

During Canada's brief history, millions of citizens have worked together to create an incredible public school system, a network of world-class public libraries, a health care system that's the envy of the world, a social safety net that protects our most vulnerable citizens, and a fine arts community that's remarkably accomplished for such a young country.

We've managed all this because Canadians believe in the power of *community*, the power to accomplish great works by working together. Many other nations have managed the same feat, so I think it's fair to say that the road to a better tomorrow isn't just starting construction; it's been a work in progress for hundreds of years.

But that doesn't mean we should be complacent, hoping that the world will steadily improve simply as a matter of course. Every human accomplishment has come about only because specific individuals, hard-working men and women, were willing to look beyond their own selfish interests and instead did something for their community.

If we really want to create a better society, then every human being must realize that he or she has a solemn responsibility to take an active role in the political, artistic, economic, and social life of our communities.

That's a tremendous privilege that far too many of us fail to exercise, and I think our civilization is all the poorer for that....

A medal from the Alberta Horticultural Association was a particularly apt honour.

Alberta Horticultural Association
Presentation of Centennial Gold Medal to Her Honour
Red Deer, August 28, 2004

WELL, I MUST SAY I AM ABSOLUTELY DELIGHTED. This honour is very special to me, because it comes from fellow gardeners, people who understand what it means to make a connection with the natural world.

It's very gratifying to be honoured by the Alberta Horticultural Association, an organization that has done such an amazing job of encouraging Albertans to garden. Everything you do really helps gardeners enjoy their hobby and find a deeper appreciation for the wonders of nature.

As gardeners, each and every one of us knows how important it is to plant healthy seeds.

And as a gardener, I believe that the future of gardening depends on planting a seed in the mind of every Albertan, a seed that says, "Get out there and support your public schools, public libraries, and the fine arts." ...

Horticulture and literacy have always gone hand in hand, and we forget that at our peril.

To paraphrase a famous saying, no garden is an island; today's gardens look magnificent not only because of our own efforts, but because of the wisdom, experimentation, and experience of those who came before us.

I can't think of a better way to celebrate Alberta's upcoming centennial than to keep learning from the men and women who built this province, and that's what this Centennial Medal will always mean to me: a recognition not just for myself, but for anyone who contributed to Alberta's gardening lore over the past century.

Thank you again for this wonderful honour. I'll treasure it always.

This brief speech at the Legislature grounds kicked off a year of preparation for the 100th birthday of Alberta as a province on September 1, 2005. The government was counting on Hole to be an important part of the celebrations, and she was looking forward to the year of events leading to the centennial.

Ready, Set, Celebrate!
Countdown to Alberta's Centennial
Alberta Legislature
September 1, 2004

ONE YEAR FROM NOW, on September 1, 2005, Alberta will be 100 years young—a bold and dynamic province with its eye on the future even as we celebrate our past.

As we celebrate this remarkable anniversary, let us honour those who made Alberta great, from the First Nations tribes to the European and Asian pioneers, from the farmers and ranchers to the teachers and librarians, from the entrepreneurs and politicians to the scientists and artists.

It took millions of people a hundred years to make this province great, and it will take all of our skill and ingenuity to keep Alberta growing and thriving in our second century.

So let us celebrate our anniversary by working together to build an even greater Alberta, with the world's best schools and libraries, a revitalized artistic community, more effective help for the poor and disenfranchised—an Alberta with a new spirit of community and caring.

We've accomplished so much in just a hundred years; let's make a promise to honour past Albertans by bringing all their hopes and dreams to life.

Of course, we should also take some time to enjoy ourselves, so I hope that all Albertans will participate in the many exciting and inspiring events to come in our Centennial year.

It's going to be magnificent, and the countdown starts right now.

A dinner for a women's shelter brought out Lois's views on the role of women in modern life.

La Salle Residence Gala
Fort Edmonton Park
Edmonton, September 24, 2004

GOOD EVENING, EVERYONE, and thank you so much for inviting me to join you once again at La Salle Residence. Far too many Albertans have had cause to seek safe harbour at La Salle, but thank goodness that harbour exists. I serve as La Salle's patron with great pride, because I know exactly how much good this organization does, and how dire things would be without it.

In times of crisis, the women of La Salle are ready and willing to provide all the support, comfort, and care in the world for the victims who appear on their doorstep. And more importantly, they provide the tools to ensure that these women are never victims again.

A loving and supportive environment, free from fear, is the only means by which a traumatized victim of senseless domestic violence can begin to get back on her feet. As I've said in the past, the women of La Salle provide that environment, and all the citizens of Alberta owe them a debt of gratitude.

What we need to do now is to become even more vocal in our support of La Salle, so more women in need will know they have a place to turn to, and also so that sympathetic Albertans will open their hearts, and their chequebooks, to support the continuing work of this crucial organization.

Giving women in need a chance to get back on their feet is the first step to restoring normalcy to shattered families, the first step towards recovery. The effects of that recovery extend beyond the affected family; they radiate outwards to touch the lives of every Albertan.

Who knows how many women and children could have fulfilled their true potential if they had only had the help that La Salle provides today? How many great artists, surgeons, entrepreneurs, or athletes spent their lives without the slightest conception of their own talents?

Let me tell you something: when a human being is deprived of a loving environment, and of the freedom to pursue his or her education, *everybody* loses. It is both a shameful waste of human resources, and a criminal abdication of our responsibilities to our fellow men and women.

With the problems facing today's civilization, we need the intelligence, the passion, the creativity of every man and woman on this planet, and yet we seem content to let so many of them waste away, often without even a clue of their own wondrous possibilities.

You know, all my life, I've had the good fortune to be inspired by remarkable women, women who had the chance to realize their potential.

I was inspired by my mother, who instilled in me the importance of public education and the fine arts, by Mary Robinson, once the United Nations Commissioner for Human Rights, and by so many others.

There's Nellie McClung, Margaret Atwood—but perhaps most importantly, all the remarkable women I've been privileged to meet and work with as a farm woman, mother, wife, school trustee, business owner, chancellor of the University of Alberta, and Lieutenant Governor.

I would never have been able to perform in any of those roles were it not for the guidance and inspiration of those women.

And in fact, it seems like every day I meet another remarkable woman who's building shelters for the homeless, or working with abused children, preparing aid packages for victims of famine, performing a beautiful piece of music at a charity event, or simply providing her students with a world-class education.

All of these women have one thing in common: they were never afraid to use their gifts and talents in the service of humanity. They recognized that one of the sacred duties of being human is to use whatever gifts we've been blessed with to not only pursue our own dreams, but to pursue the larger dream of building a safer, more peaceful, more plentiful, more equitable world.

So where does all this leave abused women, who have been denied the chance to realize their full potential? How can we ask them to give to their community, when they're trying so hard just to put their own lives back together?

Well, I believe that most women, no matter what the circumstances, want to help other people. And I think it's an important part of the healing process.

All women deserve the chance to contribute to their community, perhaps especially those who have been victimized. The important thing, in my view, is not to try to solve all the world's problems or to become some kind of superwoman.

The important thing is to do what you can, a little every day, to do your part to make the world a better place.

Even as little a thing as a smile can work wonders for a person in need. The smallest act of kindness can turn someone's life around.

That's how the world changes: bit by bit, because someone took the time to pitch in, to lend a hand, to make a difference.

Never, ever forget that your contributions matter, and that your role in building a better society is absolutely essential. The first duty of every woman, and of every man, is to our fellow human beings.

If we can remember that, then we have a pretty good chance of making some progress here on our troubled, but promising, world....

Although she was beginning to tire, the usual round of official events continued. She kept attending them and speaking at them because she believed in the importance of each.

Canadian Paraplegic Association
Red Carpet Affair
Edmonton, October 7, 2004

GOOD EVENING, AND WELCOME.

As Alberta nears its centennial, it occurs to me that when it comes to treating disabled citizens with respect, we've come a long way in one hundred years. On the *other* hand, you could also say that it's a shame it's taken us a hundred years to get here.

There is absolutely no question in my mind that Albertans with disabilities have made immense contributions to our culture, our economy, and our social fabric. But there is *also* no question that this province, and this nation, still has a long way to go before the integration of disabled citizens is complete.

There are still issues of access and intolerance to be addressed, still jobs to find for those who are willing and able to contribute but haven't yet found their niche.

I believe, however, that there is reason to celebrate our progress and to hold hope in our hearts for an even better future.

People across this nation are beginning to see that disabilities are not insurmountable barriers, and they're opening their hearts and minds to the possibilities and promise of our disabled citizens.

I think the future holds a *lot* of promise; thousands of Albertans have worked very hard to make our cities more comfortable and more accessible for those of us with special needs.

And organizations like the Canadian Paraplegic Association have done an incredible job of educating the able-bodied; without that activism, Alberta wouldn't be nearly as accessible as it has become over the past couple of decades.

When we take the time to invest in our own people, the rewards are always greater than we could have ever imagined. We need to open our eyes a little wider, so that we can see not the physical limitations of the disabled, but instead their tremendous potential.

Thank you for refusing to be silent; thank you for reaching out to play an important role in Alberta's evolution. A strong society needs to hear the voices of all its members, and as Alberta moves into its second century, your presence and participation will make us all the stronger.

Thank you, and enjoy the evening.

Harriet Winspear's 100th birthday—celebrated at a performance at the Winspear Centre—was not to be missed. Members of the audience noticed, however, that the lieutenant-governor was looking worn down. The short speech mirrored what Lois had said at two earlier events honouring Harriet Winspear's 100th.

She had also taken part in events in 2003 for Winspear's 99th birthday. Their relationship was both natural and surprising. Mrs. Winspear and her husband Francis donated the first $6 million to kick off fundraising in the 1990s for the Winspear Centre, Edmonton's top-ranked concert hall. Francis Winspear also helped kickstart the Reform Party into being in 1987 with a large financial donation. The party espoused some ideas that Lois would not have liked. But then, it was Mrs. Winspear whose birthdays she celebrated.

Harriet Winspear's 100th Birthday Celebration
Edmonton Symphony Orchestra
Edmonton, October 9, 2004

GOOD EVENING EVERYONE, and thank you for coming out tonight to celebrate the 100th birthday of a lady I think of as Edmonton's First Citizen, my dear friend Harriet Winspear.

It seems fitting that the City of Edmonton and Harriet Winspear are celebrating their 100th birthdays nearly simultaneously, for certainly it's hard to separate the city's prosperity from Harriet's generosity.

Without her, there's no question that this city's quality of life would be significantly lower.

But while Harriet's monetary gifts have been very important to Edmonton's growth, her most significant gift has been her leadership. Harriet has been an inspiration to seniors, to children, and to everyone in between.

She's shown us the value of sharing, of respecting others, of supporting education and the arts.

There's no question that Harriet's example has given thousands of people from all over Alberta the incentive and the desire to play a role in improving their community. And that, I think, is Harriet Winspear's greatest legacy.

So happy birthday, Harriet, and thank you. We've been very lucky to have you as a citizen of this province, and I hope you remain with us for many healthy, happy years to come.

After years of talking about books, CBC radio offered her the chance to recommend one of her favourites as part of a "Canada Reads" project. She was to have taken part in a panel discussion but realized that her illness was steadily making her too weak. Instead, she recorded this presentation at the CBC's Edmonton studio.

Canada Reads
CBC Studios
Edmonton, October 19, 2004

IF I WERE TO RECOMMEND A BOOK to Canadians, it would be *The Stone Diaries*, by Carol Shields. It's a challenging novel, and you may have to read it a few times to really explore its depths, but the rewards are well worth the effort.

It's the story of Daisy Goodwill, an ordinary girl from Manitoba who goes to college, marries twice, has a few children, enjoys a brief career as a newspaper columnist, suffers the loss of loved ones, and eventually finds herself in a nursing home. A seemingly ordinary life, you might think, but it's far more than that.

What's particularly interesting in this novel is the one-sided nature of many of the relationships. Keep an eye on how the male and female characters relate to each other; for example, one character builds a monument of stone to his departed wife, and in fact his stone tower makes him famous; but his wife always seemed somewhat bewildered by his attentions, and you can sense that she didn't feel much for him other than a sense of duty. The devotion in their marriage clearly flowed only in one direction. It's an interesting reversal of stereotypical romantic relationships.

There's also a good dose of dry humour in the book; one character meets a tragic end that is, nonetheless, very funny, if you're in the right frame of mind.

At one point, Daisy gets a job writing gardening columns for a local newspaper, and since I've done the same thing, that made it quite easy to identify with the character—at least on a professional level. The book includes some letters that Daisy receives from readers, and I have to admit, I've been asked the same questions. Daisy's husband Barker is also a gardener, and an academic; as a gardener and an admirer of teachers and scholars, I quite enjoyed his character.

I think Shields's message is this: *every* life—no matter how mundane it may seem from the outside—is an *extraordinary* life. And yet, at one point she also says right out that the narrator of the story—Daisy—is unreliable, so all of the events in the book should be taken with a grain of salt. Which perhaps suggests that no one should write their own life story, however extraordinary. In fact, I found it interesting that Daisy, or rather the author, glosses over many points in the main character's life, including her college experience and much of her child-rearing years. It makes you wonder about Daisy's motivations in telling her story, and if those motivations are really conscious at all.

I should add that, as you might expect from a Pulitzer Prize winning novel, the prose is exquisite; if you love language and appreciate a clever turn of phrase, you'll love this book.

The Stone Diaries is a fine novel that will have you looking back on the strange course of your own life—and it will make you wonder how you might choose to tell your own story—or if you should leave that job to someone else.

Lois almost never referred publicly to her illness. An exception was a short talk at a dinner following an investiture ceremony for the Alberta Order of Excellence. When she did talk about her illness, she tackled the subject fairly directly.

Alberta Order of Excellence
2004 Investiture Ceremony
Government House
Edmonton, October 21, 2004

THANK YOU, Mr. Chair, and thank you to our new inductees for sharing their thoughts with us so passionately and eloquently this evening.

This event is always a pleasure for me, as is the work I do throughout the year with the Alberta Order of Excellence Council.

Our intention this evening has been to provide our newest members with a ceremony and an evening that are, in some small way, reflective of the wonderful contributions they have made to their fellow Albertans and all Canadians.

If the memories they take away of this evening are even a fraction as powerful as their contributions, then we've accomplished our goal.

I think it was the wonderfully pragmatic Erma Bombeck who said, "The most important things in life aren't things."

This evening's six inductees are powerful reminders of that fact. In the end, the most powerful thing they each have to offer the world is their unique spirit and their ability to share that spirit with others.

As you all probably know, I've been dealing with health challenges over the past two years.

That experience has served to crystallize certain truths for me, as I'm sure it does for anyone who must deal with an illness.

The kindness and positive energy I've received from the people around me has served to remind time and again of the power that resides within the human spirit. It's a power that transcends any other resource a person might possess.

It's also something that needs to be fostered and carefully tended in others and in our communities in order to reach its fullest potential.

These six inductees are generous in how they share that power—in how they share the best of their spirit with the world. They also have a gift for encouraging the best to shine through in the people around them.

It's been a pleasure learning more about them and their special gifts.

Again, thank you to our inductees and thank you all for gathering together tonight to recognize and celebrate their many contributions to our province.

There was always room on the itinerary for visiting libraries and the people who helped them function. An appearance at an anniversary tea in Camrose was to be the last time Lois took part in a library event, although she did have a similar speech read for her in Red Deer on November 6. These are excerpts. The speech was about 20 minutes long.

Camrose Public Library 85th Anniversary Tea
Camrose, October 24, 2004

GOOD AFTERNOON.

It's a real pleasure to join you today, to celebrate the 85th anniversary of one of Alberta's most successful libraries.

To all those who nurtured this library over the years, who kept it stocked with books, who answered all kinds of questions, and who helped introduce countless Albertans to the joy of reading over the course of nearly a century, we owe our thanks.

We owe our thanks because librarians, and the people who support libraries—the men and women who sit on library boards, community officials, those who volunteer at libraries, and the patrons who make use of the library's wonders—are, to my mind, the unsung heroes of civilization.

These people, in their quiet way, have maintained one of civilization's great traditions: the gathering and dissemination of hard-won human wisdom. In this way, libraries have been and shall always be the engines of civilization's progress....

Without true literacy, democracy itself becomes impossible; the real battle of the 21st century, I believe, will be between those who would use ignorance to serve their own greed, and those who selflessly open the doors of knowledge to anyone who cares to listen.

By building a culture that venerates the principles of literacy, we may yet save ourselves from a grim future of literary haves and have-nots.

Libraries are the cornerstone of civil society, of the liberal democracy that we've come to cherish. We must not allow them to crumble into disuse.

That's why I strongly encourage everyone gathered here today to tell their friends and neighbours about the Lois Hole Library Legacy Program, which I hope will provide scores of books for Alberta's libraries.

Above all else, a library's book collection must have both depth and breadth; it needs to address a wide range of subjects, and it needs a sufficient number of books to give those subjects the coverage they deserve.

Books are the lifeblood of the library, and when you or your friends donate to the program, you're contributing to the legacy of literacy that took Canadians many, many decades to build.

And not only that, you can donate books in the name of anyone you like, and that person's name will be inscribed in a bookplate, placed on the inside cover of whichever book's you're donating. So when you donate to the program, you're creating a legacy not just for your library, but your own family.

I support this program because I truly believe that every Canadian has a duty to support our libraries. We owe it to ourselves, to our descendants, and to every librarian, schoolteacher, parent, and mentor who ever took it upon themselves to introduce another human being to the liberating world of literature.

Our libraries require all the love and care we can give them, for libraries don't just preserve the wisdom of the past; they contain the seeds of a better future.

For eighty-five years, the Camrose library has performed a mission that's absolutely critical to Alberta's continued prosperity: maintaining and improving the literacy of our people.

And we cannot underestimate the importance of that mission, for learning to read is the first duty of every citizen; teaching another to do so is the second; using that ability to maintain your education and the education of others is the third....

Whenever I wonder why we've been put on this Earth, the example of the men and women I've known gives me my answer: we're here to help, and to make the world a better place. Any chance we have to make a positive difference, as you have by supporting your library, should be taken: it's a blessing.

Thank you so much for coming out today, and for supporting Alberta's libraries. I hope that more and more Albertans will decide to donate books and funds to their libraries, and that they'll get more involved in library activities.

We all have a very personal stake in libraries, and so we have a responsibility to take a more active role in their maintenance and growth.

In a world of changes, contributing to the health of your library is one of the only legacies that really lasts.

And in building a legacy for your loved ones, you're also investing in a more literate, more enlightened world.

Thank you.

The Boyle Street Community Services Co-operative was renowned in Edmonton for its decades of service to inner-city poor. Lois planned to deliver this address at the dedication of a large mural painting at the co-op. Her appearance was cancelled because she entered hospital on the evening of October 26.

Boyle Street Community Services Co-operative "Metamorphosis" Mural Dedication
Edmonton, October 28, 2004

GOOD MORNING, and thank you all so much for coming out today to support people in need and to celebrate the Boyle Street Co-op's incredible service to our community. I'm very proud to help recognize some of our city's most generous and caring citizens, people who recognize that poverty is real and that it's up to us to do something about it.

Though we've worked hard in Canada to build a network of social programs that protect our citizens from economic hardship, we cannot deny that the system is far from perfect, and that every year, despite our best efforts, people fall through the cracks. But the men and women of the Boyle Street Co-Op have compensated for some of the shortfall, providing aid to those who need it most.

As Canadians and as human beings, one of our most sacred duties is to protect our neighbours, to care for them when they lack the means to care for themselves. At Boyle Street, some very special people have been doing just that for years, making a huge difference in the lives of real people, people who, thanks to you, may get the chance to realize their full potential.

Without proper food, shelter, clothing, and other basic necessities, the poor have no chance to further their education, to get better jobs, to develop their own best qualities. And that doesn't just deprive *them*; it deprives us all. To paraphrase John Donne, the suffering of one person is my own suffering; their pain diminishes us all, because we are *all* involved in humanity.

There's one other thing we can all do to help our neighbours escape the cycle of poverty: we must support our public schools and libraries. With the world becoming more and more competitive, the less fortunate desperately need the educational resources our public schools and libraries provide.

So don't be shy about asking your representatives what they're doing to improve these crucial institutions. If we hope to enjoy continued peace and prosperity, we must ensure that our schools and libraries have the tools they need to meet the tremendous challenges of the coming years.

I want to thank Alice Collett-Switzer and Phil Switzer for designing, creating and donating their remarkable mural to Boyle Street—I know it's going to serve as a beacon of hope and a symbol of positive change, a metamorphosis for Edmontonians who need it most.

Thank you.

Lois entered hospital on her doctor's advice in the last week of October after keeping up her usually hectic schedule as long as possible. The hospitalization was not announced until it became clear she would not be returning to her duties. Organizers of a Remembrance Day poppy ceremony at the Legislature Building on October 28 were not told until the last moment that she would not be attending.

Despite initial brave words from the government about her getting some needed rest, people quickly appreciated that this stay in hospital might be final. St. Albert Mayor Richard Plain said, "I don't know of any other person here in my time—three and a half decades—who has the stature and the love of the citizenry the way that Lois does."

On November 16, executives of the Royal Alexandra Hospital in Edmonton held a ceremony officially naming their new women's hospital after the lieutenant-governor.

The hospital's statement briefly captured a part of what made Lois special in many Albertans' eyes. It said her name had become "synonymous with compassion, literacy, and social justice."

She managed to take part in and speak at the ceremony, although her condition was so uncertain that a version of her speech was drafted for delivery by her son Bill. Her speech was so important to her and her family that it went through a number of drafts. With her family's aid, searching for one lasting message for the province, she settled on the theme of hope. This was her final public appearance.

The Lois Hole Women's Hospital Official Announcement

Edmonton, November 16, 2004

GOOD AFTERNOON. As you can probably imagine, having this new expansion named after me is a tremendous honour and a great thrill. Because to me, the Royal Alex has long represented the power of HOPE.

People at the Royal Alex saved the lives of my son Bill and grandson Michael, and they fixed Ted's leg after it was badly broken by a falling tractor axle—fixed it despite all of his cursing and yelling. My family and I have always been very grateful to the Royal Alex, and to Canada's public health care system in general.

Without it, our lives would have been irrevocably changed, and for the worse.

When a person discovers that they're going to have to visit the hospital, there's always some anxiety, no matter if you're going in for a routine checkup or a really serious problem. Suddenly, hope is very much on your mind. You hope everything will check out okay.

You hope your leg will heal enough for you to go back to work soon. You hope all the drugs will be covered by Alberta Health Care. You hope your pregnancy is on track. You hope you don't have anything serious. You hope the cancer will go into remission.

We've all felt that surge of emotion, and I don't need to tell you that there are two kinds of hope: the desperate hope you hang on to because you have to, and *real* hope, the uplifting hope that fills your heart when you realize that there's a good chance you might make it through this after all.

Today, the Royal Alex and the people of Alberta have provided us with a new source of hope, especially for women. Hundreds of Albertans worked very hard to get this project off the ground, and they did so because they wanted to give women from all across Western Canada a place where they will receive the very best of care, second-to-none anywhere.

I'm actually very glad that my name will be on this expansion. Not because of vanity (well—maybe just a *little* vanity), but because I hope that Albertans associate my name with fond memories and good thoughts.

I've always done my very best to make people feel comfortable, by giving away a hug or two—along with a couple of plants—and listening very carefully to what people have to say. During my time as a school trustee, at the greenhouse, as chancellor of the U of A and as Lieutenant Governor, I've always tried to put people at ease, whatever their particular circumstances.

So *my* hope is that when people come to this new hospital and see my name, they're going to have a little *extra* hope—that *real*, uplifting hope—that things will turn out okay. They'll remember how I always tried to be kind to people, and they'll know that the doctors and nurses and support staff working in this hospital will be doing their best to be kind to you, too.

I am *very* proud today. Not because this hospital is being named for me, but because *building* this hospital is a sign that Albertans remain committed to public health care.

This project in particular has been in the works for several years, and it's only become possible because Albertans from all walks of life have made it *abundantly* clear that first-class public health care is a *top* priority. Because of this widespread support, thousands of women from across the country will soon receive all the care and nurture they need.

I'm very grateful to live in a country where people place such a high value on our public institutions—not only our health care system, but our schools and universities, our libraries, the fine arts, and our social safety net. And I'm equally grateful whenever people work to keep those public institutions alive and growing.

So I'd like to say to everyone who supported the creation of this new women's hospital: you're giving Alberta a legacy to be proud of.

Thank you.

Memorial

Lois died on January 6, 2005.

A memorial service was held January 18, 2005 at the Winspear Centre in Edmonton. It was titled A Legacy of Caring. Official tributes were read by Deputy Prime Minister Anne McLellan and Premier Ralph Klein. Musical selections with particular meaning for her ended with the song "What a Wonderful World."

Her son Jim read the following address to the audience.

SINCE MY MOTHER'S DEATH, *countless* people have written or talked about her warmth, her compassion, and of course her hugs. But there was *so much* more to her. What I'll really miss is Mom's insatiable thirst for knowledge, and her love of sharing and debating *everything*.

So naturally, Mom made sure to keep up with current events and the latest books; she hated to miss out on *anything*. Mom's nightly bedtime ritual was to prop the newspaper up on her legs, flip on the TV *and* the radio, and place a book on the night table, right by her side.

Of course, after a hard day's work Mom often had a hard time staying awake. So Dad, thinking he was doing Mom a favour, would reach over and turn off the TV and the radio—and of course Mom would wake up immediately and say *"What are you doing, Ted?"* And Dad would have to turn them back on, even though he knew she'd fall asleep again in a matter of minutes. Mom believed that she could still pick up an important point or two while she was drifting off, and she hated to miss out on *any* opportunity to learn just a little more.

During her stay in the hospital, Mom would *not tolerate* losing her connection to the outside world. So I brought the newspapers to her room every morning, and we'd chat. She never wanted to talk about her health; rather, she wanted to know what was happening around the world and, of course, at the greenhouse.

I think the reason Mom was *so* committed to public service was simply because *so* much of what she learned showed *so* clearly that *so* many people needed help, and she decided to do her best to make a difference.

Mom's hugs opened our hearts—but it was her *words* that opened our *minds*. During her speeches, Mom often said—and I remember this distinctly—that the strength of a civilization is built upon the depth and breadth of its educational and literary institutions. And she was right. Mom devoted her *life* to spreading the message that education is vital. Vital not only to solving *practical* problems, but vital in producing an *ethical, compassionate* society.

Mom's only regret in life was that she didn't have more time to spread that message. Now it's up to all of us to make sure that her message isn't forgotten.

Appendix

What is a lieutenant-governor and what duties does the person holding that position perform? Lois never gave the civics lessons to adult audiences but did so many times to young students who may have been encountering the concept for the first time. This was her standard speech on the subject.

J.J. Nearing Elementary School
January 27, 2004

HELLO. I'm so glad to speak with you today about the history and the role of Alberta's Lieutenant Governor. I hope that it helps you understand the job I do, and why each province has a Lieutenant Governor.

The post of Lieutenant Governor was established by the British North America Act way back in March, 1867.
This Act united the four original Canadian provinces—Upper Canada, Lower Canada, New Brunswick, and Nova Scotia—under a central government, with each province retaining its own legislature to preside over matters not under federal jurisdiction.

In Alberta, of course, we had no Lieutenant Governors until the Federal Government, by act of the Dominion Parliament, 1905, created the province of Alberta from the Northwest Territories.

Since the Statute of Westminster of 1931, Canada has been a fully sovereign state; however, Canada has chosen to remain a member of the Commonwealth, a voluntary association of 54 independent states, representing approximately 25 per cent of the world's population. The Monarch is Head of the Commonwealth.

Plus, under section 9 of the British North America Act 1876, The Monarch is Canadian Head of State and thus, The Monarch of Canada.

It's because of Canada's membership in the Commonwealth and our ties to Great Britain that the office of Lieutenant Governor exists.

And that's because the Lieutenant Governor is the representative of the Crown in the Province and exercises The Monarch's powers and authorities with respect to Alberta.
In the early years of Confederation, Lieutenant Governors were agents of the Federal Government, and were expected to advise the Provincial Government as to the intent of Federal legislation and to ensure that Provincial legislation conformed to that of the senior government.

Over the years, however, with the gradual increase in the authority of Provincial Governments, the Lieutenant Governor's role as a Federal agent has virtually disappeared, and is now focussed primarily on their responsibilities as the Sovereign's representative and Chief Executive Officer of the Province.

One of the most important responsibilities is to ensure that the Province always has a Premier.
If this Office becomes vacant because of death or resignation, it is the Lieutenant Governor's duty to see that the post is filled.

The Lieutenant Governor has the same responsibilities if the government resigns following a defeat in the Legislature or in an election.

The Lieutenant Governor is an important element in both the Legislature and Executive Government of the Province.
The Lieutenant Governor summons, prorogues, and dissolves the Legislature, and reads the Speech from the Throne at the Opening of each Session.

With the advice of the Premier, she appoints and swears in members of the Executive Council (or Cabinet) and is guided by their advice, as long as they retain the confidence of the Legislative Assembly.

The Lieutenant Governor gives Royal Assent in The Monarch's name to all measures and bills passed by the Legislative Assembly, except on the rare occasions when "reservation" is considered necessary.

In other words, if I feel that a piece of legislation is very unwise, I have the power to send it back to the Legislature for review. However, this power has been used very rarely in Alberta, and I doubt I'll need to use it myself.

The Lieutenant Governor also signs Orders-in-council, Proclamations, and many other official documents before they have the force of law.

The Offices of the Monarch, Governor General, and Lieutenant Governor are entrenched in the Canadian Constitution, and no changes can be made to the Offices without the unanimous approval of all Provincial Legislative Assemblies, and the Senate and the House of Commons in Ottawa. So I have pretty good job security!

The Lieutenant Governor has an additional role that I find a lot of fun: he or she plays host to members of the Royal Family, visiting Heads of State, and other official visitors to the Province. This is one of my favourite parts of the job! I've met so many fascinating people from all over the world.

The Lieutenant Governor also extends hospitality to many persons from Alberta, and from other parts of Canada and abroad, at dinners, luncheons, receptions, and the annual New Year Levee, another of my favourite functions; it's held at Government House.

The Lieutenant Governor extends patronage to a wide variety of activities which contribute to the enrichment of the lives of Albertans of all ages. Basically, that means that I serve as an Honorary Patron, or supporter, of a number of worthwhile causes.

Each year, the Lieutenant Governor presents a number of awards for bravery, for outstanding public service, and for achievement: for example, the Investitures of the Order of St. John of Jerusalem, the Alberta Order of Excellence, the Duke of Edinburgh Awards, the Royal Life Saving Society Canada, and other organizations.

The Lieutenant Governor attends many dinners, cultural events, and military and civilian ceremonies. The Lieutenant Governor also opens buildings and conferences, addresses gatherings of various kinds, and visits schools, community events, and military establishments.

As a result, I travel extensively throughout the province. My schedule can get pretty busy at times, but I love meeting Albertans from the biggest cities to the tiniest hamlets.

The Lieutenant Governor is appointed by the Governor General, on the advice of the Prime Minister of Canada, for a period of not less than five years.[28]

I can say from experience that former Prime Minister Jean Chrétien took the responsibility of choosing Alberta's Lieutenant Governor seriously. Understanding the politics in Alberta, he personally telephoned to offer me the position—and that's a story in itself.

I was chancellor of the University of Alberta at the time, and the call caught me completely off-guard. We were in a senate meeting, and I was summoned from the room to take "an important call." The prime minister's offer came out of the blue, especially because at least a year remained on the term of then-Lieutenant Governor Bud Olson. People didn't yet know that ill health would soon cause him to leave the post.

I was astounded—and thrilled. But I already had a job. After thanking the Prime Minister profusely, I added, "But I'm chancellor of the University of Alberta."

To which he responded, "Just quit!"

But it wasn't that easy. I was honoured to serve as chancellor for Alberta's namesake university, because I believe places of learning are among the most important institutions in this province. I dearly loved the role, and there was work I still wanted to accomplish. Could I do both? Given the demands in each case, frankly no. So I would need to choose.

But I didn't say yes—not right then. I think the prime minister was a bit taken aback by that. But as I told him, I needed to go home and talk it over with Ted and the boys. That's how all big decisions are made in our family. Plus I wanted time to be sure the outcomes would match what I wanted to accomplish with the next years of my life.

The prime minister understood. "Certainly," he said. "Let me know your answer within a week."

So I took the offer home. We hashed out the pros and cons over lunch, and then over supper, and again over lunch—until the answer became clear.

The answer, as you now know, was yes. Not because of the added stature, or pay, or perks. But because being Lieutenant Governor of Alberta allows me to connect with all sorts of people, in all walks of

life. Young people such as you as well as the university students I
knew as chancellor. And farmers, and politicians and business people.
I have the opportunity to remind Albertans about things that I think
matter most: public education, public healthcare, libraries and
the arts.

Because of the Lieutenant Governor's constitutional position as head of the Executive Government of the Province, the Lieutenant Governor is not involved in political activity. This apolitical position permits the Lieutenant Governor to represent Alberta on ceremonial and state occasions.

In other words, even though I have political preferences like anyone else, I'm not really supposed to express them too loudly.

The primary role of the Lieutenant Governor is to promote Canadian values. During a visit to Canada in 1973, Her Majesty The Queen observed that "...the Crown is an idea more than a person, and I would like the crown to represent everything that is best and most admired in the Canadian ideal."

The Canadian Crown is a distinctive and essential part of Canada's heritage and character, and thus a focus of national pride. It is an important symbol of unity, serving to bind Canadians together in their common ideals and aspirations.

It is viable proof of the vitality of our traditions, the permanence of our institutions, and the continuity of national life.

As representative of the Crown in Alberta, the Lieutenant Governor is both personification and custodian of these traditions and ideals. And *that* really is my favourite part of the job.

I think our country is something rare and precious, and so I always do my best to defend Canadian values.

But what are "Canadian values," exactly? The phrase means different things to different people, so in the hopes of giving you some food for thought today, I'd like to offer what I feel are the most important Canadian values.

First, there is literacy. Only a society of well-read individuals with keen critical thinking skills, can maintain and improve our free and democratic society. Citizens of a democracy should read every day. They should use and support their public libraries and public schools.

They should question authority, and they should, in turn, question those who question authority. And they must always be willing to think, and to think hard.

Then, there is empathy, that is, caring for other people. A democracy cannot function unless its people are concerned with the welfare of their fellow citizens.

Charity is not enough; we must work towards addressing the inequalities in our society, towards bridging the gap between rich and poor. There's a saying I quite like: "when we all do better, we *all* do better."

In other words, the more help we give the less fortunate, the more we resolve issues of discrimination, the better off everyone—the rich, the middle class, and the poor alike—will be.

Thirdly, there is creativity—both using it and appreciating it, particularly when it comes to the arts.

Good books, plays, movies, operas, photographs, paintings, and all the other forms of artistic expression provide valuable insights on contemporary culture, insights citizens can use to examine the most important issues of the day. Canadian citizens, therefore, have a vested interest in supporting the fine arts.

Those are some of the Canadian values that I cherish, and as you continue your studies, I encourage you to discuss and explore the other values that are essential to a fair, prosperous, and free society.

So that's my job! As you can imagine, it's quite a task, living up to the ideals that the role demands, but I do my best.

I was very honoured when the Prime Minister asked me to fill this role, and I'm very proud to serve the province in this way. Besides, it's a lot of fun!

Before I go, I want you to know how proud I am of your accomplishments here, and how happy I am that you're studying the various branches of government in our country.

You know, it's very important that each of you learns about how our government works; you folks, after all, are our future leaders.

Thank you again.

Notes

Lois Hole seldom included the texts of the stories she told in the speeches themselves. More often than not, she merely included a note that indicated which story she wanted to tell. Many of the stories were favourites that had appeared previously in *I'll Never Marry a Farmer*. We have reproduced the stories here with the permission of The Hole Family. In some cases, the tense of the story needed to be changed to acknowledge, for instance, the death of Lois's husband, Ted.

1   In this speech, Lois's notes simply said: "WOODWARD'S STORY GOES HERE." She improvised three stories for the occasion.

2   This story first appeared as "Time for Lunch?" in Lois Hole, *I'll Never Marry A Farmer*, 130 (St. Albert, Canada: Hole's, 1998).

        Lois's note to herself in the typescript reads: "Angle—Perhaps you could emphasize how important these regular meals are to your family's health and well-being."

3   This story first appeared as "Society's Loss" in Lois Hole, *I'll Never Marry A Farmer*, 150.

4   This story first appeared as "Grandma Hole—A Life Well Lived," in Lois Hole, *I'll Never Marry A Farmer*, 82.

5   This story first appeared as "A Woman of the Soil" in Lois Hole, *I'll Never Marry A Farmer*, 62-63.

6   This story first appeared as "The Beet Incident" in Lois Hole, *I'll Never Marry A Farmer*, 121.

7   This story first appeared as "A Woman of the Soil" in Lois Hole, *I'll Never Marry A Farmer*, 62-63.

        Lois's note in the typescript reads: "Here, tell some of your favourite stories about Mrs. Durocher, focussing on what you learned from her."

8   At this point, the speech contains the following note: "This might be a good spot to mention what kinds of things you were reading at the time, especially if they were by Canadian authors—Farley Mowat, etc.—and why you liked them." Below is the story Lois told on this occasion.

Lois was a huge Carol Shields fan. In fact, in August 2004, she agreed to participate in the CBC's January 2005 Canada Reads—and chose Carol Shields as the author she wanted to promote. Her secretary, Sandra Kereliuk, recalls the shortlist being narrowed down to two favourite works by Carol Shields, *Stone Diaries* and *Larry's Party*. Ill health later forced a decision to forewarn the CBC that Lois wouldn't be participating in Canada Reads "due to other commitments."

9   This story first appeared as "The Innovator" in Lois Hole, *I'll Never Marry A Farmer*, 104-05.

In the typescript of the speech, Lois's notes to herself read: "Focus on how Ted used his keen wits and creativity to improve the family business...the roll bar on the tractor, new varieties, the carrot lifter, the razor-seeder."

10   This story first appeared as "You can't Give 'em Away?" in Lois Hole, *I'll Never Marry A Farmer*, 84.

11   This story first appeared as "Never Push a Pig" in Lois Hole, *I'll Never Marry A Farmer*, 144.

12   This story first appeared as "Caught Red-Handed" in Lois Hole, *I'll Never Marry A Farmer*, 141.

13   This story first appeared as "One Gardener's Secret" in Lois Hole, *I'll Never Marry A Farmer*, 87.

14   The note in Lois's speech reads: "Story about Bill and Terry and the Break-in."

15   This story first appeared as "The Pea Bandits" in Lois Hole, *I'll Never Marry A Farmer*, 108.

16   The note in the speech simply states: "Do you have an example you could use here?

17   This story first appeared as "The most Important Job" in Lois Hole, *I'll Never Marry A Farmer*, 124.

18   This story first appeared as "Never Push a Pig?" in Lois Hole, *I'll Never Marry A Farmer*, 144.

Lois's note in the text reads: "Focus on how you used a child-hood experience to help you out later; if you hadn't seen the stock-yards when you were younger, you wouldn't have known how to help Ted get the pigs loaded."

19 The note in the text reads: "Do you have a favourite Canadian painting or artist you'd like to talk about? This would be a good spot to say so."

20 This story first appeared as "Never Push a Pig?" in Lois Hole, *I'll Never Marry A Farmer*, 144.

21 The note in the text reads: "Story of your plane ride to meet the Queen, and if time allows, your story of the audience itself."

22 The note in the text reads: "Story: Sharing the bathwater with your brothers, using dishwater for roses, and maybe the "vinegar coffee" story."

23 This story first appeared as "Career Day" in Lois Hole, *I'll Never Marry A Farmer*, 64.

24 This story first appeared as "Dig a Little Deeper" in Lois Hole, *I'll Never Marry A Farmer*, 101.

25 This story first appeared as "Mrs. Sernowski's Potatoes" in Lois Hole, *I'll Never Marry A Farmer*, 79-80.

26 This story first appeared as "The Innovator" in Lois Hole, *I'll Never Marry A Farmer*, 104-05.

27 This story first appeared as "The Innovator" in Lois Hole, *I'll Never Marry A Farmer*, 104-05.

28 The note to Lois reads: [You may want to tell the story of your phone call from the Prime Minister here.]

Index

Most facilities named are located in Edmonton, and most towns are in Alberta; where this is not the case and where the location is known, it has been provided. Numerals followed by r denote pages containing information cited in earlier speeches. Numerals appearing in italics denote pages containing a photograph.

hair length, 208

Hall, James Norman. *See* Nordhoff, Charles, and James Norman Hall, *The Bounty Trilogy*

Hancock, Dave, xxxv, xli, 289, 290

handwriting, 137-38

Hanukkah, 284

happiness, 5, 14, 106, 112, 154, 255, 309

Harry Ainlay High School, 325

heads of state, 353

health care, xv, xvi, 323, 346-47. *See also* Douglas, T.C. "Tommy"; institutions, public

contribution to quality of life of, 40

costs of before Medicare, 91-92

preventative, 73

privatization of (*See* Bill 11)

public support of, xxxi, xxxii, 28, 237, 282

role of women in, 90-93

stereotypes surrounding, 90

for terminally ill, 269, 272-73

health care providers, 44, 179-80, 272 (*See also* nursing)

hearing protection, 54, 224-25r, 271r

hedges, 81

Hendrix, Jimi, 261, 265

Henry, Laura, xxvi, 14

herbal remedies, 32, 33, 41, 43r

herbs, 68

Heritage Park, Calgary, 322

heroes, heroism, 135-36, 231-32. *See also* role models

Hewlett-Packard, 199

Highgrove House, UK, 247

High Level, 325

Hilton, Charles, 125

Hiroshima, Japan, 325

history, 86. *See also* United Empire Loyalists; World War II

importance of learning, 36, 214

preservation of, 238

Hitler, Adolf, 264

HIV/AIDS, xxix, 323

hockey players, compared to teachers and librarians, 141, 218-19r, 297r

Hole, Annie King, 30-31

Hole, Bill, xxii, xlix, 52, 345

"arrest" of, 72-73

catching of garden raiders, 87

childhood and youth, xxiii, 104, 114, 212

experience in opera, 258-60

involvement in family business, xviii, 5-6, 19, 253

philanthropy and volunteerism of, 27, 93-94

Hole, Edward (Ted) Glancefield, xxxi, 32, 67, 128, 349. *See also* beets story; pigs in the chute story; vinegar coffee story

appreciation of art, 125

Mazankowski, Don, 182
McClung, Nellie, 261, 330r
McDougall United Church,
    277-78
McLachlin, Beverley, 199
McLellan, Anne, 349
McTavish Business School, xxii
mealtimes, 18-20, 30, 162
media, 89, 239, 296, 308
medical research, 10
medicine. *See* health care
Medicine Hat, xxxix, xlvii
Medicine Hat Exhibition and
    Stampede, 249
Meiji University, Tokyo, 81
mental illness, 44
mental state, effect of plants on,
    117
Metamorphosis Mural, 343
Métis, 26-27, 32, 94-95. *See also*
    Durocher, Peter; Durocher,
    Virginie; Stanley-Venne,
    Muriel
Mewburn Veterans' Centre, 69
Military Communications and
    Electronics Museum,
    Kingston, ON, 238
Miller, Florence, xxxix, xlvii
minorities, 172. *See also*
    multiculturalism
Misericordia Hospital,
    Edmonton, 108-9
Mitchell, W.O., 199
Monarchist League of Canada,
    183
monarchy (Crown)
    concept of, 355

loyalty to, 36
role of, 184-86, 351-52
mothers. *See* farm women;
    Veregin, Elsa Norsten
Motorola Canada, 199
movie stars, 218-19
Mulhurst Bay, 54
Mulhurst Bay Ladies' Day and
    Quilt Show, 52
multiculturalism, 55
    as a benefit to Canada, 40-41,
        131, 181-82
    continued efforts toward,
        81-84, 121-22, 285
    in schools, 73-74, 218
municipalities, twinning of, 121
murals, 343, 344
Murchison, Clint W., 261, 262
museums, 238
music, 16-17, 23, 34, 35, 218-19,
    227, 236, 349. *See also*
    Edmonton Symphony
    Orchestra; Johann Strauss
    Foundation; opera; pianos;
    pipe organs
    festivals, 277-78
    in nature, 229
Mutiny on the Bounty. See
    Nordhoff, Charles, and
    James Norman Hall, *The
    Bounty Trilogy*
Mynarski, Andrew, 182
Myrnham Alzheimer Home
    Development Association,
    269, 273

pipe organs, 231
Pitcairn Island, 49
Pittman, Cst. Arthur, 135
Plain, Richard, 345
plants. *See also* farming;
    gardening; landscaping;
    market gardening
    effect on mental state, 117
    medicinal, 32, 33, 41, 43*r*
playwrights. *See* Stoppard, Tom
Plutarch, 309
pneumonia, 91
poetry. *See* Byron, Lord; Wesley,
    John
police, 135. *See also* Royal
    Canadian Mounted Police
Polish Canadian Women's
    Federation, 181
Polish Canadians, 181–82
politics. *See also* Alberta
    government; Klein, Ralph
    as a career, 110
    elites in, 306
    L. Hole's lack of aspiration to,
        xxiv
    participation of artists and
        educators in, 297
pop music, 218–19
populism, xvii, xix
potatoes, 81, 211–12
poverty, 276
    effects of, 93, 94–95
    elimination of, 282–83,
        343–44
    loss of potential through,
        262–63

Prairie Oat Growers and
    Canadian Grains, 62
prayer, 114–15
prayer breakfasts, 29–33, 114,
    304
pregnancy, out-of-wedlock, 155
prejudice, 26–27, 93, 206–7
    based on physical appearance,
        207–9
    interfaith, 109, 114–15
Premier's Prayer Breakfast, 29
Prime Minister, 354
privacy commissioners, 181
Progressive Conservative Party,
    xvi. *See also* Alberta
    government; Klein, Ralph
prosperity, global, 285
provinces, jurisdiction of, xxxiv
puppies for free story, 56

Quality of Life commission, 101
Queen of Hugs, ix. *See also* hugs
Queen's Golden Jubilee. *See*
    Elizabeth II, Queen,
    Golden Jubilee
quilting, 52

racism, 83, 301. *See also*
    prejudice
radicalism, 203, 208, 231*r*, 256*r*
radio, 252. *See also* CBC
Radwanski, George, 181, 182
railways, 125, 126
R.A.R.E. (Retired and Retired
    Early) of Ascension
    Lutheran Church, 230
rationing, 69

Wilson, Mike, 260

Winspear, Francis, 334

Winspear, Harriet, xxii, 231, *286*, 334‑35

Winspear Centre, xli, 231, 334, 349

WISEST (Women in Scholarship, Engineering, Science and Technology), 46‑47

WITT. *See* Women in Trades and Technology

Wizard of Oz, The, 138

Wolfensohn, James, 261, 262

Wolff, Moe, *78*

Woman of the Year Award, *xiv*

women, xxvii‑xxix, 182. *See also* farm women
achievement of potential of, 171‑72, 329‑31
businesses (*See also* Cowgirl Cattle Company)
careers, 97, 312
community support of, 155‑56
contribution to family/ community, 27‑28, 30, 46, 90‑92, 151
education of, 146, 171
as role models, 261‑62, 330
rural (*See* farm women)

Women of Distinction Award. *See* YWCA Women of Distinction Award

Women in Trades and Technology, 97, 99

Women's Day. *See* International Women's Day

women's shelters, 26, 108, 109, 154, 329

Woods, Earl, xviii

Woodward's, xxii, 5‑6, 58

words, Canadian spelling and pronunciation of, 110

World Bank. *See* Wolfensohn, James

World War II, 69, 97, 182

writing. *See also* handwriting; *Lois Hole's Northern Flower Gardening: Perennial Favorites; Lois Hole's Vegetable Favorites*; speeches
advice on, 143‑44
biographical, 337 (*See also I'll Never Marry a Farmer*)

Young Alberta Book Society, 48

Yugoslavian Canadians, 9

Yukon. *See* Northwest Territories and Yukon Radio Systems Memorial

Yunick, Albina, 210

Yunick, Alex, xxv, 210‑11

YWCA Women of Distinction Award, xlvi

Zon, Cathy, 103

zucchini, 8